Jade

The young, wise ruler of the Nation of the Dragon King. In contrast to his cool and suave demeanor, he has a soft spot for all things cute and cuddly. He dotes on Ruri not only in cat form, but human form as well, and has given her his dragonheart, proof of dragonkin matehood.

Character Introductions

THE WHITE CAT'S REVENGE AS PLOTTED FROM THE DRAGON KING'S LAP:
VOLUME 5

by: KUREHA
Illustrations by Yamigo
Translated by David Evelyn
Edited by Suzanne Seals
Layout by Jennifer Elgabrowny
English Print Cover by Kai Kyou

First published in Japan in 2018 by Frontier Works Inc.
Publication rights for this English edition arranged through Frontier Works Inc., Tokyo
English translation © 2021 J-Novel Club LLC

Managing Director: Samuel Pinansky
Light Novel Line Manager: Chi Tran
Managing Editor: Jan Mitsuko Cash
Managing Translator: Kristi Fernandez
QA Manager: Hannah N. Carter
Marketing Manager: Stephanie Hii
Project Manager: Nikki Lapshinoff

ISBN: 978-1-7183-1999-8
Printed in Korea
First Printing: October 2022
10 9 8 7 6 5 4 3 2 1

Contents

Contents

 **Prologue**

"Hnghhhh..." Ruri grunted, stretching her arms toward the clear blue sky and working out the stiffness in her muscles from the long trip so far. The spirits by her side mimicked her actions despite having no need to do so. It warmed a corner of her heart to see them.

Ruri and her party had set off for the Nation of the Dragon King from the Nation of the Beast King. They stopped at the same lake she visited on her way over and began setting up camp.

On the initial trip, Arman and Celestine had nonchalantly sat off to the side, as royalty, while everyone else vigorously worked around them. Unlike those two, Jade was running around with the soldiers to prepare the campsite. Joshua had mentioned that Jade would likely join in on the prep work in spite of being a ruler himself, and that guess was absolutely correct. Even on the off chance that he would leave all the work to everyone else like Arman did, it was doubtful that anyone would object. In any case, it was probably more in character for Jade to be leading the efforts.

Ruri beamed as she watched Jade actively and energetically work alongside the others despite his status. In fact, Heat seemed kinglier as he sat underneath the shade of a tree, making the soldiers prepare him a drink and ordering them around. Everyone watched his hedonistic display with exasperation, but not a soul spoke up because they knew how futile that would be. There was also the fact that it benefited them more if he stayed still rather than needlessly moving around.

Ruri knew she would just slow everyone down with the physical labor, so she volunteered to handle the cooking and made soup. Once the campsite was about finished, she called for everyone and they all started their meal. However, in another turn from the Nation of the Beast King, everyone sat together around the pot—king and soldier alike.

Ruri started to dish out the soup. If a Beloved were to do something like this in the Nation of the Beast King, it would sap the color right from the people's faces. However, this sense of harmony and togetherness was comforting to Ruri. She ate and told Jade about her time in the Nation of the Beast King until Joshua changed the subject.

"Still, I sure am glad that the Church of God's Light stuff is all wrapped up. If they had their eyes set on the tournament season, there would have been all sorts of trouble."

Everyone nodded in unanimous agreement—except Ruri, who hadn't a clue what he was talking about.

"Tournament? What tournament?" she asked.

"Aah, you don't know, do you, Ruri? The Nation of the Dragon King is going to be holding a tournament pretty soon. A fight to determine the Dragon King."

"Wait, determine the Dragon King?" Ruri repeated, turning to look at Jade.

Jade nodded and elaborated, "Our rules state that only the strongest of all dragonkin can be the Dragon King. Once every thirty years, a tournament is held to determine the king. I won said tournament last time."

"So does that mean you're going to enter this tournament too, Jade-sama?"

"It's a Dragon King's duty to enter. The tournament itself is open entry—any dragonkin can participate."

"Then, what if you happen to lose…?"

"My title as king would go to the winner and they would be the next Dragon King."

Now that she really thought about it, Ruri had never seen Jade actually fight before. He mentioned that a lot of the soldiers, those confident in their abilities, would enter the competition. This made her recall the carnage that unfolded daily on the castle's training grounds. She started to doubt whether Jade, who spent most of his time pushing papers, could beat those battle-hardened monsters. Ruri looked at Jade less out of concern and more out of sheer doubt.

That was when Ewan scoffed at her and said, "Hmph, what are you so worried about? His Majesty became the Dragon King in the first place. No dragonkin around stands a chance."

"Oh, I see. So, hey, are you and Joshua going to enter too?"

"Neither of us intend to. We know the limits of our own abilities. Plus, I'll be too busy cheering on brother."

It seemed Ewan wasn't particularly interested in the throne. He probably found his beloved brother, Finn, far more important than a title anyway. She could just picture Ewan loudly cheering from the stands.

"So, Finn-san is entering?"

"Of course he is," Ewan answered, his head held high as if he were talking about himself. "After all, he is the second most likely candidate to win the tournament after His Majesty. If brother doesn't enter, who will?"

This wasn't just a younger brother being biased. Joshua even endorsed Finn, saying, "It's just as Ewan said. Realistically speaking, the finals are probably going to be a one-on-one between His Majesty and Finn. I'd get insta-killed even if I *did* enter."

"You getting insta-killed aside, if you were to become king, I could see that doing a number on Claus-san's stomach." Ruri envisioned Claus's plight and the scores of people booing at those results.

"Shoot, if I were king, my first order of business would be bumpin' up the number of holidays and givin' people more time off. Don'tcha think I've been working too much? I think it's 'bout time to let me take some time off already."

Right after the attempt on Ruri's life, Joshua ended up going with her to the Nation of the Beast King and had been working as Ruri's bodyguard ever since. Given that he was never totally loyal to his professional duties, he was probably feeling the urge to start slacking off. That was why he was appealing to Jade, who was sitting beside him, in a roundabout way for time off. However, Jade was either oblivious to Joshua's hopeful gaze or chose to ignore it because he started to talk about a completely different topic.

"Citizens are allowed to watch the tournament. While it takes place, the capital city opens up shops and stalls, turning the whole thing into a festival of sorts. You ought to enjoy it."

"You mean I can go into town?" Ruri asked. This was good news for her, but she hesitated since going into the crowded town could still be dangerous. However, Jade, the most likely to oppose, gave his permission instead, much to Ruri's surprise.

"The matters with the Church of God's Light are all wrapped up. And Lord Kotaro seems to have a barrier in place around you, so I see no issues with you going. Well, with a security detail, that is."

Ruri was pumping her fists in joy, in her mind anyway. She wanted to enjoy the festivities, but she also had ambitions of her own—ambitions to build a hot spring in the Nation of the Dragon King. Gaining permission to go into the city was a great help for that. Now she could stop trying to think of excuses to go.

And it was mostly all thanks to Kotaro. Ruri gave him a nice thorough pat on the head to show her appreciation.

Return to the Nation of the Dragon King

He loved her more than anyone else.

He was always by her side. She was in a position of immense responsibility, but he would always support her and keep by her side even when she could feel the weight almost crush her. She thought he would remain by her side forever, acting as her support in both public and private. However, after being stricken with illness, he was taken before her very eyes all too easily.

She couldn't bear it. She couldn't possibly accept the fact that he was dead—that he was gone—even if she had no other choice *but* to accept it.

However, she had the power; she had the knowledge. She could make things work out if she used them. She could get back her time with him. Those thoughts stirred in her mind. They stirred and continued to stir.

Even if it meant harming others, if it allowed her to get him back, then so be it…

"It's the Nation of the Dragon King. We're back!" Ruri declared. The vast ocean lay before their eyes, the water glittering from the sun shining above. The sea breeze trailed over Ruri's skin, carrying the smell of salty water with it. The weather was excellent, and many boats were entering the harbor. It was certainly a sight for sore eyes. Ruri's excitement started to rise just seeing it.

"*Ruri, don't lean over. It's dangerous.*"

"Yes, sir." Even though Ruri could fly with magic in the event she fell, she listened to Jade's instructions and re-seated herself on his back.

Ruri and her party had flown back from the Nation of the Beast King. They were heading straight for the castle without taking any detours outside of their lake stop. Once they arrived, they descended toward the terrace on the castle's highest point, Sector One. The terrace was so wide that Jade and the others could easily line up in a row while still in their dragon forms.

"Whew, we're finally here," Ruri said as she hopped off of Jade. Even though she hadn't been flying herself, she sighed and stretched in exhaustion. Jade and the other dragonkin reverted back to their human forms one by one, signaling that their long journey was over. It brought a smile to Ruri's face.

"Ruri, I need to get to the office, but what about you?" Jade asked.

"I'm going to go tell Euclase that I'm back. I want to introduce Heat-sama as well."

"I see. You should take a look around the castle while you're at it. It's been fixed up quite nicely."

"I will."

Jade took Finn and walked toward the royal office.

"Come on, Heat-sama, let's go see Euclase."

"And who is that, pray tell?" Heat asked.

"They're the chancellor of this nation. We need to get you introduced if you're going to be living in this castle. After all, we don't know *what* you're liable to do moving forward."

Heat being who he was, it was inevitable that he would raise some sort of stink sooner or later. The hassle and cleanup of it all would inevitably fall on Euclase's shoulders. Introducing him was probably the best option. He would need Euclase to remember his face if he was going to be walking around the castle, and he would need to have Euclase prepare a room for him in the castle if he intended on living here.

Heat grumbled with a sulky look on his face, possibly finding the whole thing annoying, but he obediently followed. With Kotaro and the other spirits in tow, they all headed to Euclase's office.

"Oh, wow, it really is all fixed up!"

True to Jade's words, the once half-destroyed castle interior was repaired. It was even more beautiful than before. Ruri was very impressed they managed to do this given the dreadful state it was in when she left.

As Ruri admired the renovated surroundings, they reached Euclase's office. She raised her hand to knock on the door, but as soon as she did, she heard a furious yell from inside.

"What in the blazes are you doing?! How did *every single one of you* let it slip past you?!"

"A thousand apologies!"

The one screaming their head off was Euclase; they seemed to be in the middle of reprimanding someone. Euclase's irritation was palpable from the other side of the door. With the unwelcoming aura permeating her skin, Ruri timidly knocked on the door.

"*What*?!" answered Euclase, sounding irritated.

Ruri softly opened the door and poked her head in.

"Oh, if it isn't you, Ruri. You're back home?"

"Yes. Is now a good time?"

"Yes, certainly," Euclase said, greeting Ruri with a smile— before immediately turning that smile upside down and glaring at the soldier standing nearby. "Send out our available ships and catch them on the double. You'll besmirch the name of the navy otherwise!"

"Y-Yes! Right away!" replied the poor soldier as he scrambled out of the room.

Ruri watched as he exited and then turned back to Euclase only to find…

"How beautiful!" Heat exclaimed. His eyes were sparkling and he was holding Euclase's hand. "I have rarely laid eyes on an individual with such immense beauty as yourself."

"Oh, is that so?" Euclase replied. Heat's compliment seemed to catch them off guard, but their cheeks soon flushed in a somewhat satisfied manner.

"I knew coming to the Nation of the Dragon King was the right idea. To think I would run into someone so beautiful. You are exquisite and to my liking."

Although Heat was ecstatic over the beautiful Euclase before him, Ruri had an unfortunate announcement.

"Heat-sama, I hate to break it to you, but despite appearances, Euclase-san is a man…"

"How rude! I have the heart of a noble maiden!" Euclase quickly corrected, but the fact still remained.

Since Heat was a lover of beautiful women, Euclase was outside of his demographic—or, at least, they should have been. However…

"Hah, don't make me laugh, brat. Be they man or woman, it is but a trifle for a spirit such as myself. Their *beauty* is all I care about."

"Huh? So, it's fine?" Euclase was prettier and more feminine than any woman, so much so that some men ended up in tears after they learned the situation. However, seeing how Heat would hit on any woman that suited his fancy, regardless of age—a fact that Ruri found a tad too unscrupulous—he was probably well past the point of caring.

"Your name is Euclase, is it, O beautiful one? Your name is just as beautiful as you are."

"Oh my, such flattery."

"Heat-sama, didn't you say the same thing to Celestine-san?" Ruri asked. It seemed that anyone was fair game to this womanizing spirit.

Euclase seemed to be in such a good mood that it was hard to imagine they were the same person chewing out that soldier just a second ago. But it seemed as though Euclase was getting curious as to who this mystery man was—albeit a touch late.

Euclase looked at him from head to toe. "By the way, Ruri, who might this gentleman be?"

"Ah, right. This is the woman-loving supreme-level Spirit of Fire," Ruri explained.

With their hand still in Heat's tender grasp, Euclase's eyes bulged. "Supreme-level spirit?! You gained *another* one?! How many do you intend on collecting? Do you just add a new one every time you go *anywhere*?"

"I wish I knew that myself," Ruri said, just as clueless. Out of the twelve spirits, she already had five of them, which was nearly half. She never planned for any of it, so she wondered how it even turned out like this. This many supreme-level spirits in one nation was probably unprecedented as well.

"Plus, they're in a person's body this time around, I see," Euclase noted. Considering that Kotaro, Rin, and Chi were all in animal forms, it was probably no wonder Euclase felt something was out of place.

"He can technically turn into a penguin since he's inhabiting a demi-human's body," explained Ruri.

"I am *not* a fan of that form," added Heat.

"But I think the dragonkin would like it," said Ruri. "Why not transform into a penguin later? I'm sure you'll garner some interest—man, woman, young, and old alike."

"Yes, I suppose the dragonkin would be fond of you," Euclase said. The dragonkin always craved the touch of small animals, so they would probably treat Heat like an idol. Euclase couldn't refute that either.

"All of that aside, did something happen? I could hear your voice all the way from outside, Euclase-san."

"Ah, that. There's a bit of a problem. There have been many eyewitness reports of suspicious ships for the past few days. I mobilized the navy, but they narrowly managed to escape apprehension. If you happen to go look, Ruri, keep on your guard. Though, I doubt anyone could do anything to you with the supreme-level Spirit of Water by your side."

"That's true. Picking a fight with Rin on the open seas is practically a death wish. I don't have any plans to go out to sea at the moment, but I will be careful nonetheless." She wasn't seabound, and the Nation of the Dragon King's navy was excellent even in comparison to other nations. The suspicious ship would likely be caught in due time.

Ruri then added, "Apparently, Heat-sama will be living here in the castle from now on, so would you mind preparing a room for him?"

"No, not at all. I'll send out the orders. It will be in Sector One if that's all right."

The royal guest rooms were in Sector Two, but since it wasn't clear what Heat might do, putting him within eyeshot was for the best. Ruri couldn't stand to see a repeat of what happened in the Nation of the Beast King, where an entire sector became his personal harem.

Ruri nodded, agreeing. "Okay, I would appreciate that. Heat-sama, let's go."

"I'm staying here," Heat said. He was apparently very much into Euclase and was eager to get to know them better.

Ruri worried that Heat would interrupt Euclase's work, but Euclase agreed and said they wanted to talk a little more. The chance to speak to a supreme-level spirit was rare, after all. Ruri wasn't completely sure, but it also seemed as though Euclase wanted to speak to him about something as chancellor of the nation. Heat knew the most about the Church of God's Light's activities, so maybe Euclase wanted to talk about the incident involving the organization.

"There is something I want to ask you about as well, Ruri," Euclase added.

"What might that be?"

"About you and His Majesty. That necklace of yours."

The necklace—Ruri had only learned it was a dragonheart not too long ago. Although, being a dragonkin themselves, Euclase naturally knew what it was from the start.

Seeing the alarmed look on Ruri's face, Euclase heaved a long sigh. "From your reaction, I assume nothing has progressed. I'll ask you about it later, then. You may go."

Knowing she wouldn't stand a chance if Euclase were to question her more thoroughly, Ruri left Heat behind and rushed out of the room with the other spirits in tow.

As she walked the halls down to Jade's office, she passed by the dragonkin who worked in the castle.

"Lady Beloved, welcome back."

"Yes, welcome back."

"Thanks. Glad to be back."

Being greeted by each person she met made her feel back at home and in her element. She had missed this casualness in the Nation of the Beast King. Over there, people would treat her with reverence, and no one would simply talk to her. The ones who did were so nervous about showing the slightest bit of disrespect that it made Ruri just as nervous around them. On the other hand, in the castle of the Nation of the Dragon King, there was none of that. The casual demeanor of the dragonkin gave her peace of mind.

Ruri definitely thought the Nation of the Dragon King suited her better. Not to say that the overly polite treatment she'd received was *bad*, but she liked living in a more carefree way, which was why she gladly welcomed the casual attitudes of the dragonkin. However...

"Lady Beloved, please give us your healing!"

"Excuse me?"

Several dragonkin stood in Ruri's way—male and female alike—as they all appealed to her.

"Because you were away, we've started to show withdrawal symptoms."

"We need to gaze upon that soft and fluffy form of yours once every day."

"We tried petting strays in the meantime, but they would run away from us."

These people were apparently Ruri's cat-form admirers. She took a good look around to see the hopeful eyes of many focused squarely on her.

Smaller animals innately disliked dragonkin, but the majority of dragonkin, most notably Jade, loved anything small and cuddly. They would usually find healing in watching cat-Ruri on her walks around the castle. But with Ruri gone on her trip, it seemed they'd all come down with a cuddle deficiency.

They pleaded with her.

"Please, turn into the cat! Turn into your cat form, please!"

"There's no small animal around that *won't* run away from us, milady!"

"I want to see the cuteness up close, not from afar!"

"Well, I suppose that's fine." All of them were so desperate. She worried about any work they should be doing right now, but since they were practically begging her, she decided to oblige. She took out the bracelet, put it on, and transformed into a white cat.

"M-May I pet you?"

"Oh, sure. But not too rough, okay?"

Ruri agreed to let them touch her, bringing a delighted smile to the dragonkin's face. The dragonkin controlled the strength of their grip, delicately stroking Ruri's head in utter joy.

"Aah, this soft and cuddly sensation can't be beat."

"Hey, I'm next. Me!"

"And I'm next after the both of you."

Before long, a line had formed in order to admire Ruri. She preferred things being more casual, but an extreme lack of restraint might be an issue. Every last one of them viewed Ruri not as a Beloved, but as a house cat. However, they were all so thrilled that she gave in and allowed them to rub their hands all over her head. She had to wonder why they were so shy if they liked fluffy creatures this much. Then again, maybe it was their shyness spurring them on to get closer.

Once they finished petting Ruri, all of the dragonkin went back to work with satisfied smiles on their faces, leaving a very exhausted Ruri behind. The spirits around her petted her tired head and consoled her.

"You sure are popular, Ruri."

"Pet, pet~"

"Good job~"

"Whew, it's finally over..." Ruri said, pawing her way to Jade's office still in cat form. Like normal, she went in by herself, while Kotaro remained outside.

Ever since the Church of God's Light had been apprehended, Kotaro had loosened his guard a few degrees. Before, he was so on edge that he wouldn't even let an ant come close to Ruri, but now he had mellowed out. Not enough to take away the barrier that was still affixed around her, but mellow all the same.

Ruri jumped up in Jade's lap. Despite returning to the kingdom just today, he was scanning over documents that had apparently piled up in his absence. Jade accepted it like it was the norm and petted Ruri's tiny head as she curled up on his lap. This once ordinary part of her daily life felt much more special after her stint away, making her realize that she was finally back to her peaceful existence. Whenever she thought about the business with the dragonheart, she had the urge to roll around on the floor in distress, but for now, she simply closed her eyes and put it out of her mind.

The Ghost Dwelling in a Pocket Space

It had already been a few days since Ruri and her party returned from the Nation of the Beast King. In the renovated Sector One, everyone's lives started to return to how they once were.

As Jade worked away in his completely refurbished office, the sound of rushing footsteps echoed outside in the hall. The sounds got closer and closer, reaching the front of the office before long. Then, without so much as a knock, someone flung the door open.

"We have a situation, Your Majesty!"

"You're causing a racket, Agate," Jade warned. He couldn't help but wonder about Agate's youthful exuberance in spite of his age. In fact, it almost felt as though he wasn't growing weak from aging, but *powering up* instead. He was especially gung ho when it came time to talk about Jade marrying, where he would display an unbelievable amount of gusto.

Jade simply had to reproach Agate for his lack of manners, entering the royal office without so much as knocking, but the next words out of the old man's mouth made Jade's pen stop in place.

"My apologies. However, there are more pressing issues. Master Quartz has made his return!"

Jade's eyes opened wide. "Master Quartz? Are you sure?!"

"Indeed I am. He landed on the terrace just a moment ago and Euclase is seeing to him right now—Ah, wait, Your Majesty!"

Jade rushed out of the room before Agate had a chance to finish his sentence. People watched in bewilderment as he stormed through the halls, but he darted past all of them, unfazed.

A crowd had formed at the terrace, and at its center was the man Agate had mentioned. He was exchanging banter with Euclase. Seeing this, joy surfaced on Jade's face.

"Master Quartz!" Jade called.

Hearing his name, the man turned and smiled broadly. "Hey there, Jade. Been a while."

A tinge of disappointment crossed over Jade's otherwise happy expression. "'Hey there, been a while,' nothing, Master Quartz. Where have you been wandering about for the past few decades? You could have *at least* written just one letter. Everyone has been worried about you," Jade said, using this chance to launch his complaints.

However, instead of offering an answer, Quartz gave a hearty laugh in reply. "Ha ha! Now, now. I'm back now, so that's all that matters. All that aside, I heard a Beloved showed up here."

"Indeed, one has."

"In my travels across the lands, you see, I happened to overhear news of the Beloved, so I hurried back here."

"You've come back to meet Ruri? But you never came back all this time for any other reason," Jade said, his eyes filled with dissatisfaction. He had never even received a single letter.

"Don't get all pouty at me, now. This is a huge event, isn't it? I felt inclined to get a look at them."

"In any case, let us go to my room. I'd like to sit down and talk," Jade suggested.

"Yes, let's do that."

Ruri had gone to Lydia's and was helping her erase rooms without owners. As new rooms were spawning one after another, so too were rooms with owners lost to time. Each room either signified a new life brought into the world or a new life taken from it. Since pocket spaces could only be opened by their owners, they had no choice but to erase what lay inside along with the room, which was why they took out anything useful first.

Ruri was averse to this at first, but there was no way to pass items along to the deceased's families since you couldn't figure out what belonged to who. And just erasing the possessions from existence seemed like a waste. Those facts gave Ruri a change of heart. She would check the rooms and search for anything that seemed useful. Anything she needed, she would bring back to her own pocket space. However, finding useful items wasn't the easiest task in the world.

"Too bad. This room doesn't seem to have anything," Ruri said, closing the door to a room after peeking in and seeing that it was practically empty.

Many people who realized they were on death's door would bestow their belongings to others while still alive. After all, a pocket space could only be opened by the owner themselves. That meant there were a lot of rooms that were virtually empty. At the same time, there was no small extent of those who died without bestowing anything. Ruri would search through those rooms, and once she was done, she would have Lydia erase them.

"Not much worthwhile today, huh, Lydia?"

"*Yes, well, these days do happen. There are many rooms, after all.*"

"Rats, here I was hoping to sell anything that looked valuable to help fund my hot spring too."

Ruri had pledged to build a hot spring once she got back to the Nation of the Dragon King since having an earth, water, and fire spirit made that possible. However, it would cost money to acquire the land and build the facilities for the spring. The realistic nature of her problem saddened her.

"*Your hot springs are one thing, but isn't there something more pressing you should be caring about, Ruri?*" Lydia asked.

"What do you mean?" Ruri asked.

"*I mean that. The dragonheart,*" Lydia replied, pointing at the necklace dangling from Ruri's neck. It was a scale the same shade of green as Jade's eyes.

Jade's kind eyes popped into Ruri's mind, sending her heart aflutter.

"*That should take priority over the springs. You haven't given him an answer yet, correct?*" Lydia asked, as Ruri's romance was a point of interest for her.

"No. I mean, I know you're right, but…" Ruri stammered, acting indecisive.

"*Oh my,*" Lydia said, putting her hand on her cheek and cocking her head. "*Did you plan on turning him down, by any chance?*"

Ruri had never been asked that question in such a straightforward manner before, and she couldn't hide her unrest.

"N-No, that wasn't the plan. It's just…"

"*Then why not answer him already?*" Lydia nonchalantly suggested. Things weren't that simple, however.

Ruri's face was painted in distress. "Uuuugh~! I know I should. I know I should, but…!" Ruri groaned, clutching her head.

She realized she was delaying the inevitable. She had been so very careful not to sway any conversation in that direction that it oftentimes made things awkward. Jade was bound to suspect something sooner or later. No, in fact, he probably already did.

"Listen, I just don't know how to break the ice. And it's not like he confessed to me in the first place; he just gave me the dragonheart. He might end up thinking I'm being too self-conscious…"

"*What are you talking about? Giving someone a dragonheart is the biggest form of confession for dragonkin.*"

"Hmm…" She had been told that many times in the past by both Celestine and Rin, but to Ruri, who was raised in a world without dragonkin, it was more important to convey things of this nature in words. Even if told via an item, it wouldn't click because the recipient wouldn't have any idea of how valuable that item was, obscuring the point. Knowing that any possible mistake in judgment would bring shame made it hard to tread forward.

However, Rin told her up and down that a dragonheart held great importance, so Ruri knew. She knew, but…

"Gaaaah, what should I dooo?! Lydia!"

"*Asking me won't get you anywhere. It's all on you whether you accept his feelings or not.*"

"Ugh~"

"*Do you even like the king in the first place?*"

"Well, um…"

"*You should start from there, shouldn't you?*"

She did like Jade. Or rather, it would be strange if she didn't have feelings for him considering how much he doted on her. Things would be fine if he had any noticeable bad qualities, but he was personable, very handsome, a king, and especially kind to her. Jade was someone with great status, fame, looks, and personality.

Knowing that someone like that might be in love with her, even if someone else were to show up, she would immediately compare them to Jade. She found Jade's presence extremely comfortable, but she couldn't say for sure whether it was simply because their mana wavelengths were compatible.

Ruri pondered for a while and then answered, "Okay, I'll think about it after I make my hot springs." She had decided to delay it for the time being.

Lydia threw her an exasperated look. Ruri tried not to glance her way as she resumed sorting the rooms.

"*That's called 'escapism,' you know.*"

Ruri pretended not to hear her as she absorbed herself in sorting through the rooms as a means to run from her problems. That was when she heard a sound from out of nowhere, causing her to stop what she was doing.

"A song?"

It wasn't just any sound—it had a melody. These faint notes were coming from a female voice, producing a tender yet forlorn song that traveled through Ruri's ears. However, the only ones here were Ruri and Lydia, neither of whom were speaking.

Could it have been her imagination? This was a place where only the Spirit of Time, Lydia, and her contract-bearer, Ruri, could enter. There shouldn't be anyone else around. Ruri looked back to what she was working on, but she started to hear the song once again.

As if being tempted, she started walking in search of the source. "Here?" she asked, her search leading her inside a dark room that didn't have an owner. Curious if anyone was actually inside, she reached for the door—but that was when it happened.

"*Ruri, don't!*"

Just as Ruri was about to open the door, Lydia stood in front of it to stop her.

Ruri was perplexed by her frantic display. "What's the matter, Lydia? This is a song, right? Is someone here?" she asked, even though that shouldn't be. Not only had she never heard of anyone else being in this pocket space, she knew extended periods of time here affected one's psyche. It wasn't an ideal place to sing a ditty without a care in the world.

Nevertheless, it was there. Ruri listened to the beautiful song in vacant admiration.

"That is the singing of the ghost that dwells in this room, so you should by no means open it."

"G-G-Ghost?!" stammered Ruri. She immediately backed away from the door. There were two things Ruri absolutely hated—bugs and *ghosts*.

"The owner of this pocket space died several decades ago, but after some time, I started to hear a voice coming from the vacant room. I initially thought the owner put a living person inside or something of the sort before their death, but I didn't feel the presence of a living being. I became curious, so I peeked inside. And that's when I saw it."

"S-Saw what?" Ruri questioned. Lydia's creepy tone coupled with her serious expression caused Ruri to gulp loudly.

"The transparent form of a woman!"

"There's no twist to this, right? Like it being a spirit all along?"

"No twist. No other spirits aside from myself can enter here. It was terrifying. So since then, I've made this room off-limits."

"Can't you deal with it?"

"Deal with it how?"

"Like exorcising it or something?" Ruri suggested. Spirits filled the role of God in this world, so it didn't seem like a stretch to think they could purify or exorcise a soul. "Oh, or couldn't you just get rid of it, room and all?"

Lydia, however, strongly disapproved. *"No way. What would happen if I got haunted as a result?"*

How could a *spirit* be afraid of a *ghost*?

As the two conversed, the song continued. Ruri was afraid of ghosts, but the music was beautiful. The pleasant-sounding and memorable melody comforted her. She listened to the song, forgetting all about her fears. It even compelled her to start singing the same song herself.

According to Lydia, the ghost had been staying here over the course of decades. Ruri wondered what ran through her mind in her many years of being here. At the very least, she couldn't imagine someone with such a beautiful singing voice would be spiteful and haunt others.

The Previous Dragon King

Ruri returned from Lydia's domain and headed off to see Jade. She was anxious about meeting him face-to-face, but it was to gain permission to go into the city. She peeked inside of his office, where he usually was, but he was nowhere to be found. She searched all around until she managed to find him in his personal quarters.

"Oh, so this is where you were, Jade-sama."

"Ah, Ruri. Just in time. I was just about to send for you," Jade said, his cheeks pulling up into a tender smile.

His expression seemed much sweeter than usual, but perhaps her newfound knowledge about the meaning behind the dragonheart she'd received influenced her perception. She still wasn't prepared to accept that meaning at face value, though. Although her heart was in disarray, she pretended to be none the wiser.

"What for?" Ruri asked, cocking her head. Then she noticed an unfamiliar man sitting across from Jade. His hair was somewhere between silver and white, shoulder-length and glistening, and his eyes were a deep purple that practically sucked you in. The coloring of both only emphasized his almost inhuman beauty.

(*Holy cow, he's so handsome. Neck and neck with Jade-sama, in fact. Who is he?*)

He made eye contact, and the corners of his mouth rose into a sweet, soft smile—like an angel. Ruri bowed her head slightly, in lieu of a verbal response, as her heart began racing. The man rose from his seat, took her hand, and gently kissed the back of it.

"A pleasure to meet you. Your name is Ruri? Might you be the Beloved?"

Ruri silently nodded, cheeks flushed. She was completely taken in by the man before her. Jade, on the other hand, grimaced in displeasure and rose from his chair, yelling, "Master Quartz!"

Despite Jade's tone, the man paid him no mind and smiled playfully. "Oh, come now. Where's the harm? It's not as if she's your mate, right?" he said, hitting the nail on the head and silencing Jade. Jade was determined to put up a fight regardless and profusely wiped the back of Ruri's hand.

The man watched Jade in great delight, nodding to himself as if he comprehended something. "I see. I see. You've finally found yourself someone good, haven't you, Jade? Oh, is that thing around Ruri's neck a dragonheart? Boy, it was just the other day you were yea high, but look at you now—all grown up."

"'Yea high'? And when was that, pray tell?" Jade quipped.

Wanting to skirt around the topic of the dragonheart, Ruri quickly interjected, "U-Um, excuse me! Sir, who might you be?"

Both of them looked her way at the same time.

"Yes, I still haven't properly introduced myself. I am Quartz. It's a pleasure," Quartz said, presenting his hand and flashing an angelic smile charming enough to captivate all the ladies of the world.

Ruri took his hand out of instinct. She assumed he was a dragonkin based on his handsome features, but the only thing she knew was that and his name. It wasn't until Jade elaborated further that Ruri's eyes went wide in surprise.

"Master Quartz was the Dragon King before me," Jade said.

"Huh? He is a *Dragon King*?!" Ruri blurted.

"Former," Quartz corrected. "I left the Nation of the Dragon King for quite some time, but I came back once I heard news of a Beloved. And it seems that doing so has proved unexpectedly insightful. I actually planned on leaving again once I met you, but I think I'll stay around for a while longer instead."

"Oh, really?!" Jade asked, looking extremely happy. There was an innocent charm to his joy, almost like a puppy fawning over its owner. It seemed he was being more straightforward with his emotions than usual. Perhaps that was just how much Quartz meant to Jade. Nevertheless, Ruri recognized this slight change in Jade's attitude. In fact, it vaguely reminded her of a certain someone.

"Really. I have a feeling that things might get amusing," Quartz said, bouncing his eyes from Ruri to Jade with a playful wink. "Speaking of which, didn't you come here for some specific reason? You were looking for Jade, weren't you?"

"Oh, right! I almost forgot. I wanted to get permission to go out into the city."

"For shopping?" Jade asked.

"Yes, *technically* shopping. I plan on buying some land to build my hot spring."

Realizing that Ruri's plans weren't just empty talk and she was actually going to go through with it, a look of exhaustion crossed Jade's face. "So, you were serious about that, huh?"

"Of course I'm serious! I'm going to popularize hot springs in the Nation of the Dragon King!"

"Hot Springs, eh?" Quartz said. "I've taken a dip in the ones in the Nation of the Beast King. They're mighty fine. Makes you feel great. But is there a spring in the Nation of the Dragon King?"

Quartz was the first dragonkin to show a positive reaction, and it boosted Ruri's excitement level. She was glad to have gained the backing of a like-minded individual. After all, the Nation of the Dragon King's people wouldn't understand the wonders of hot springs even if she explained it to them. They'd always reply that it was easier to clean themselves with magic. Although Ruri worried whether a nation like this would be receptive to hot springs, she was sure there were people who would be charmed by them like Quartz.

"I can apparently make it happen with the power of the spirits. I'd like to build it in the best spot in town so everyone can use it," Ruri explained.

Unable to fully comprehend the appeal, Jade remained totally indifferent. "Well, the idea has merits and I don't necessarily mind, but I'm assigning security to you if you're going into town." Even with Kotaro's barrier in place, Jade needed to make sure she didn't walk around by herself willy-nilly.

Ruri didn't protest; she knew this would be a given. "In that case, maybe I should ask Joshua." Since Joshua wasn't really a stickler for following security to the letter, she knew she could enjoy herself without feeling cramped.

Jade, however, opposed the idea. "No, Joshua can't."

"Why is that?"

"He's currently on a different assignment, meaning he's not in the Nation of the Dragon King at the moment. If you're going to pick, I'd suggest Ewan since Finn is most likely tied up with preparations for the tournament."

"Oh, Joshua's not here?" Despite all that pleading for some time off, Joshua was already out on a different task. Ruri could just picture him now, down in the dumps after throwing a fit over his predicament. Despite all his quibbling, he ultimately couldn't get out of work. Poor guy couldn't catch a break.

CHAPTER 3: THE PREVIOUS DRAGON KING

"Then I will ask Ewan," said Ruri.

"Yes, do so," said Jade.

"If you get the spring up, let me know," Quartz added. "I'll come take a dip."

"Yes, sir," Ruri replied. Then she left the room and headed toward Sector Five to meet Ewan.

Passions were running higher than usual at the Sector Five training grounds. It *wasn't* Ruri's imagination either; there was definitely more blood flying through the air than usual. She had gotten used to the sight of the dragonkin training, but even she felt the urge to about-face and leave. Everyone was probably getting fired up over the forthcoming tournament.

Ruri scanned the training grounds until she found Ewan and walked over to him.

"Ewan, I have a favor to ask. Do you mind?"

"What? I'm busy here," Ewan snipped.

"Well, you sure don't look it," Ruri replied. Ewan didn't seem to be doing anything aside from looking on as the soldiers trained. To be frank, he looked totally free.

"I'm supervising. These guys are getting way too riled up with the tournament around the corner. They're likely to destroy the castle if they go out of control, so someone has to be here to jump in and stop them."

"Ah, that makes sense," Ruri said. The carnage unfolding throughout the grounds convinced her of the merit in his role.

"So, what's this 'favor'?" Ewan asked.

"I want to go into town. Jade-sama said I could as long as I have security, so I'd like it if you came along."

"Why don't you ask Joshua or someone else?"

"He's out at the moment. Apparently, he's on assignment."

"He's always coming and going, huh? Where's he off to this time?"

"Not sure," Ruri said. She had only been told that he was out.

That was when Finn, who was also supervising the training grounds, joined the conversation. "If you're talking about Joshua, then he went to Yadacain."

"Yadacain?"

Ewan explained, "It's the small island nation across the sea from the Nation of the Dragon King. It's ruled by *witches*—users of *sorcery* passed through the ages. It's also a nation forsaken by the spirits—at least, by all accounts, that is."

The ominous words sprinkled throughout Ewan's explanation caught Ruri's attention. "What do you mean 'a nation forsaken by the spirits'?"

"I'm sure you remember the Spirit Slayer magic," Finn said. "The witches of Yadacain created it. The Spirit Slayer wiped out so many spirits that the world deemed it taboo, but the witches of Yadacain persisted in using it. Therefore, spirits stopped going near Yadacain, and it's now known as a nation forsaken by the spirits."

Spirit Slayer—the magic that tormented Ruri up till now—and the witches who crafted it... Only one thing popped into Ruri's mind.

"Hey, do the witches and the Spirit Slayer have any connection with the Church of God's Light?"

Finn's face tensed as he replied, "That I do not know. However, His Majesty suspects there is some sort of connection with Yadacain, hence why Joshua has gone off to investigate."

Joshua must have been entrusted with investigating Yadacain because he had firsthand knowledge of the incident in the Nation of the Beast King.

"But brother, will Joshua be all right?" asked Ewan. "I doubt he'll be able to do much espionage in Yadacain."

"What do you mean?" Ruri asked.

Ewan elaborated, "In the past, we had diplomatic relations with Yadacain. But ever since they began using Spirit Slayer and closed off their nation, we've ceased all interaction with them and severed our ties. We've sent a few of our intelligence operatives into Yadacain, but they've all complained about not being able to gather much information. Their people are extremely wary toward strangers—a possible result of prolonged isolation. That's why we barely know anything about Yadacain as it is."

"Doesn't that mean they'll suspect something if they find Joshua?" Ruri asked. "He's an outsider to them, so that can't be all right, can it? What if something bad happens to him?"

Joshua would most likely be able to manage considering who he was, but that wasn't absolutely certain. That nation produced Spirit Slayer magic, making them a dangerous threat—even more so given their possible ties with the Church of God's Light. The fact that no one had any idea what the nation was like due to the sparsity of information also spurred concerns.

"It will be all right. Joshua is an excellent intelligence operative. He'll be coming home looking just as aloof as usual in no time," Finn said, reassuringly patting Ruri on the head. "So, you'll be going into town, yes? Ewan, keep a good eye on Ruri."

"Of course, brother. No one will lay a finger on her with me around!"

"Right, I'm counting on you."

Ruri noticed that Ewan, brother complex extraordinaire, practically wagged a nonexistent tail in joy. She pondered over the sense of déjà vu she got from looking at Ewan's expression until she placed it—she had seen that *exact* same face not even a moment ago.

"Oh, it's Jade-sama."

"What's the deal with you? What about His Majesty?" Ewan asked.

"Nothing. It's just that I met the former Dragon King, Quartz-sama, a moment ago. The reaction Jade-sama had with him resembles you when you interact with Finn-san," Ruri explained, noting that their absolute faith in the person they admired came across in their attitudes to an egregious degree.

"The previous Dragon King? I heard he just made his return. I've never met him before, though."

Ewan didn't seem to be very familiar with Quartz. Finn, however, flashed a wry grin. "His Majesty is like Ewan, is he? I suppose that comes with the territory. Master Quartz is to His Majesty as I am to Ewan. Due to the strength of his mana, His Majesty wasn't adept at controlling his power. But since controlling mana is Master Quartz's forte, he essentially took care of His Majesty. Because of that, His Majesty adores Master Quartz like an older brother."

"Oh wow…" Ruri said, now comprehending the situation.

Jade would probably grimace to be compared to someone with such extreme brotherly adoration like Ewan, but the way he looked at Quartz indeed fit the bill. He wasn't as blatant as Ewan by any means, but it was still apparent.

"If Quartz-sama is the former Dragon King and Jade-sama is the current one, then that means Jade-sama beat Quartz-sama in the tournament, right?" Ruri asked, thinking about how she would have liked to see that fight.

However, Finn denied her assumption, replying, "No, the two never fought."

"But the winner becomes the next Dragon King, don't they? Jade-sama said that a Dragon King's entry is their duty."

Finn frowned, but Ewan didn't notice it and went on to explain, "His Former Majesty didn't have a complete reign. In other words, he abdicated the throne without ever entering the tournament. So the two never faced each other in battle, and His Majesty won the tournament, becoming the next Dragon King. Apparently, His Former Majesty then left the nation and went to parts unknown until now."

"Why did he abdicate the throne?" Ruri asked.

"Who knows? That was before I started working in the castle. Brother might know, though," Ewan said, looking over at Finn. That was when he finally noticed the displeased expression on his brother's face. "Brother?"

"Well, let's just say things were complicated with Master Quartz. Very complicated."

Both Ruri and Ewan looked at each other in confusion. However, suspecting that something had happened, and that Finn would rather not speak about it, they decided they shouldn't pry any further and both ended up keeping their mouths shut.

4 Building a Hot Spring

Ruri sorted through the pocket space rooms with Lydia. She wanted to scrounge up the costs for building her hot springs, but she wasn't able to come up with anything worthwhile. The rooms she searched didn't really yield much. That being the case, she would need to sell some of the items in her own space.

She had the option of selling the valuable old money from the First Dragon King's era to Euclase, but she wasn't really fond of that idea. She wanted to avoid anything related to the First Dragon King, Weidt—for Lydia's sake. Lydia had said she didn't mind if Ruri used them, but Ruri could tell from Lydia's words that she still held Weidt dear even to this day. Her relationship didn't seem like the type others could encroach on. It wasn't one of furious romantic attachment, but one of trust, respect, and affection. Given that, Ruri found it unlikely that Lydia would ever forget Weidt, now or forever. Part of her even felt a little envious—considering herself and Jade. She just couldn't bring herself to tamper with any mementos of him.

There was a wealth of items unrelated to Weidt, but she couldn't discern what was worth money on her own. While the quickest way to solve that problem would be to bring a merchant into the pocket space, that wasn't feasible. As such, she racked her brain over which item to sell.

Actually, there were definitely some things that clearly looked like they'd fetch a high price, but there were also items embossed with the emblems and family crests of other nations.

She was worried the owner's descendants would show up if she tried to sell any of them. Not to mention, if anyone asked her where she got her merchandise, she couldn't very well tell them she took it from other people's rooms.

Although she had many paintings, furnishings, and pieces of jewelry with no distinguishable owner, she'd probably need a sizable sum of money to purchase land in the center of the capital. She would have to sell off a considerable amount of these wares to afford that. Selling off one or two probably wouldn't raise suspicions, but if a Beloved started selling valuable items in bulk, then it would naturally raise doubts as to where she got such a huge collection in the first place—and give rise to some unsavory rumors. Even with that spear she sold when she arrived in the capital, people questioned where she obtained it. She managed to smooth things over by saying it was a spirit's mischief, but that same excuse wouldn't work forever.

Perhaps she could sell them via Euclase? Or perhaps she could travel to other nations to sell them? She probably wouldn't be found out that way.

Ruri folded her arms and considered her options. Lydia saw this and spoke up.

"You're free to do as you please with what I gave you, but if it bothers you that much regardless, why not ask Chi for help?"

"Why Chi?"

"Chi is the Spirit of Earth. He can produce a wealth of gemstones. All you would have to do is sell them off."

Chi had once unearthed a bevy of gemstones because he was bored. Those would definitely sell for a high price.

"Oh, that is an option. Ah, but...no, something about it feels like cheating," Ruri said. It didn't feel right; it was practically like begging Chi for money.

41

"*Where's the harm? Weidt did it all the time. Said he didn't have the capital to build a nation otherwise. In fact, he had Chi create them without any semblance of the reserve you show, Ruri, so I don't think you'll hurt his feelings by asking either.*"

"The First Dragon King did that…?"

His philosophy was to use whatever was usable. Quite the *easygoing* attitude, for lack of a better word. Ruri would've loved a chance to talk to him and see what kind of person he actually was.

"*I'll tell Chi, so why not go and give it a shot?*" Lydia suggested.

"Right, okay. I'll do just that. Thank you, Lydia."

Ruri exited the pocket space and found the spirits assembled as if they'd been waiting for her this entire time.

Ruri asked, "Do you guys know where Chi is right now?"

"*Hmm, I think in the garden!*" one replied.

"*He's spinning round and round in the garden!*" another added.

"'Round and round'?"

Chi was prone to some very bizarre behavior, but Ruri had to wonder what he was doing from that description. Thinking he might've heard the situation from Lydia and was crafting gemstones, Ruri rushed to the garden. There, Chi was indeed spinning around in circles, but she also spotted Kotaro and Heat there as well.

"What are you three doing?" she asked.

"*Oh, hey, that you, Ruri? Ol' Fire here said he wanted some gemstones, so here I am.*"

"You too, Heat-sama?" She didn't know what use a spirit like Heat would have with gemstones. It was especially odd considering he had no interest in anything like that.

Once Chi stopped spinning, Heat gave an order to Kotaro. "All right, Wind, now dig!"

"*Right,*" Kotaro replied.

Ruri thought that *Heat* should've been the one digging them up since *he* wanted them, but she kept that to herself.

Kotaro proceeded to dig with his front legs like a puppy in the park, unearthing scores of glittering gemstones. Spotting the one that glittered the most, Heat picked it up and smirked in satisfaction.

"Heat-sama, what do you plan to do with those gemstones?"

"I'm about to go on a date. A gift is necessary for a beautiful woman."

"Ah, right…" It seemed Heat was enjoying life in the Nation of the Dragon King. Not even a few days had passed and he'd already found himself a girl to date. Ruri wanted to ask whatever happened to Euclase.

After getting what he came for, Heat happily sauntered off.

"Ruri, you need some too, right? Lydia filled me in. I made a bigger batch, so you can take whatever you like. If it's not enough, just let me know."

"Thank you, Chi," Ruri said before graciously picking up the gems.

Knowing that she would need Euclase and their vast knowledge of things of this nature, Ruri brought the gemstones over to them in order to find out their worth. Euclase's eyes lit up when they saw the gemstones of various shapes and sizes. Then Euclase checked their quality like a pro appraiser.

Once Euclase told her that she had enough to buy a plot of land in the center of the capital, they started separating out the bigger stones. By Euclase's account, what they pulled aside would be more than enough if sold. That left the smaller gemstones—relatively small, at least. They were still big enough to make into jewelry or accessories.

As she thought of the possibilities, Agate and the other elders abruptly entered the room. It seemed they'd overheard their conversation because they came asking if they could have the remaining gems. Since she had no real plans to use them, Ruri gave them to the elders, much to their great delight.

When she asked whether they would make them into jewelry for someone, all of them cryptically grinned at her. They smiled and said it would be a surprise for later, but it was clear they were up to something.

While Ruri was curious as to what they'd use the stones for, she decided she shouldn't delve any deeper than she already had. However, it seemed Euclase had a hunch as to what they had in store.

Gemstones in hand, Ruri set out for the city with Ewan and several other soldiers. Jade hadn't felt comfortable sending Ewan on his own to protect Ruri, so he'd sent soldiers as well. He did this because while Ruri usually disguised herself before going into town, she'd decided not to hide her rare platinum blond hair and entourage of spirits—essentially showing people she was a Beloved. It was a good way to stir up a commotion, but that seemed to be the point behind Ruri's actions. It would be good publicity if people knew that a Beloved was out and about with a specific purpose in mind. Essentially, she was planning to let word of a Beloved-built hot spring spread before its grand opening in order to attract potential patrons.

"What's the first stop?" Ewan asked.

"First up is a realtor!" Ruri replied, absolutely brimming with excitement. Since she had a limited knowledge of businesses in the capital, she asked Ewan and her soldier accompaniment to help her. They led her to a realtor that managed many of the properties in the capital.

"Well, this is a delight. Greetings and welcome. It is an honor to have the great Lady Beloved at our humble establishment. What kind of property might you be looking for?"

The real estate agent had looked confused and shocked that a Beloved had entered the shop, but as soon as he realized he was in the presence of an honored guest, he fixed his expression. Professionalism was this business's middle name; it made sense why Ewan and the others had recommended it.

"I'd like a large plot of land, somewhere in the middle of the capital, with as much traffic as possible."

"Are you seeking a secondary residence?"

"No, I'm trying to build a hot spring."

"A hot spring, you say, milady?" the real estate agent repeated, bewildered. His bafflement was understandable since the Nation of the Dragon King had no hot spring source. He would have never suspected that Ruri planned on building the spring from the ground up—source and all.

"Yes, a hot spring. I want to build a public bathhouse similar to the springs in the Nation of the Beast King, so that everyone can enjoy it. Not only that, but I was hoping to include some recreational facilities as well," Ruri explained. She basically wanted to build a hot spring amusement park.

After hearing her request, the agent went into the back, brought out a stack of papers with properties, and began looking for appropriate locations.

"Let's see. This is a tad tiny. This is farther from the center of the capital. And this one is..." The agent trailed off. After some scrounging, he returned with a few papers from the stack. "These are three properties I can show you. Shall we go and see them now?"

"Yes, if you'd be so kind."

With that, they went off to the first property. It was located in the heart of the capital and had the best flow of traffic. It was a perfect plot to build on. There was only one issue; there was barely any space to be had. She could probably build an average-sized bathhouse, but nothing like the grandiose facility Ruri had in mind. The second site was pretty far from the center of the capital, but it was wide enough to comfortably build the amusement park Ruri envisioned. The issue here? There was little traffic. The third site was closer to the capital than the second and had a healthy traffic flow, but it was even smaller than the first site.

"Hmm..." Ruri hummed after looking at all three properties. It seemed that things weren't going to go exactly how she planned after all. She would have to decide whether to prioritize space or traffic.

The most important point was that cramped wasn't going to cut it. This world was oppressively devoid of many forms of amusement, so Ruri's desire to construct an amusement park outweighed the spring itself. The plot would need to be a decent size in order to construct a facility like that.

This requirement made it a toss-up between the second and third properties. In terms of space, the second won, but there was already a lavish manor on the plot and she'd have to demolish it in order to build her springs. It would be a waste of a perfectly fine building. On the other hand, while the third was a little tinier than she'd hoped for, it was an empty lot more conducive to new construction.

"Okay, I've made up my mind! I'll go with the third," Ruri said decidedly.

"Thank you very much. In that case, I shall get the contract paperwork for you."

After Ruri signed the papers, it was time to actually pay. However, this property was what you'd expect out of land in the heart of the capital. It was as expensive as it was expansive.

Ruri presented the agent with a pouch stuffed with gemstones. She laid aside enough to pay with, but she still had plenty of the stones Chi gave her. She planned to do some shopping with the rest afterward.

"Is this enough? If you need currency instead, I can always go and get them exchanged."

The agent peeked into the pouch and his eyes widened. "If I might be so brazen to ask, wherever did you find such large gemstones?"

Ruri debated on how to reply, but she ultimately decided to give him a vague answer. If she simply told the agent that she had Chi make them for her, it might encourage people to kidnap Chi in the future. Not that Chi would be easy to kidnap, but she *was* afraid of him willfully allowing it because it was "interesting."

Ruri smiled sweetly and said, "A blessing of the spirits." Her answer seemed to satisfy the agent, more or less. "Is it not enough?"

"No, with the added value of their origin, this is *more* than enough, I assure you. No need to have them exchanged. This will be sufficient payment."

And just like that, Ruri successfully acquired her land. However, this was only the groundwork. Things had only just begun.

Ruri's next stop was a builder's office. She could certainly create a building via magic, but she planned on constructing a *big* building. To craft material with magic required an abundance of imagination.

It was spirit magic—telling a spirit your vision of a material item and invoking their magic. Ruri could manage to build a small shed, but she didn't have the imagination needed to craft something big and wide. In order to make something more detailed, she decided it would be more reliable to draft out blueprints and get professionals to do the building for her.

As far as the type of contractors, she figured the end result would be more satisfactory if she hired people who had experience with hot springs. After she made that clear to Ewan, he led her to an office run by the Nation of the Beast King.

Once she explained that she wanted to build a hot spring, the contractor trembled in delight. "I can't believe it! A hot spring in this nation?! This is like a dream come true. Aah, when I came here, I was taken aback by the fact that not only do they not have hot springs, but they didn't *bathe* at all. I built a bath in my own house since there was no natural spring to be had, but I was sad no one appreciated the value of soaking your body in hot water. Indeed, indeed, if I can bathe in a spring without returning to my homeland, I will dedicate all I can toward your cause, Lady Beloved. If you would inform me first when it is completed, I will also assist you with spreading the good word."

He had probably been starved for a hot spring this entire time. His mouth was running full blast and showed no signs of stopping. Then again, if he loved hot springs this much, then he would most likely do a thorough job of designing the building.

The manager started right away, drafting Ruri's design per her specifications and excitingly discussing what the facility should have.

"It has to have an outdoor bedrock bath," Ruri added. "Also, I was thinking about planting some trees and having an open-air bath where you sit in nature…"

"That is superb. In that case, we could have a bathtub made out of trees situated here."

Ruri burned with an unparalleled passion for constructing a hot spring, and the designer pined for hot springs to bathe in. Ideas that greatly reflected their own tastes came out of both of them one after another.

Standing in the back, Ewan and the soldiers watched on in confusion, but Ruri was overcome with a sense of accomplishment.

"Well then, it will take about a week's time to take these requests and make a proper blueprint out of them. I will be sure to create something that will satisfy you, indeed."

"Thank you. I look forward to it."

They had such a rousing planning session that it had already gotten dark. Promising that she would be back in a week, Ruri and her party decided to go back to the castle for the day.

5 Groveling

After a week had passed, Ruri went to the builder's office to check the blueprints as agreed. She saw the plans were finished and everything had been carried out to her liking. In fact, that was an understatement. The designer's enthusiasm oozed out of every single intricate detail. Honestly speaking, the results exceeded her initial expectations. With things taking shape as they were, reality started to kick in and Ruri became even more excited than before.

With a solemn pledge to see this plan to completion, the builder began construction immediately. Ruri left the actual building to the pros; she only came to check on the progress from time to time. Still, there was one big issue she needed to handle in order to complete the hot spring—the hot spring itself. You certainly couldn't bathe in hot water if there was none to be had. In order to build the springs, she needed the power of water, earth, and fire spirits. For water, there was Rin. For earth, she had Chi. And for fire…

Apparently, any fire spirit would do but in order to match the power of supreme-level spirits like Rin and Chi, it was more convenient to ask another supreme-level spirit. That was why Ruri reluctantly went to visit Heat, who was in his personal room in Sector One. Normally, he'd be walking around the castle talking to girls he passed by. Now that he knew his penguin form was popular among the dragonkin ladies, he would parade around for no real reason other than to enjoy the enamored cries of the women around him.

CHAPTER 5: GROVELING

Ruri figured Heat would be enjoying some quiet time in his quarters around now. However, contrary to her belief, he had brought several women back to his room and made them wait on him and serve him wine.

Whether he was in the Nation of the Beast King or Dragon King, Heat hadn't cooled down one bit. While Ruri wanted to lay into him for being a womanizing cad, she needed his powers to help build the spring, so she tried to walk on eggshells. She went up to Heat, sat on her knees, and put both her hands in front of her. She was literally groveling before him.

"What is the big idea here, brat?" Heat asked.

"Heat-sama, I have a favor to ask of you…"

"Denied," Heat replied in an unapproachable, frigid manner. Nonetheless, Ruri wasn't going to let that discourage her one bit. Her dream was within grasp. She had no time to lose heart.

"The thing is, I want to build a hot spring in the capital. I heard I can build one with the power of water, earth, and fire. Rin and Chi said they'd help out, so all I need now is…a fire spirit. So, I beg of you, please! Help me out!"

"Nope," Heat replied so fast that she barely had time to process it.

Despite her gumption, Ruri felt discouragement rearing its head. Nevertheless, she wasn't giving up—not by a long shot.

Heat paid no attention to Ruri, as if to say he had no further interest in her. He instead turned to the girls and prompted them to pour him liquor.

"Oh, shall I pour that for you?" Ruri offered, reaching for the wine bottle on the table. However, Heat brushed her hand away, not wanting her to touch it. Ruri couldn't help but pout in displeasure.

"*You* pouring it would sour the wine."

"Oh, don't be so mean; why don't you just help out? You're not doing anything anyway, right? Once it's done, I'll let you have the first dip! Come on, come on."

"I'm busy. I don't have the time."

He was busy, all right—busy chasing the tail of any woman who crossed his path.

Ruri decided to try a slightly more forward approach. "Hot springs do wonders for your *beauty*, meaning the *ladies* will surely come flocking. And when they do, they'll most likely be very *grateful* to you for building the spring, Heat-sama. Why, you might even be *more* popular than you are now."

Heat's cheeks rose at that prospect. Ruri felt she was on to something, so she kept it up.

"Say, all of you would like a dip in a hot spring too, wouldn't you?" Ruri asked, involving the girls by Heat's side. They were surprised the ball was suddenly in their court, but they seemed to understand how desperate Ruri was. The astute girls complied, acting as the allies Ruri needed.

"Yes, well, I have never personally soaked in hot water, but I am quite interested now that I've heard its beauty benefits. I would certainly like to experience it," said one girl.

"Will you be making a hot spring? Then again, I shouldn't be surprised. Only one individual is capable of such an outstanding feat, and that is you, O Spirit of Fire. You have my utmost respect," said another.

Yet another added, "Yes, indeed. Very impressive."

Every single girl began to shower Heat with excessive praise. It was clear it was working too, considering his expression. A man harsh toward Ruri yet a pushover for other women—that was Heat in a nutshell.

"I see," Heat muttered, pretending to think before looking back at Ruri. "Well, if you're that sure, then I'll play along and assist you in this endeavor."

(Hell yeah!) Ruri thought, pumping her arms in victory.

"Oh, thank you!" she added, verbalizing her insurmountable gratitude toward the group of ladies, the real MVPs in all of this.

"We will call it even if you were to allow us to touch your paw pads later," said one of the women, holding out her hands and wriggling her fingers in a greedy manner. It seemed they too were fluffy animal lovers. Still, if that would serve as an appropriate thanks, then Ruri was happy to do it.

Heat would go on to assist in her plan, but he wasn't going to make it easy.

"However," he started, clearing his throat, "I have one condition."

"Condition?"

"I want to go to an establishment called Knies."

"Pardon?"

"I said I want to go to Knies. Are you hard of hearing?"

"But where is this 'Knies'?"

"I don't know, but I heard it's a garden of dreams, one that any man would desire to go to at least once. If you take me there, then I will consider building your hot spring."

"Aw, what?" Ruri asked, at a loss for what to do. It wasn't like she could say, "Oh, sure," and just take him there. In fact, she didn't even know *where* or *what* it was he was talking about. What in the world was a *"garden of dreams"* anyway?

"Do any of you know where it is?" Ruri asked the other ladies, but they only responded with bewildered expressions. Ruri was just as confused, but since all she needed to do was take him there, she couldn't very well afford to say no. "Okay, then. I'll gather a little information, so just hold tight."

"Don't leave me waiting too long."

Ruri hurried toward Sector Five, toward Ewan who was in the training grounds.

"Hey, Ewan! Have you ever been to a place called 'Knies'?!"

Ewan did a spit take. Even the soldiers fighting around them stopped what they were doing and stared at Ruri.

"*Excuse me*?! What are you talking about?"

"Never mind that. Have you or not?"

"I have *not*," Ewan refuted, his cheeks flushing red.

Ruri slumped where she stood. "Ugh, you're useless."

"Why are you asking that anyway?!"

"Because Heat-sama said he wants to go. It's part of a deal so he'll help build my hot spring. What kind of business is Knies anyway?"

"You asked me not knowing?"

"Because Heat-sama asked. What kind of place is it?"

Ewan sighed, explaining, "It's a restaurant where you booze around while ladies serve and entertain you. It's the classiest establishment in the capital, and it's members only, so it's not a place where anyone can go. In order to get in, you need a member to introduce you."

Women serving and entertaining? It sounded like some kind of cabaret club.

"It's members only? So, that's why he asked me, then," Ruri surmised. She assumed Heat had already tried to get in but couldn't because he wasn't a member. "Ewan, I want to go there."

"Don't be absurd. I just told you that you have to be a member, didn't I? Well, I'm not, so I *can't* take you there," Ewan replied.

Ruri clicked her tongue. Realizing that Ewan wasn't going to be any help, she tried asking the other soldiers nearby, but none of them gave her a favorable response. That was no wonder. Knies was more of a high-class establishment than she'd thought—definitely not your run-of-the-mill restaurant. Their unreasonably high prices made it impossible for a common soldier to go, nor could they become members in the first place.

"Isn't there anybody?" Ruri asked, but she received no reply.

Right when she considered turning to Agate, with his wealth of life experience, Quartz just so happened to show up.

"Oh, what's everyone gathered around for?" he asked. A nearby soldier whispered an explanation to Quartz. "Oh, you want to go to Knies, Ruri?"

"Less me and more Heat-sama. He's the Spirit of Fire, but he said he wants to go. Quartz-sama, have you ever been to Knies?"

There was no way he'd answer truthfully, or so Ruri thought, but Quartz subverted her expectations and nonchalantly answered, "I have."

"Wait, you have?!" Ruri asked, incredulous.

"Yup, sure have," Quartz said, nodding. "If he wants to go so badly, then should I introduce him? I'm a member, after all."

"Would you? Thank you so much."

"All right, then we'll head there tonight. You should come along, Ruri."

"I appreciate it, sir!"

Ewan and the soldiers listening from the sidelines all wondered if this was a good idea. Knies was in the nightlife district, a place surrounded by brothels and the like. It wasn't a place a young lady should visit.

"Should we stop her?" asked one soldier.

"No. I mean, Master Quartz is accompanying her," replied another.

Another soldier suggested, "Maybe we should report this to His Majesty?"

The worried soldiers all went to Jade to report the news, but Jade replied that Ruri would be fine so long as Quartz was with her.

That night, Quartz took Ruri and Heat to Knies. This certain back street in the capital, said to house brothels, had a completely different atmosphere than the commercial district bustling with people during the day. Ladies were trying to attract patrons into their shops, dressed in outfits skimpy enough to put the Nation of the Beast King's attire to shame.

Ruri had followed along out of sheer curiosity, but she felt out of her element. Knowing she wouldn't last if she were left behind here, she made sure not to get separated from Quartz. Although Heat seemed likely to follow the female hawkers, Ruri got him back on track and they reached a certain elegant-looking building, glittering with dazzling lights.

"This is it. The place I used to go to ages ago and the most high-class establishment in the capital," Quartz noted as he entered the building without a moment's hesitation. Ruri hurried along after him.

"My, my. If it isn't you, Master Quartz! I see you've made your return to the kingdom." They were greeted by an elderly woman, whose eyes lit up as soon as she saw Quartz. She seemed to be an acquaintance of his and welcomed him warmly.

"Hey there, Madam. It's been quite a spell," he said in a friendly manner.

"Indeed it has. It seems you have some guests with you tonight," the madam observed, turning her eyes over to Ruri and Heat behind him. Making eye contact, Ruri gave a formal bow.

"Oh yeah, this is the Beloved and the Spirit of Fire," Quartz added.

"Oh me, oh my. *You* coming here was enough of a shock, but having a couple as distinguished as a Beloved and a spirit visit our establishment is such a joyous occasion. Now then, I cannot very well allow such honored guests to stand around forever. Please, allow me to show you to your seats."

The interior was what you would expect from the classiest establishment in all the capital. Everything from the floor to the ceiling was lavish and luxurious. The furnishings looked exquisite and expensive. For all that, the place wasn't gaudy; it was all refinement.

After Ruri's party arrived at a room, women started to bring them loads of booze and food.

"Please, please. Enjoy yourself," said the madam, filling their glasses to the brim with wine. Then women began to dance in front of them, accompanied by instruments. It was less like a cabaret show and more like a personal geisha performance.

Ruri looked to her side to see Heat wearing a dopey expression and letting the women serve him as he drank. He seemed to be having a ball. She hoped that he'd stay in a good mood. The rest depended on how the girls working here panned out. Living up to this establishment's reputation, the girls carried themselves with style and offered very courteous service.

Ruri figured that Quartz would be just as much of a womanizer as Heat since he'd said he used to frequent this establishment. Nevertheless, he wasn't flirting with any of the girls. Instead, he was sipping his wine with silent grace.

"Quartz-sama, did you come here often?"

"Long ago, yes. Back when I was still king. Isn't that right, Madam?" Quartz mused, looking at the proprietor.

She smiled sweetly as she poured his glass and answered, "Indeed, you surely did. When you would drop by, you'd always partake in this manner. That reminds me, Master Jade and Master Finn are not here with you tonight, I see."

Ruri couldn't help but blurt, "Huh?! Jade-sama would come here too?"

"Yes, Master Quartz would visit with both in tow very often."

This establishment was by no means seedy, but Ruri couldn't quite feel easy hearing that Jade "very often" came to a place where he'd been constantly surrounded by beautiful women. Picturing Jade where Heat was, up close and personal with the young ladies here, made her brow tense. She wanted to believe that his personality wouldn't allow him to flirt and act goofy, but Jade was as handsome as they came. Even without asking any of the ladies to, they probably coddled him like mad. The thought of him nestled up to another woman frustrated her to no end.

Perhaps noticing the mixed feelings on Ruri's face, Quartz explained, "I like drinking with a group of people rather than on my own. Jade and Finn are so dead serious all the time that not many women would come near them. They simply accompanied me here."

Ruri let out a sigh of relief. That made sense. After constantly running away from Agate's advances to find him a bride, there was no way that Jade would ever cling to and flirt with another woman. Even though she knew that, she couldn't hide her relief. Nonetheless, Ruri was confident that she was the only one Jade would cling to. It filled her with an odd sense of superiority.

Seeing that Ruri was clearly reassured, Quartz's lips curled into a smile. "It would seem that Jade's feelings aren't unrequited. How far have you two gone, by the way?"

"'How far'?" Ruri echoed, putting her lips to her glass.

"Have you at least kissed?"

Immediately, liquor came spraying out of Ruri's mouth as she stammered, "Wh-Wh-What are you talking about?! I have done no such thing!"

"Oh, you haven't? Jade is a surprisingly passive romancer, huh?" Quartz said, delivering a devastating amount of damage to Ruri in an aloof, nonchalant tone.

Quartz asked, "But you do have feelings for him, don't you?"

"Am I that easy to figure out?" Ruri replied. Was it written on her face that clearly? She knew exactly what she felt just a second ago. It was jealousy.

"I wouldn't necessarily say that. But your face right now is the spitting image of Seraphie's when she found out that I visited this place, so I just assumed that to be the case."

"Seraphie?" Ruri asked.

"My mate."

"Oh, wow. So you have a mate yourself? Where is she now? Did she come back with you to the Nation of the Dragon King?" Ruri wondered what the woman who won over someone as dashing as Quartz was like. It was extremely intriguing. There weren't many women around her married to dragonkin, so she hoped to maybe pick her brain about a few things. She soon regretted asking her *insensitive* question, though.

"Seraphie died. Quite a long time ago, in fact."

"Oh..." Ruri's face stiffened. The madam most likely knew as well since she silently cast her eyes downward. "I'm sorry, um, I just..." Ruri mumbled.

Quartz, on the other hand, seemed unaffected. He smiled and patted Ruri on the head. "No need to worry. What's in the past is in the past. Besides, I actually need to thank you."

"Why, sir?"

"Ever since Seraphie passed, this nation, that castle...they all remind me of her, so I've had a tough time returning. That's why I didn't come back this entire time. But after hearing about you, a Beloved, I felt the urge to finally return home."

Ruri hesitantly asked, "And remembering her now doesn't hurt you?"

"No, I'm actually more comfortable than I thought. That aside, judging from Jade and Agate's reactions, I regret not coming back sooner. Agate bawled his eyes out when he saw me."

Agate had served as Quartz's aide during his time as king. It made sense why Quartz's return most likely overjoyed Agate as well as Jade.

"I could tell by looking at Jade-sama," Ruri offered. "His face and attitude screamed that he really cares for you, Quartz-sama. He is truly happy that you made your return home."

"It's really nice to know that someone out there cares about you, eh?" Quartz replied with a sweet and kind smile. He likely considered Jade someone very important to him, like a little brother perhaps.

Afterward, the liquor continued to flow and Ruri found herself getting more drunk by the second—talkatively drunk. She babbled incoherently about things in her own world and events that had happened after she was summoned to this one. Quartz listened to every word with a smile well into the wee hours of the night.

Constructing a Hot Spring

6

"It's really flowing!"

Water started to gush from the ground with billowing clouds of steam, signifying that it was hot.

After Ruri took Heat to Knies per his wishes, he made good on his promise. He must have really enjoyed himself. He'd been in a good mood ever since boozing with women surrounding him. Even after he returned to the castle, he remained in high spirits, basking in the afterglow of the experience.

Per their agreement, Ruri asked him to build the hot spring, and despite his usual arrogant attitude, he willingly complied. Honestly speaking, part of Ruri had doubted that her idea would actually come about, but the spirits truly exceeded human standards. She was surprised and impressed as she watched water gush up from the ground, releasing hot steam in its wake.

Construction workers and onlookers who'd caught wind of the Beloved's plan stood all around. They gazed in surprise as hot water erupted from the earth. Impressively enough, the manager of the building office from the Nation of the Beast King seemed to be even *more* ecstatic than Ruri. He would undoubtedly be one of the spring's regular patrons. Furthermore, news of the spring would spread by word of mouth from those who saw this scene. It would serve as a good advertisement.

With the most important part out of the way, the motivated manager urged his workers to get the lead out and hustle. At this rate, the building might be completed ahead of schedule.

Ruri hurried over to the commercial district, looking as if she were late to something. She was raring to start the next phase of her project.

Since she was now frequently visiting town, the townspeople had gotten used to seeing her. This made it easier for her to get around because it caused less of a commotion than when she first started coming. It seemed to also make life easier for Ewan and the other soldiers guarding her.

As Ruri walked through the commercial district, she looked around, searching for something.

"Maybe she still hasn't come back yet?" Ruri wondered aloud. Her search was unexpectedly proving to be difficult, but before long, she managed to find the person she was looking for.

"Amarna-san!"

Amarna stopped opening up shop and lifted her head. "Oh, if it isn't you, Lady Beloved. Good afternoon."

"Good afternoon. I thought you'd be back to the kingdom by now. I'm glad you are."

Amarna had been in the Nation of the Beast King at the same time Ruri had been. When Ruri met her there, Amarna had mentioned that she would be returning to the Nation of the Dragon King soon. This gave Ruri a good idea of the time frame.

"Might you need something from me?" Amarna asked.

"Yes, I need you to help me with something, Amarna-san!"

"Help you? I'd love to, but I have work I must attend to…"

Amarna was a penny-pincher. She wouldn't work unless it meant she could line her pockets. Despite the smile on her face, she couldn't hide the fact that she was annoyed by the request. However, her penny-pinching ways were exactly why Ruri was confident she would accept her offer.

"Would you like to manage a hot spring with me?"

"Manage a hot spring?"

"Yes, I'm building one as we speak," Ruri said, launching into a fiery explanation about the hot spring under construction.

"So I see. A mixed hot spring and amusement facility? While I'm not sure what to think about the spring, I believe the attractions will bring in many people. Amusement is a valuable asset."

"Right, right. But running it all by myself would be way too hard. I also can't walk around the city without security detail, meaning I can't always be around. That's where you come in, Amarna-san. I'll be the owner, and you'll be my manager. What do you say? Please?"

"But why me?" Amarna asked.

"Well, for one thing, there aren't any other merchants that I know. And since you were in the Nation of the Beast King for a while, I presume you know a fair share about hot springs."

"Well, I did pick up a little from my stay over there, yes. And I was intrigued by hot springs and their ability to draw in tourists."

Amarna had gone all the way to the Nation of the Beast King so she could make money. She was also aware of the power hot baths had to attract people. That was why it had to be Amarna. It was hard to entrust the people of the Nation of the Dragon King with a hot spring when the idea itself wasn't known to the public yet. She wanted someone with a certain degree of familiarity to aid her.

"By the way, this would be your salary," Ruri said, writing a value on a piece of paper and slipping it over to Amarna. Amarna's eyes bulged out of her skull. "I can throw in a bonus depending on turnover. Plus, you can sell your merchandise within the facilities. All of those sales would go directly to you."

The merchant's eyes sparkled. She quickly grasped Ruri's hand, saying, "A pleasure to be doing business with you, boss. I will carry out my duties as manager to the fullest!"

Ruri grasped Amarna's hand back. "Let's spread the good word of hot springs all over this kingdom!"

"Yes, we will be raking in the cash!"

Now with her somewhat money-hungry manager secured, Ruri jumped right into management talk with Amarna.

"There are going to be amusement facilities in addition to the springs themselves, correct?" Amarna asked. "I believe that will make for quite a large establishment, but do you plan on hiring other people?"

Ruri nodded. "I think I would need to. But who would want to work in a place so foreign to them?" Ruri pondered.

"No, the fact it's being run by a Beloved makes it more likely that people will be fighting for the opportunity to work there."

This facility would be run by a Beloved herself. Many would come pawing for the job, even if the establishment was a tad suspicious, as long as it meant getting acquainted with a Beloved. Amarna assured it would practically cause riots. While it was nice to know there was no shortage of workers, Ruri didn't want to incite fighting in the streets because of it.

"Still, we'll need other personnel," Ruri stated. It would be difficult for Amarna to run the place all by herself.

Amarna then proposed, rather formally, "Lady Beloved, would you consider hiring people from the slums?"

"Slums? There are slums in the royal capital?"

"Why, yes, of course. The bigger the city, the greater the gap between the rich and the poor. Although the nation has various countermeasures set in place, it's difficult to escape poverty once you've fallen into it. I used to be from the slums myself. I may lead a normal life now, but that is a privilege only a handful can obtain."

Ruri wondered if this was the reason Amarna was so money-hungry. She must have worked very hard to escape a life of poverty.

Amarna continued, "If you have no issue with people from the slums, would you mind giving them a chance to work their way up?"

"No, I wouldn't mind. But slums or not, I need people who are honest workers, so I'd like to interview them."

"Yes, understandable," Amarna said, nodding. "I'll go and find some promising candidates, then. Believe it or not, I have some clout in the slums. I would appreciate you meeting with whoever I bring in."

"Yes, absolutely. I'll talk to you later, then."

They then parted ways that day, making plans to meet later.

When the day finally came to conduct the interviews, Amarna brought a selection of people, male and female alike. They were all younger than Ruri expected. Rather, half of them looked like children, which took her aback.

"Amarna-san, are these children..." Ruri started.

"Yes, the candidates!" Amarna excitedly answered.

"But they're *children*, aren't they? Shouldn't kids this age be going to school, not working?" Ruri asked, knowing that the hot spring would essentially operate during the daytime. These children looked like they'd be preoccupied with school, so it was unlikely they'd be able to work.

"No, these children don't attend school; they're regular workers."

Ruri allowed Amarna to explain in detail. The realistic plight of the poor in this world made her want to rub her temples. If their parents were poor, children started working at an early age to help support their families. Because of this, they neither attended school nor received a proper education. And without that education, they wouldn't be able to find decent jobs, which would toss them into the vicious, inescapable cycle of poverty.

However, working with a Beloved would raise their stock. Amarna wanted to hire them because it would increase their chances of getting decent work in the future. Every child Ruri spoke to came across as serious and diligent. None of them were lazy by any stretch of the imagination. One good chance might change their lives drastically. This was probably a little two-faced of her, but if her desire to create a hot spring could help someone else, then it was like killing two birds with one stone. Ruri decided to hire all of them.

There was just one problem. All of them were uneducated. So uneducated, in fact, that they struggled with simple addition. She couldn't let them calculate money. Customer service also proved a tad difficult.

Ruri racked her brain. It was hard to turn any of them down when Amarna practically begged her to hire them. These were very motivated children, and Ruri wanted to give them positions. After some thought, she came to a simple conclusion—if they're not educated, why not educate them?

The hot spring was still under construction, and luck would have it that it would take a little more time for it to be completed. She could simply use that time to educate the kids so they were equipped to serve patrons. First, she would teach them math so that they could calculate money properly. Then, she would teach them how to write while Amarna taught them customer service etiquette. This would make it easier for them to find their next job when they were ready to move on.

Before all that, though, she needed to do something about their appearances. None of them had the money for new clothes, so they were all in tattered, patchwork outfits.

Ruri had made up her mind. If she was going to do this, she knew she couldn't go halfway. She needed to go all in and give these kids a complete makeover.

Ever since the Church of God's Light issue was resolved, life had been relatively peaceful in the capital. There had been a few small skirmishes here and there, but no major crimes or notable conflicts to report.

In contrast to the peaceful capital, the castle was preparing for the upcoming tournament and things were hectic. The busiest among all of them was Jade, who was swamped with paperwork as usual. He was giving off such a negative aura that his frustration was virtually palpable. The reason? He had come down with an acute case of Ruri Deficiency. His busy schedule played a part, but that wasn't the entire reason. It was because he barely got any petting time in with Ruri over the past few days.

Normally, Ruri would be curled up on his lap while he worked. It was the only thing that helped him work through the monotony of tedious deskwork with peace of mind. However, in recent days, Ruri had been going out to make her supposed hot spring and rarely stopped by the royal office.

69

Jade couldn't shake the feeling that she was using this project as an excuse to avoid him, but digging any deeper into it only made him sadder, so he kept it to himself. After all, if she was avoiding him, there was only one reason he could think of. He started to think that perhaps he'd been too hasty in handing over his dragonheart after all. Jade wanted to feel secure letting Ruri go off elsewhere, but if she was avoiding him, then that made everything he did pointless.

Jade naturally had no intention of letting Ruri slip away from him, but he was growing impatient from lack of petting time. This was compounded by the fact that Jade was too busy to go and see her. If it weren't for that, he'd go into town with her and be there twenty-four seven. He knew that no one would try to court Ruri while she had his dragonheart, but Ewan reported that she was getting along quite well with the construction workers. He was not at all amused by the fact that she was getting cozy with random men who-knows-where.

Jade's wish would be for her to just stay in the castle, but Ruri was such an active person that it seemed entirely unlikely. "Maybe I should confine her," he muttered aloud. Jade knew that some dragonkin wouldn't let their mates out of the house, to keep them from the prying eyes of other men, and he finally understood how they felt.

Jade's whispered desire fell upon the quiet office. Claus, who was also working in the same room, heard it clearly though.

"Your Majesty, you've let quite a dangerous comment slip from your mouth."

"It was a joke."

No, anyone with eyes could see the dead serious look on his face.

"Even if you were able to confine Ruri, the spirits would immediately aid in her escape, Sire."

"Yes, I'm well aware," snapped Jade. He sometimes wished Ruri was a regular human being, but he wouldn't admit it.

"She's finally back home after all this time too. I swear, that Ruri…" Jade lamented, his hopes of spending time with her dashed because of her active pursuit of building a hot spring. He found the sight of Ruri happily running back and forth charming, but he wanted her to slow down and sit still as well.

"I can understand how Master Quartz felt," Jade admitted.

"Yes, even among dragonkin, the way he treated his mate was especially overcareful."

Quartz, the former Dragon King, had a mate of his own and was famous for carefully keeping her away from any men—his aides included. In fact, he didn't let another man lay eyes on her, not even after she had passed.

"It's a relief to see him doing well," Claus whispered.

Jade knew whom he was referring to and gave a small nod.

When Quartz had lost his mate, he started to waste away to an unsightly degree. Everyone feared that he might take his own life. They placed him under constant surveillance to ensure that wouldn't come to pass. Be that as it may, what kept Quartz alive was a promise he shared with his mate. That promise made him give up the throne and leave the Nation of the Dragon King.

Everyone knew it was an extremely rash and unrealistic promise, but Quartz had faith. He had faith it would be fulfilled. In fact, it might have been the only thing he had to cling to. After all, that promise was the only ray of hope Quartz had.

Once Quartz decided he would leave the kingdom, all of his aides expressed concern. They were afraid he'd just go on to vanish without a trace. But everyone feared that stopping Quartz, who was clinging to his last thread of hope, would break him mentally.

No one could oppose him because of that, so all they could do was watch him fly off into the sunset. That was just how much Quartz's mate meant to him.

Both Jade and Claus remembered the events of that time well. They lamented that they hadn't been able to do anything to help him.

Quartz's loss and departure wound up affecting Jade greatly from then on. He started to fear the male dragonkin's nature to dedicate that much to their mate. He thought maybe it would be best if he didn't have a mate at all if that was the trouble it caused. As a result, he'd continuously rebuffed the elders and their hopes of matrimony. However, he ended up finding Ruri, rendering his efforts useless. He had no idea what it would all yield, but now that he had Ruri, Jade was painfully aware of how Quartz felt when he lost his mate.

After pondering what would have happened if he was in Quartz's shoes, Jade felt it was a miracle that Quartz came back with the smile he'd lost when he initially left. Jade couldn't comprehend how much pain he must have endured in order to regain his smile.

Just then, there was a knock at the door and in came the man himself—Quartz.

"Hello, hello, hello! Hard at work, are we?" Quartz greeted in an awfully cheerful tone.

Upon closer inspection, Quartz's clothes were covered in vicious bloodstains. Ruri would have shrieked her head off if she were in the office. Nevertheless, Jade and Claus were unconcerned. His wounds were nothing by dragonkin standards. Still, the bloodstains had them curious.

"What happened to your outfit, if I may ask?" Claus inquired.

"There were a lot of hot-blooded soldiers in the training grounds, you see. I was just giving them some practice in preparation for the tournament," Quartz explained.

"And there were no…casualties, I take it?" Claus asked, slightly concerned. Although he was the *former* king, he was still the individual who'd claimed the honor by defeating the dragonkin general, someone who loved the thrill of battle more than eating three square meals a day. Needless to say, he was amazingly skilled.

"I'm no fool. I know how to hold back. Granted, I don't think they'll be walking upright for a while. Anyway, that didn't provide me with enough exercise, so I dropped by to see if Jade could help me out, but…" Quartz trailed off, his eyes moving over to the stacks of papers piled on Jade's desk. "That seems like a no-go, eh?"

Jade nodded, looking regretful. "Yes, correct. And thanks to all this work, I can't even spend time with Ruri."

"Inevitable, what with the tournament on the horizon, yeah," Quartz concurred. "But are you going to be all right as you are? If you don't maintain your physique, I'm worried Finn might end up wiping the floor with you in the tournament."

"You needn't worry for me. I've been exercising my body in between work." As the current Dragon King, he couldn't put on a disgraceful fight. Since Finn was the top contender, he was much more dedicated to training than Jade. Jade couldn't afford to lose to him.

"Well, that's good, then. By the way, what's Ruri up to?" Quartz asked.

"She said she's teaching children in town. She's educating them so she can hire them to work at her hot spring," Jade replied.

"Well, that sounds like she's up to something fun. I guess I should go check on how she's doing. I'll make sure to have fun for you, Jade," Quartz teased.

Jade couldn't be with her right now even if he wanted. If he could, he would throw everything by the wayside just to go to her, but Jade's character wouldn't allow for that. The fact that Quartz made that comment with that knowledge in mind was playfully mean-spirited.

Jade's hand tensed so much from that remark that he snapped the pen he was holding in two.

"Welp, keep up the good work!" Quartz said as he walked off at a jaunty pace, leaving Jade to his bitterness.

7 Making Merriment

The children's "employee training" education was going well. With their honest nature and ambition, they took their studies seriously and were improving at a rapid pace. That being said, they could have just gone to school if studying was the only purpose here. Any free time they had was spent working in order to sustain themselves. That was why this study session was really job training. It was simply necessary for work, and since studying was part of the job, she compensated them modestly for their time. They got to study and got paid for it.

That reminded Ruri of something. She'd heard that in impoverished nations in her world, in order to incentivize working children to go to school, they would set up a school lunch system so they'd come for the goal of eating a hot meal. In that case, if the Nation of the Dragon King introduced something similar, the poorer children would likely attend so they could eat a decent meal. Ruri thought it might be an idea worth pitching to Jade.

But before talking to Jade, who would have the final say, Ruri figured she should probably run it by the nation's chancellor, Euclase. She went straight to Euclase and discussed taking money out of the budget set aside for Beloveds. Her thought was that if this turned out to be a model case, then it would be easier for the nation to introduce it as common practice. This was the money that Euclase had said to spend as she wished, after all. She didn't like the idea of spending taxpayer money on herself, but if she used it on volunteers, then it made things much easier. Euclase consented, seeing no problem in her experiment or the use of Beloved funds.

Ruri immediately proposed the introduction of lunch services at a school near the slums, where the poorer children would normally go if they didn't have to work. Euclase took steps to implement her plan, and Ruri's experimental school lunch program was approved. Euclase also wasted no time implementing other necessities, such as cooks and facilities for them to utilize. The talented chancellor was the epitome of tactful decision-making.

Considering Euclase was working for her benefit amidst the busy tournament season, Ruri wanted to thank them somehow. Though it was initially her idea, Ruri felt a little regretful that she was completely relying on Euclase. The only thing she did was make the suggestion and pay for it—and the money wasn't even from her, but from the taxpayers.

In an attempt to do something of merit, Ruri went to the slums and went door to door, telling people that she had created a school lunch program. Once she did, the children who struggled for a day's meal started to funnel into classes, little by little. She knew that not *everyone* would just suddenly start attending. Nevertheless, the only thing she could do was pray that the number would continue to grow. She hoped they would receive an even better education and find even better jobs. Then again, she doubted it would work out *that* great, but if it could help change even a handful of their lives, then it was a cause for celebration.

The best thing would be to hire the children from the slums at her hot spring, but Ruri didn't have room for any more employees. She'd already hired a bigger amount than needed out of pity for them. She wondered if she could call on the businesses in the royal capital to place them with jobs. But coming from a Beloved, she worried it would end up being less of a request and more of a threat. Almost no member of the general public would refuse a Beloved's wishes. That wouldn't work to *anyone's* benefit; it might just worsen people's perception of the slums. Also, that was probably more of the government's territory, not Ruri's. It seemed unlikely they'd take action in this busy season, though, so she would have to wait a while before proposing a new idea.

Ruri had no power other than her moniker as a Beloved, but she wanted to do whatever she could to help. This nation was already Ruri's home away from home. Nothing would please her more than to see her knowledge from her world help to better serve this land.

Construction of the hot spring had been coming along smoothly and was nearing completion. What Ruri needed to think about now was *what kind* of entertainment the facility would offer.

By default, there were attractions in this world. However, theme parks didn't exist, only street performances, plays, and things of that nature. And in typical port town tradition, they used the ocean for a variety of leisure activities—swimming competitions, fishing competitions, whatever they could manage. To be honest, though, it wasn't enough for someone born in a place rich with entertainment like Ruri. An amusement facility was something she'd been craving for quite some time.

The question now was what kind she should make. The lack of electricity was a huge factor. Most of the entertainment in Ruri's world used electricity. Magic existed in its place, but it was a toss-up between things that could be substituted with magic and things that required neither electricity nor magic. Ruri racked her brain in order to come up with something that would fall into the right category.

The first thing that came to mind was a zoo. But that would require zookeepers. Not only that, but since there were already beastmen in this world, no one would be that curious about animals. So she scratched that idea. She didn't have the technology to make thrill rides, so any kind of attractions you rode were off the table as well.

She thought of perhaps having a mascot costume like at a theme park, so she had one custom-made at a tailor. Her explanation didn't translate over very well and the costume turned out a bit homely, but it would do for now. After that, she asked the flower spirits to fill the facility with rare flowers not common to the area, turning the location into a florid paradise so beautiful it could garner fame on its own.

She still had no activities for attractions, though. In terms of old-school amusement, bowling, pinball, and shooting galleries came to mind. Making those seemed entirely doable. She could swap out the guns for bows and arrows. She had a few of those in her pocket space, and people of this world were familiar with them. Then she decided to ask a woodworker to make a non-electric pinball cabinet. She used drawings and gestures to illustrate her point, and after several rounds of prototyping, they finally came up with something satisfactory.

"Okay, could you make me ten more cabinets?" Ruri requested.

"Sure thing. But would you mind if we made a few for ourselves?"

It seemed that the woodworkers liked the new device. They were playing with the cabinet with great interest, shouting out which of them was next to examine it. If this was how they were acting, then it would likely be a hit with customers as well.

"That's fine. In exchange, I'd like you to make something else," Ruri said, pulling out a piece of paper and proceeding to draw a picture of a bowling ball and pins. "There are ten of these pins, and there are holes in this ball to fit your fingers in, you see…"

"Mm-hmm, mm-hmm. If that's all, I think we can make these pretty quick."

A few days later, after seeing the finished product, she set them up in front of the curious builders. She stood the pins upright, rolled the ball, and knocked them down. Once she performed the extremely simplistic series of actions, the woodworkers showed interest in this invention as well.

"Hey, let me get a try!"

"Me too!"

As Ruri watched the craftsmen gleefully resetting the pins like a flock of happy children, she realized that resetting manually every time would probably get annoying. But when the person next in line was about to go stand the pins back up, another of the workers called for him to stop.

"What are you doing? Use magic instead of doing it by hand," he said, using wind magic to make the fallen pins stand upright.

Ruri had seen the light. "You're a *genius*, mister!" she exclaimed. She had completely forgotten about the existence of magic. It was relatively easy to reset the pins that way. She put in an order for more bowling pins and balls, and the woodworkers agreed to make a few for themselves.

As things proceeded swimmingly, Ruri figured her safest bet for amusement was probably tabletop games—card games, Reversi, The Game of Life, and whatnot. There were things similar to cards and chess in this world as well, but they were basically games meant for adults, and they were often used for bets.

The adults in this nation did a lot of betting. There was even an official bet set up for who would win the upcoming tournament. The most popular wager of course was Jade, followed by Finn and the others. In that case, if she introduced *betting* in her amusement facilities, perhaps the people of this world would have an easier time accepting the idea as a whole.

With that thought in mind, Ruri came up with the idea of letting people bet on the outcome of sporting events. Horse and cycling races were the first ideas to come to her, but raising horses was a handful and bicycles didn't exist for there to even *be* cycling races. There was sports betting in Ruri's world as well, and that was the image she was working from. However, she felt that if it turned into gambling, then it was bound to cause conflicts. If they really did like gambling as much as she suspected, they would have a lot of zeal for it. If she made a misstep in the process, it could mean a lot of unnecessary hassle.

She decided to give up on the whole betting angle. Instead, it seemed better if people played a regular sport with no strings attached. She thought about what kind of sport she should make. No matter how silly, if it had a ball, it could be a sport. She needed one with simple rules that anyone could follow without the need for a lot of equipment.

She asked the spirits, who knew of her world, for ideas. "What do you guys think?"

"*Soccer!*"

"*Baseball!*"

"*Tennis!*"

"Hmm..." None of their suggestions struck a chord with Ruri. All of them had pretty difficult rules. Plus, you needed equipment—rackets, mitts, bats.

"*Dodgeball, then!*"

"Oh, that's it!"

The rules were easy to understand; if you got hit, you were out. It was easy to teach and easy to learn. All you needed was a single ball.

She explained the rules to the children in the slums and let them play, proving that people who didn't know the rules could play right away.

"Okay, okay. Things are smooth sailing." That seemed like enough attractions for now. She could just add more later if necessary.

The next order of business was meal prep. Enjoying the hot spring and the attractions would probably work up an appetite. But rather than a hearty meal you had to sit down for, a light meal you could eat while walking would be much better. She needed food like what would be sold at a food stall—something easy enough for her child staff to make on their own with a high turnover rate. What she came up with was...

"Hmm, corn dogs would be easy to eat. Also, there's ikayaki, yakitori, and, oh! Can't forget takoyaki!"

She figured she would need a griddle first, so she went to the ironworks and asked them to make a griddle with a bunch of round holes. With that, they could make the doughy, octopus-filled balls. The ironworker who took her order was baffled by her need for such a strange griddle, but it was an essential tool for making takoyaki.

Next, Ruri went to the commercial district to look for ingredients. She found sausage, chicken, and seafood. But for some reason, she couldn't find the ingredient she wanted most—octopus! They had squid, but octopus was nowhere to be found.

She went to a store that handled seafood and asked, "Do you have any octopus?"

"What's an octopus?" they replied.

"An octopus is an octopus. You know, eight legs with suction pads on the bottom?" Ruri explained.

The only response she got was the shopkeeper's blank stare. She went to another store and got the same answer.

She vented her frustration to Ewan, who was with her, asking, "What's the deal, Ewan? *Why is there no octopus*?!"

"Don't ask me. The hell is an 'octopus'?" he asked in reply.

It was an idea beyond comprehension. She never would have imagined that octopuses didn't exist in this world even though they had squids.

"What should I do? Substitute it with squid? No, takoyaki needs that plump and chewy texture of octopus."

As she agonized over what to do, a voice called out to her from behind. When she turned around, she saw Quartz, who was not supposed to be here.

"Master Quartz, what are you doing here?"

"I heard you were up to something interesting, so I came to check it out myself. But when you weren't over at the spring, I asked around and heard you were here. Since your hair stands out so much, it was easy to find you." So Quartz said, but his own head of platinum blond hair was just as easy to spot from a distance.

Seeing Quartz jogged Ruri's memory. Quartz supposedly had been bouncing from nation to nation ever since he'd left the Nation of the Dragon King. If he saw that many nations in his travels, he just might know of octopuses.

"Master Quartz, do you know what an octopus is?"

"Octopus? No, afraid I've never heard of it."

"It's a wriggly sea creature, similar to a squid, but with a lot of legs with suction cups on the underside. It has white meat that's chewy and plump and very delicious," she explained.

Quartz pondered her description for a moment. Just when Ruri was about to give up on octopus altogether, Quartz seemed to remember something.

"Would you be referring to a kraken, by any chance?" he asked.

"Kraken?" Ruri replied.

"It's a monster that dwells in the sea. It has many legs like a squid that are lined with suction cups. Yeah, if it resembles a squid, but actually isn't, it must be a kraken."

"Is it delicious? Can you catch it in the Nation of the Dragon King?"

"I've had it and it tastes great. Though, I'm not too sure if you can catch them. I mean, they're so humongous that any normal person would go down with their ship if they ever tried. I think it would be hard to catch one unless you are a dragonkin in dragon form. Also, krakens crop up very rarely out at sea."

"Aww, you're kidding..." Ruri slumped in disappointment.

Just then, something came to Ewan's mind. "I heard the navy boys say that a kraken has been showing up in the seas around the capital lately."

"Really?!" Ruri asked, excitedly.

"Yeah, according to one of them, suspicious ships have been spotted near the capital as of late, and every time the navy tries to capture them, a kraken shows up and blocks their way. And that's the reason why they've let every single suspicious ship slip away. I think he said something about going on a full-scale Kraken hunt soon."

"Okay, then count me in too!" Ruri exclaimed, pumping her fist to the sky.

Ewan slapped her across the head with his hand. "You freakin' dummy. No way we'd let you do something so dangerous! Not when there's suspicious ships out and about. You need to be more self-aware regarding your status as a Beloved!"

"Okay, but then I won't be able to get any octopus. And I want myself some takoyaki!"

Ewan just shook his head. "I'll tell the guys in the navy to bring the damn thing back for you, then. There, be satisfied with that."

Reluctant as Ruri was, she had no choice but to agree—despite her curiosity to see the hunt as it happened.

Why He Quit Being King

Quartz wanted to see how the hot spring facilities were progressing, so he headed to the construction site. The exterior frame of the facility was nearly finished; all that remained was to complete the interior.

"Wow, incredible. It looks almost done, I see," Quartz commented.

"Yes. The entertainment facility is almost finished as well," Ruri explained. "All that's left is staff training, and that's also coming along."

"You said you'd hired kids from the slums?"

"That's right. But all of them are ambitious, hard-working employees."

They all were diligently studying, learning how to serve customers so they could function in front of potential patrons without fear. Perhaps that was thanks to the money-hungry Amarna, who put education before work.

"It seems you're working hard on a lot of fronts, Ruri, even though this is actually something the nation itself should be tackling."

"Well, I only put in the suggestion. Euclase-san did most of the legwork." In fact, the nation had overseen and carried out much of the work since the chancellor was the one pulling the strings.

"Still, the hot spring isn't the only thing that needs your care. You need to give Jade some of that care as well, or else he'll keep sulking."

"Jade-sama?" Ruri asked. "Why is that?"

"He said he couldn't spend time with you because you're going out every day," Quartz said with a chuckle, even though he'd recently been teasing Jade about his predicament.

"I mean, It's not that I've been neglecting him. Plus, Jade seems to be busy preparing for the tournament."

Ruri had been thinking about how little time she'd spent with Jade lately, but when she'd seen how busy he was, she'd figured it was best to limit her visits and not disturb him. Ruri had been missing him, but if he felt the same, it was probably a good idea to make some more time for him.

"Speaking of the tournament," Ruri started, "will you be participating, Quartz-sama?"

"Me? No, I won't be. I already abdicated the throne. It's too late for me to go butting in." Quartz's gentle expression turned slightly sorrowful. "After all, I'm the one who ran away from that position. I can't go back."

"So...why did you quit being king, if you don't mind me asking?"

Ruri knew it was an insensitive question, and she didn't know if it was safe to ask, but she felt she *needed* to ask it anyway, especially after seeing Quartz looking so sad. He had been smiling ever since they'd met, but every now and then his expression would take a somber turn—as it had just now. She guessed that something earth-shattering must have happened to make him give up the throne.

"Hey, Ruri. You like Jade, don't you?" Quartz asked.

"Yes," Ruri replied concisely. Ruri had been intentionally vague before, but after seeing the look on Quartz's face, she decided now wasn't the time to fudge the truth.

"What would you do if Jade were to suddenly disappear?"

Ruri was surprised by his question, but Quartz looked far too serious to reply jokingly, so she answered truthfully. "I would be sad, of course."

"Yeah, I figured. But your sadness is hypothetical. I actually did lose my mate—my beloved, my one and only," Quartz said as he looked toward the sky, his eyes steeped in sorrow. "Being a dragonkin is a burden, you know? Once you find your mate, they become your everything and you can't find it in yourself to look at anyone else. She was my other half, and there'll be no other. Losing her was as if my body had been torn apart. I fell into darkness and despair with Seraphie gone."

Hearing Quartz speak about his mate greatly affected Ruri. Her heart sank. Everyone had always told her about a dragonkin's love for their mate, but just hearing it probably wasn't enough to comprehend it.

"I thought we would die together," Quartz said, the words practically straining the words from his throat. "I pleaded for her not to leave me alone. I asked to follow her into death. But I couldn't— because of Seraphie's last request. She begged me on her deathbed not to follow her after she passed. I couldn't help but find it cruel. I couldn't continue to live in a world without her."

Ruri had thought that Quartz hadn't been able to put his mate in the past yet. He still loved her and suffered from her absence.

"She promised me something, however," Quartz stated.

"What kind of promise was that?" Ruri asked.

"She said, 'I assure you I will come back reborn, so come search for me.'"

"Reborn? But that seems…"

Was that possible? Supposing someone was reborn as a different person and lived somewhere in this world, would one even be able to find them?

"I know what you want to say. But the spirits told me that it's not impossible. A person may die, but their soul cycles through and is born anew. The quality of that soul's mana doesn't change when it's reborn, so finding the new owner isn't an impossible task—from what I've been told. No one knows when they'll be born, but the spirits told me I stood a chance with my long dragonkin lifespan."

Ruri wondered whether there would be a point in finding Seraphie if she didn't remember who Quartz was, but she couldn't say that aloud since Quartz's eyes held such honest belief.

"I decided to look for her—something I couldn't do if I remained king. After all, she wouldn't necessarily be born here in the Nation of the Dragon King. I can't do my kingly duties if I'm traveling around to different nations, so I stepped down. I threw it all away to find my one and only, my other half. The cleanup after I suddenly exited the throne must've been enormous. I feel sorry for the vassals in my court I left behind. That's why I haven't been able to come back to the Nation of the Dragon King."

Quartz smirked, adding that he had no incentive to return unless he heard news of a Beloved—a statement he'd made before he left.

"I'll keep looking for Seraphie. Forever until I find her, in fact," Quartz said. His determination and persistence were virtually palpable.

Quartz turned to face Ruri and smiled sweetly. The depression that had tinged his face was gone. He was back to his usual calm and gentle demeanor.

"Ruri, that's just how absolute the existence of a mate is for dragonkin."

Quartz gently tapped on the glass sphere encasing Jade's scale hanging around Ruri's neck. Ruri cocked her head, unsure of what he meant by that.

"I don't know what you're hesitating over, but I can tell you that he didn't give this to you half-heartedly. That is how we dragonkin operate. Don't make him wait too long, okay?" Quartz said, obviously referring to Jade.

Ruri felt at a loss as the conversation suddenly shifted to her. "It's not that I'm keeping him waiting... It's just that I wonder if it's true. Like, maybe he mistakenly likes me. Maybe he really just likes me as an extension of a pet because he has a fondness for small animals."

"Impossible," Quartz asserted. "This dragonheart carries more weight than that. He would only give this to someone he has set as his one and only, someone irreplaceable."

Rin and Celestine had told her as much before, but it was more convincing coming from a fellow dragonkin such as Quartz.

"But he just gave me the dragonheart without telling me he loved me," Ruri added.

"Is that what's been bugging you? Maybe Jade was just scared to tell you himself. Maybe he felt that your heart wasn't quite there yet and you'd reject him. But he wants you to be aware of it. He doesn't want to give it to someone else. He can't say it out loud, but he wants you to notice. That may be why he decided to give you the dragonheart."

"But I'd prefer it if he just told me, clear and straightforward."

"In that case, you should tell him that. Despite appearances, he is a wimp at heart. You should *make him* make it clear to you."

Ruri felt like all the escape paths were blocked off. "Ughh, but how do I break the ice?" she asked.

"It's just a matter of feeling and momentum. I mean, that seems to be your specialty. Right, Ruri?"

To be fair, Ruri was prone to deciding things based on feeling and momentum.

"Don't worry. I give you my guarantee, so just give it a shot," Quartz retorted.

"Well, that's one shot I don't think I should take…" Ruri replied, racking her brain.

Ruri couldn't deny that she'd been avoiding him and using the hot spring as an excuse as of late, but she couldn't just keep dancing around the subject forever. Despite knowing that she would have to come to grips with the dragonheart matter at some point, she kept putting it off. Hearing about Quartz's deep love for his mate, however, made her realize she needed to stop running away from this issue and give it the consideration it deserved.

At the same time, Ruri also felt somewhat angry with Jade. He should have given her a thorough rundown on dragonkin mating habits like Quartz just did. If Jade had done that, Ruri probably would have reacted and felt much differently than she did now.

"This is all Jade's fault to begin with, isn't it? I'm not from this world, you know. If he gives me a scale and tells me it's a 'good luck charm,' how in the world am I supposed to know that it's a dragonheart? Women absolutely want it in words!"

"Men are romantics and women are realists, so yeah… Well, if you have something to say, then you should just be direct about it. He needs to understand how a woman's heart works."

"That is really true. Jade-sama never uses enough of his words!"

"Jade has always been like that. Not really much you can do about it. That reminds me of something similar that happened to me in the past…" Quartz started as he began to launch into old stories and complaints about Jade from the past.

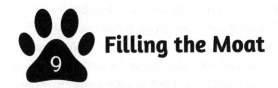

Filling the Moat

Ruri had decided to give Jade proper consideration, but she found herself at Lydia's for some reason. Well, the reason was clear. She was going to ride the momentum all the way to Jade, but along the way she hesitated and couldn't bring herself to see him. She went to Lydia's to get away. And there she sat cross-legged in front of the room where the ghost dwelled, listening to the haunting tune that seeped through the door.

"*Ruri, what are you doing?*" Lydia asked.

"Gathering my mind."

Puzzled, Lydia watched Ruri as she sat and practiced this mysterious method called "meditation."

"I'm trying to process my feelings before I go talk to Jade-sama," Ruri said.

Ruri wasn't quite ready to accept Jade's feelings. At this rate, she could speak to him as many times as she liked, but chances were that she would stop short and run away.

When all was said and done, what did Jade mean to her? Her heart raced whenever she looked into those jadeite eyes. She was captivated by the sweet, charming smile meant for her eyes only.

The elders would bring Jade portraits of potential brides, and seeing them would make her irrationally irritable at the thought of one of them becoming Jade's queen. If she already knew that much, wasn't that more than enough? That was the question.

"Oh my, you're finally ready to put this matter to rest, then? But why are you in front of this room again?" asked Lydia.

"Well, because listening to this song puts me at ease."

Since she'd first heard this ghost's song, she'd been frequently returning to this room in hopes of listening to the melody etched in her mind. Not every visit yielded her a listen, unfortunately enough. However, she seemed to be in luck this time around. The song had poured out from the room at just the right time, so she'd decided to stay and listen to it as "meditation." Their voice was always so beautiful; it felt like it was cleansing her mind. After reeling from the idea of going to Jade, it helped calm her down a great deal.

Ruri didn't know why she was being so wishy-washy. After learning that Jade had given her a dragonheart, she was overwhelmingly bewildered. Now that she had calmed down, though, what else was there? She asked herself this question and realized that she was honestly...happy. She liked being with Jade. Being by his side was comforting, and she wanted to stay there.

It hadn't started out that way, but before Ruri knew it, being with Jade had become the status quo. She tried to ignore it during her stay in the Nation of the Beast King, but she missed having him near her. The sense of longing churned up a murky feeling in her heart. That was a testament to how natural it felt being with Jade in the Nation of the Dragon King.

Ruri pondered over her course of action. A dragonheart was incredibly important to a dragonkin. Quartz had even mentioned how it wasn't some half-hearted gesture. But was Ruri ready to accept Jade's feelings? That question weighed on her mind. She could return the dragonheart, but part of her didn't want to do that. She didn't want to give back Jade's show of affection. Then should she accept it? A part of her was still conflicted about *that* as well.

After hearing about Quartz's deep, binding love for his mate, Ruri felt her feelings still weren't ready to be taken out of the oven. She thought it would be better to give it just a *little* more thought.

"Hmm, hmm, hmm, hmmmm."

After she left Lydia's, Ruri hummed a little ditty as she strolled to her room at the castle. The ditty in question was the ghost's song. It had lingered in her ears, and as a result, her vocal cords naturally reproduced it.

As she continued to hum, she heard the distant sound of footsteps hurrying down the hall. Ruri stopped in her tracks and turned around to see Quartz running from around the corner. He looked desperate.

"What's wrong with you, Quartz-sama? Why are you in such a hurry?"

"Oh, it's you, Ruri. Did you just hear a song coming from somewhere?"

"A song? Well, I was just humming to myself, but that's it."

"You? No, it can't be. I must've heard wrong..." Quartz mumbled to himself, coming to some sort of conclusion on his own. The only word to describe the look on his face was—despair.

Ruri cocked her head and asked, "Is something the matter?"

A moment later, Quartz reverted back to his usual gentle smile. "No, it's nothing. I must've been thinking too hard and misheard you. Anyway, did you go to Jade's place? I was convinced you were going to let the momentum carry you there."

"I thought about going in there like that, but I wanted to think it over before I gave him my answer."

"Well, that's smart. It's best to give it proper thought. Dragonkin can get extremely jealous, so I would suggest not going in with any second thoughts. That would be torture for Jade."

"Yes, don't worry. I'll give it the proper consideration," Ruri said, hoping she didn't regret her eventual answer.

"I'm looking forward to your wedding."

"Wait, *wedding*? That seems like quite a big leap," Ruri replied. She found his comment odd considering they hadn't even started *dating* yet.

"No, I don't think so. Once you accept Jade's feelings, Agate and the others will be so beside themselves with joy that they'll skip straight to the wedding. And it will be an extravagant one, I'm sure."

Agate had been nagging Jade to marry for some time now. He seemed gung ho about Jade rushing headlong into a wedding if he found himself a mate. Ruri had wondered why he hadn't been bugging Jade about a wife lately, but that was because he knew that Jade had given Ruri his dragonheart. They were instead busy working on *something else*—something Ruri was still not privy to.

"By the way, what was your ceremony like, Quartz-sama?" Ruri asked, curious to hear the former king's firsthand experience.

"We had a modest ceremony."

"Really? A king's wedding? *Modest*?" Quartz's explanation was surprising. Ruri had imagined that a royal wedding would be quite a grand affair, especially for the king of a superpower nation.

"Well, I suppose it would be common procedure to invite a lot of guests. But I didn't want anyone else to see Seraphie in all her beauty, so we held it with just us."

"Oh, I see." Quartz seemed to be enjoying himself as he recalled that moment, so Ruri fought to keep her cheeks from twitching. From what she'd heard so far, Ruri secretly thought that Quartz had a bit of a yandere temperament. Perhaps because they were destined to love the same mate for life, dragonkin were said to get very attached and possessive. Quartz seemed the typical dragonkin in that way.

So, what would Jade do, then? Quartz had told her that he rarely let his mate out into the open, so would Jade end up keeping *her* from leaving her room as well? Ruri thought she'd need to check with Jade about this matter.

As she walked to her room with Quartz, she noticed that people were coming and going from the room next to Jade's.

"Why?" Ruri questioned, curiously peeking in. The room was supposed to be unoccupied, but she saw that they were removing items from it.

"Huh? Is someone moving in?" Ruri wondered aloud. She caught a person working and asked, "Why are you moving things out?"

"We're redecorating the room by order of Lord Agate."

"And who is it moving in?"

"I was told you are, Lady Beloved."

"What? *Me*?" Ruri's current room was right across from Jade's. Why would she need to move *even closer* when they were already so close? It made no sense.

Quartz, however, seemed to understand the situation. "Yeesh, that Agate. They haven't even had the wedding yet. He's being too hasty."

"Care to explain?" Ruri prompted.

"The king's quarters and this room are adjoined. Both bedrooms are connected via a single door, meaning you don't have to go outside to go to and fro. It's the 'queen's quarters,' as it were."

"The *queen's quarters*?!"

"It seems they're filling the proverbial moat to keep you from running away," Quartz explained.

"Agate-san..." Ruri trailed off. She remembered that Agate had been asking her detailed questions about curtain colors and furniture preferences. *This* was the reason why. All this time, he had been steadily fashioning a net to prevent Ruri from escaping.

10 Hot Spring Completed

"At last! At long last! The hot spring is done!" Ruri exclaimed.

The long-awaited spring was finally completed. The path to this point had been indeed long. Planning, construction, personnel training—everything had been worked up from scratch, and the equipment for the amusement facilities had been crafted by hand. Granted, Ruri hadn't done much herself—she'd hired others to do most of the work—but she had been waiting for this day on bated breath.

"We did it, Amarna-san!"

"Indeed, completed at long last!"

Ruri and Amarna took each other's hands and rejoiced.

"All right, time for the inaugural bath!"

Ruri decided to take a bath to celebrate its completion. She extended an invitation to the slum children who had assisted with the construction. They had been helping out a lot ever since Ruri tasked them with inspecting the new equipment in the recreation facilities. As thanks for instating a lunch program in school, they would help out in any way they could when they found time between school and work. It really made a difference in the long run. Admittedly, though, some of them were probably just doing it for the sweets Ruri gave out as a token of appreciation.

In addition to the children, she also invited the construction workers and the various craftsmen responsible for the equipment. She had actually invited Heat to join as well, but he'd become disinterested once he'd learned that the women's and men's baths were separate. At first, he'd asserted that there wouldn't be a problem since he was a spirit. But Ruri flatly refused, insisting she couldn't allow a womanizer with the body of a man in the women's bath. His situation was different from Kotaro's or Chi's.

She stepped into the Nation of the Dragon King's first hot spring with everyone. Ruri lathered the heads of the slum children with shampoo and washed them. It seemed that this was their first time bathing and they were confused about how it worked.

This raised a good point. If she didn't write down any kind of instructions, the customers might get confused as well. After all, they didn't even know how to use the shampoo or conditioner—both of which, as a note, had been imported from the Nation of the Beast King. Ruri had tracked down stores in the Nation of the Dragon King that carried them, but they didn't sell well considering no one in the kingdom bathed. All the products had been sitting on the shelves for ages.

As she taught the children how to bathe, Ruri considered the idea of including an explanation at the reception desk. The women's side was fine at the moment because Ruri was there, but she did worry about the men's side...until she remembered. The man with more unbridled passion for hot springs than anyone else—the building manager from the Nation of the Beast King—was in the men's bath. He must have been giving the boys a thorough lecture on how to use the spring.

"Lady Beloved, hot springs feel good," one of the children commented.

"They do, don't they?" Ruri replied.

The slum kids wore rosy smiles as they soaked in the perfectly hot water. Embracing the atmosphere, Ruri put a towel on her head.

The children copied her by putting towels on their heads as well. As she giggled at the sight, water came splashing onto Ruri's face.

"Wa—pft!" While some of the children soaked in somber silence, others mistook the large bathing area as a playground. They were swimming around and getting into splash fights.

"Hey, there! A hot spring is for relaxing, not for splashing and swimming!"

Ruri prompted the obedient children to soak in the hot water peacefully. Since she would always give them sweets, they had learned that they should listen to Ruri and so they complied.

Once the hot spring was open to the general public, however, more children might crop up, mistaking the bath for a big playground. It would be necessary to teach people bathing etiquette. She might also need to consider banning those with especially bad manners. No one likely wanted to be banned from an establishment built by a Beloved, so it should prove to be quite a potent strategy.

"Maybe I should put up warning signs all over the facility in addition to the explanation at reception. It would be good if they all behaved well, but it might be difficult at first because people who don't know anything about the place will come here."

Even in her world, foreigners with no knowledge on how to properly enter a bath had been a problem because of their manners. The same situation was to be expected here.

"Though, it'd be a good idea for someone to warn them or show them by example."

She considered having the children fill that role since customers would be less likely to make a fuss if children warned them. However, they had work and school themselves.

"I guess I'll wait and see, then."

She didn't know how much a Beloved's power would correlate to the people's manners, so she figured she could afford to wait and see just how bad they would be. If they ended up being *too* bad, a warning from Ruri herself was bound to straighten them out.

As Ruri pondered over that matter, she heard one of the children say, "Lady Beloved, my head's starting to feel all woozy." Her face was flushed red and she was obviously having a hot flash.

"Whoa, hurry and get out of the water! Everyone else too!"

It seemed the child had soaked a little too long. She wasn't used to bathing in hot water. That extended to the other children as well, as they showed signs of lightheadedness. They didn't know the limit since it was their first time, so Ruri hurried them out of the bath and gave them some water to drink.

She was relieved to see that none of the children got to the point of collapse. However, in the men's bath, since they were keeping up with the hot-spring-loving manager, apparently many of the kids got heat exhaustion. Perhaps because he was teaching them how to bathe, even some of the adults got lightheaded as a result of sitting in the unfamiliar water for so long trying to follow his example. This was bound to happen if you stuck a bunch of rookies with a professional.

The lobby, where people could relax after their bath, wound up being a convalescence room for the heat-exhausted adults and children. Out of all of those that went to the men's side, the manager was the only one doing just fine. The girls on Ruri's side of the bath recovered quickly since their symptoms were only mild. They were running around handing out water to the heat-stricken boys.

"Hmm, maybe we need a warning to tell people to soak in moderation."

Once everyone had recovered, Ruri began to make food. She was making takoyaki, the dish she planned on serving once the spring officially opened. Since she hadn't been able to get octopus yet, she put cheese in the batter instead.

The children looked at the strange griddle riddled with holes with great interest—as did the adults, who clapped at the sight of her flipping the dough with the awl.

"What an odd shape."

"I've never seen food shaped like this."

The Nation of the Dragon King was a nation of many races and creeds as well as an international port city with a wide variety of different foods and ingredients. One of those ingredients, Ruri discovered, was a seasoning that resembled Japanese katsu sauce. Praise be to this great melting pot of a nation! She never imagined she would encounter katsu sauce in a different world. Not only was takoyaki possible now, but so was everyone's favorite smorgasbord of batter, cabbage, and meat—okonomiyaki.

After Ruri finished grilling up the balls of batter, she finished them off with a layer of sauce.

"Oh, these are delicious."

"I could see myself packing a few of these away."

The taste was generally well-received, but Ruri found it lacking. She was used to the real deal. However, as long as there was no octopus, there was no choice but to go with cheese for a while.

Discounting the mass hot flash, everyone enjoyed the hot spring. Ruri determined that the nation's people would like the experience too.

It was time for the grand opening, and it wasn't long before people started to trickle in.

The day before, Ruri had paid the slum children to walk around town with signs. Maybe the advertisement had helped because there was a satisfactory number of customers for the first day. There was even a group that stayed all night—a group of passionate hot spring lovers who hailed from the Nation of the Beast King. They ran to the hot spring as soon as it opened to the public.

The children she hired as personnel seemed to be doing well too. She looked at the child working the reception desk, and despite there being some room for improvement, there were no problems so far. She even went to check on the child in charge of cooking to see they were doing a good job of both serving the customers and cooking as taught.

However, there was a bit of a problem at the amusement facilities. Not a huge problem, of course, but the kids there were pretty swamped with customers. To Ruri, the hot spring was the main attraction. But that didn't register with the Nation of the Dragon King's people, who weren't accustomed to the concept of bathing. A great deal of people came out of curiosity since it was the first day, but it was fewer than expected. The people flocked more toward the entertainment facilities.

Amarna was ecstatic to sell so much merchandise due to the massive influx of people. She was even more excited than usual. On the other hand, the kids were feeling topsy-turvy and couldn't handle things all that well. The crowds were pretty big, and the kids were trying to serve customers, even though they were sniffling and tearing up.

This was *bad news.*

Facilities like these were a rare commodity in a nation where sources of entertainment as a whole were scarce. Adults and children alike were flooding in to play pinball and bowling. Some were cutting in line and yelling for people to hurry up. If things kept up like this, it could develop into a massive commotion.

Ruri took out a whistle she had for just this occasion, took a deep breath, and blew into it, producing a loud *tweeeeeet.*

The uproar stopped all at once. All eyes curiously turned to Ruri.

"Line up properly! No cutting in line! If you can't wait patiently, you'll be barred from entry!" That was Ruri's final say on the matter, and there wasn't anyone around who would still raise a fuss after hearing a Beloved's warning.

Once they had quieted down, Ruri decided to move up the scheduled time for sports in an attempt to thin out the number of people. She went to the plaza in the center of the building, between the hot spring and the recreational facilities, and drew a simple line in the ground. The children that Ruri had asked to participate were all standing in a row, dressed in clothes with numbers on them. Little by little, people gathered to see what she was up to.

"We'll now be playing a game. Since it's one that doesn't exist in the Nation of the Dragon King, I'll first explain the rules."

Ruri gave a brief explanation of dodgeball and asked the kids to put on a demonstration. The rules were simple: if you were hit, you were out. They were so simple, in fact, that the children picked up on them immediately. Seeing how it was a game that only needed a single ball to play, it could possibly spread within the Nation of the Dragon King, mainly among the younger generation.

Ruri asked for participants for the next game, but mainly just the children raised their hands. Some adults also participated, but they took the game more seriously. Whenever they pegged a child with a ball, the other children would meet them with a chorus of boos.

In a world where entertainment was scarce, it was safe to say that the grand opening was a rousing success. However, Ruri decided to add more little by little so that people didn't get bored with the still-limited number of entertainment options. Sure, there was better entertainment in Ruri's world compared to this selection, but there was also a limit to what she could recreate. She was a little worried that she would run out of material.

After a few days, it was clear that the hot spring didn't attract as many people as the entertainment facilities. The trade-off to all this was that they gained a dedicated fan base, and there were quite a few regular customers that frequented every day—the building manager from the Nation of the Beast King among them. He apparently had his own bath at home, but the spring must have been leagues better. Ruri didn't want it to get so popular she wouldn't have time for a dip herself, so it was probably for the best that it was a little empty.

"Maybe I should invite Chelsie-san too, while I'm at it," Ruri said aloud. She wanted Chelsie to experience the hot spring she so painstakingly created. There was no better time than the present. Instead of just pondering, Ruri rushed off to Jade to ask for his permission.

11 Grandfather

"Jade-sama, may I step out for a bit?" Ruri asked as soon as she entered Jade's office.

Jade was in the middle of a break from work, relaxing with a drink in his hand. He put his cup down and waved for Ruri to come over. She approached without any forethought, and once she was in front of him, he pulled her hand and cradled her in his lap.

"Wha? Huh?!" Ruri screamed. Jade's abrupt behavior threw her into a panic. She wouldn't have minded if she had been in cat form, but as a human she was far too self-conscious. She could feel her face flush immediately.

She tried to get off of him, but Jade firmly held her in place, preventing her escape. Their faces were much closer than when she was a cat. Jade's face, smiling softly, was so close that she felt both happy and embarrassed to look directly at it. She could tell he was enjoying her reaction.

"Where are you going this time?" Jade asked.

"Ch-Chelsie-san's house. I want her to experience the hot spring for herself, so I was going to invite her to the royal capital."

"Chelsie's, you say? That's all well and good, but one thing, Ruri."

"Yes?"

Jade suspiciously stroked her cheek, startling her. What on earth was wrong with him today? He normally would never do something like this.

"You've been leaving me behind too much lately, haven't you? Do what you must with your hot spring, but if you abandon me for much longer, I'm going to want to lock you up."

Ruri jumped in an almost exaggerated manner.

Jade fiddled with the dragonheart around her neck, saying, "I assume you already know the meaning behind this, right?"

"Erm, well…"

"I don't care how long I have to wait, but don't leave me waiting too long."

Although she'd complained to Quartz, talking his ear off about it, Ruri had never expected Jade to be the first to address the matter. He wanted an answer soon. But at least he wasn't asking for it right away. Knowing that she had some time to think it over brought Ruri a tiny bit of relief.

Ruri decided to take the opportunity to ask Jade a few questions. "So, Jade-sama? The, um, person who becomes your mate will be your de facto queen, yes?"

"Yes."

"What is the queen supposed to do?"

"Nothing."

"What? Nothing? But isn't the queen supposed to have a lot of responsibilities? I'm practically clueless, but things like…helping you in your work or entertaining other nations?"

"Well, a normal queen of a normal nation would be involved in diplomacy and national politics, but you're a Beloved. Allowing a Beloved to get involved is out of the question. Your words are seen as the spirits' words, meaning people would comply with *whatever you say*. If that were to happen, the political landscape would be utter chaos."

Even if a political amateur were to propose an unnecessary policy, someone would normally shoot it down. But if said amateur was a Beloved, then no one could simply refute their suggestion. It would usher in a wave of political chaos. Barring Beloveds from politics ensured stability. No other country with a Beloved allowed them a say.

"Dragonkin are kings in the relationship anyway. They wouldn't let their mates out without permission. There have even been kings who *never* let their mates out in public."

"Are you talking about Quartz-sama, by any chance?"

"That's right. Master Quartz kept his mate extremely sheltered. I believe Agate had met her before, but few ever saw what she looked like. I've never even seen her. But that's not an uncommon occurrence for dragonkin."

"Does that mean that *you* also operate the same way, Jade-sama…?" Ruri asked, even more frightened of possibly being confined to the castle.

"What, will you let me shelter you like that?" Jade asked, his lips turning up into a grin.

Ruri felt like a cat staring a carnivorous beast in the face, but she shook her head as hard as she could. "I'm not trying to deny the affection that dragonkin have toward their mates, but I think everything should be done in moderation." She wanted to avoid total confinement if possible. She knew she'd try to escape no matter how fond of Jade she was.

"I see. Well, I'm always open to the idea if you'd like."

"I-I'll pass on that."

Jade was only half-joking, but his comment had flustered Ruri. He chuckled and said, "I didn't think that you'd stay still, Ruri. You can do whatever you want, however you want. Just don't do anything too dangerous. And make sure not to forget me too much, of course."

Jade didn't seem to be as possessive as Quartz despite being from the same race. In fact, he knew Ruri well and always put her first. His request not to forget about him was somewhat sweet in its own way.

"O-Okay," Ruri simply uttered, hot under the collar.

Jade's face then moved closer and closer until his lips met her forehead.

"Whoa, whoa, whoa!"

Ruri panicked at Jade's abrupt gesture, her cheeks blushing. She really had no idea what was going on with him today. He was being extremely forward.

"What has gotten into you, Jade-sama? You're acting strange today."

"Master Quartz told me that I'm not getting my feelings across clearly. So I've decided to take a more proactive approach."

"Quartz-sama, how could you?!" Ruri cursed. She wished she'd never talked to him about her love life the other day.

"I thought I should take it slow, which is what I've done so far. But if you want, I don't have to limit myself like that."

"No, please, take it slow!" Ruri said, her poor heart almost giving out. Even as she spoke, it was beating like a wild drum.

How did things end up like this? She had just come to ask for permission to go to Chelsie's, but now she felt herself in mortal peril.

"I'll be leaving for Chelsie's now!" Ruri exclaimed, hopping off of Jade's lap. He let her go without any resistance.

Once she left the room, she found Agate standing in front of her with a broad, suggestive smile. "What is it, Agate-san?" she asked.

"Dragonkin are very jealous beings, you know. You should be very, *very* careful. Still, I'm glad you two are on good terms."

Ruri didn't know what he'd heard from listening in, but she contained her urge to yell in embarrassment and instead rushed off without responding.

Ruri hopped aboard Kotaro and took to the skies. Once they were airborne, she remembered Jade's kiss earlier and clutched her head in anguish.

"*Is something the matter, Ruri?*" Kotaro asked. Her strange behavior worried him.

"O-Oh, nothing," Ruri said, choosing to fudge the truth rather than dare utter what had just happened moments ago.

Since Jade hadn't said anything about the dragonheart until then, he'd caught her completely off guard. He wasn't playing fair with his surprise display of proactive behavior, especially with that forehead kiss.

Ruri gently touched the spot his lips met and blushed. She was embarrassed to admit that part of her didn't mind it in the slightest.

"He said that I could do whatever I want…"

Jade would surely accept Ruri no matter how she conducted herself. A tiny part of her thought it might be okay to be sheltered as long as it was Jade doing it—but she kept that secret.

She slapped her blushing cheeks to get herself together as Rin watched her in bewilderment.

Chi was back at the castle, but since Kotaro and Rin were with her, Ruri was going out without a dragonkin escort. She wouldn't go to Chelsie's with anyone other than the spirits in the first place, but she had been going into town so much lately that a dragonkin security detail had become the norm. She felt free for the first time in a long while.

Ruri had thought that a guard escort was over the top, but there was no arguing against it. She'd felt cramped, but seeing as how she had been assaulted once before, it did give her a vague sense of relief. However, her views remained the same as before, and she didn't want to bring a host of soldiers on a casual trip to Chelsie's house. She was glad that Jade hadn't told her to bring guards along.

Kotaro was delighted by this. Ruri had been so busy with the hot spring lately that she hadn't been able to spend quality time with him and the other spirits. Chelsie's place would be free of disturbances. Ruri would talk to Chelsie, of course, but she could spend the rest of her time with him and the others.

After a few hours, they finally reached the forest where Chelsie dwelled.

Nowadays, Ruri had become so busy that she hadn't been able to visit, so it was her first time in a long time seeing the scenery around her. Not a single thing had changed from when she'd called this forest her home. The scenery reminded her of her peaceful life in those days, instantly flooding her with nostalgia.

"Oh, Chelsie-saaan!"

Since only acquaintances would drop by a place this remote, Chelsie usually left the front door unlocked. Ruri ran right into the house without a moment's delay. However, she saw something she didn't expect—there were *a lot* of spirits around. She went into the back of the house looking for Chelsie, but instead she met an unfamiliar older man. She stopped dead in her tracks.

"Huh?" The surprisingly well-built older man looked at Ruri and furrowed his brow. "Who the hell are you?"

"Um, I might ask you the same question…"

Ruri first thought that she'd entered into the wrong house, but Chelsie's house *was* the only house around, so that definitely wasn't it. In that case, who was this old man?

"Me? I'm Andal. You could say I'm Chelsie's husband of sorts."

"Husband…" Chelsie had never been never married, meaning she was a single mother with three sons, including Claus. However, since she had children, she had to have had a partner. The partner in question was the former king of the Nation of the Beast King and Arman's father.

"Are you the former Beast King?" Ruri asked.

"Aye, I am, but who are you? My kids and grandkids are all guys, so you aren't any grandkid of mine."

"I'm Ruri, sir."

The old man placed his hand on his chin as if the name rang a bell. "So, you're the 'Ruri' that Beryl spoke of, eh?"

"Huh?"

"Someone here?" asked another voice. It wasn't Chelsie's voice either, but another male voice.

Surprised that there were even more people here, Ruri turned around and her eyes opened wide in surprise. There stood an elderly man with blond hair, blue eyes, and a sculpted physique.

"Huh? Wha? What?" Ruri stammered in shock. "Grandpa?!"

"Ooh, my lovely granddaughter! How have you been doing all this time?"

Ruri's grandfather, Beryl, came toward her with his beefy, muscular arms spread wide and embraced her firmly.

"Grk… Can't…breathe…"

It was less a firm embrace and more a muscular stranglehold—one that was cutting off Ruri's oxygen supply.

"I give, give," Ruri said. She was starting to fear that her guts would pop out if the hug went on any longer. He let go of her and she breathed a sigh of relief. "I thought I was a goner…"

"Sorry, sorry. I was so darned happy that I squeezed a little *too* tight," Beryl said.

Although it was more than just *a little*, now wasn't the time to nitpick over that.

"Why are *you* here, Grandpa?!"

"'Why'? Didn't I tell you that I'd be coming to this world?"

"That's not what I meant. I meant *when* did you come?! Why are you at Chelsie-san's house?! Are mom and dad with you?!" Ruri questions came out in rapid succession.

"Shut up! What's with all the damn commotion?!" Chelsie shouted, entering the room. "Oh, Ruri. You're here?"

"Chelsie-saaan! Please explain what's going on!"

Chelsie was about to ask what Ruri was talking about, but once she spotted Beryl, she figured it out immediately. "Okay, just settle down, child."

Chelsie urged Ruri to take a seat and went to prepare a cup of tea for her. In the meantime, Beryl greeted the spirits.

"So, you two are Kotaro and Rin, are you? Neither of you had physical forms in the other world, so I had no idea."

"*Yes, it's been quite some time,*" Rin replied.

"*Glad to see you're doing well,*" Kotaro added.

Rin and Kotaro had taken a trip to Ruri's world to deliver a message before, so they were on familiar terms. But seeing as how they'd both left their bodies in this world before they'd left, Beryl didn't pick up on who they were right away.

113

After drinking her tea and regaining her composure, Ruri turned to face Beryl once more. "Grandpa, exactly *when* did you get to this world?"

"Aah, when was it? Half a year ago, I believe?"

"Half a year ago?! What've you been doing all this time?!"

"I was wandering around, trying to get to the nation you were in, and that's when I ran into Andal here. The two of us hit it off and went journeying together. Then he suggested I meet his missus before we set off to meet you. When we arrived, we learned that you had crashed here for a spell. So we accepted her hospitality and stayed here for a few days, hearing stories of your life here in this world."

Ruri's jaw was practically on the floor. "Why did you never tell me? You could've let me know right away if you'd used the spirits as messengers."

Beryl had just as many spirits hanging around him as Ruri. She'd never seen any of them before, so she suspected they were her grandfather's entourage.

"Well, I wanted to show up and surprise you, y'see," Beryl said with a hearty laugh.

Ruri could feel herself crumbling on the inside. He was far too reckless, trying to reach her on his own in a different world without even relying on her. Even she would have keeled over dead in the middle of nowhere if it weren't for Chelsie. She simply had to admire her grandfather's tenacity for coming here with only the clothes on his back. It was unreal that he had been able to travel for half a year like that. Then again, perhaps his luck in meeting Andal along the way also played a part.

"Wait, why didn't you just have them bring you to the Nation of the Dragon King when you came over here from the other side?" Ruri asked. It would have saved him half a year's worth of trekking.

"They told me it's because no one knows where the paths lead to. There was no guarantee I'd conveniently fall into the same place you were. I ended up close to a place called the Nation of the Spirit King."

"Oh, right. Well, I'm glad you managed to make it this long safely."

"There are people here who can see spirits, unlike in our world, y'know. They called me a 'Beloved' or whatever and set me up with food and shelter. Never had anybody *worship* me before, so you can guess my surprise. But I managed to get by thanks to it."

"Spirit-based religion is big here in this world, yeah," Ruri commented.

Beryl had conveniently landed in a place where the people could see spirits and worshiped them. If he had been transported to a nation with a population that couldn't see spirits, like Ruri had when she wound up in Nadasha, then things would have ended up ugly.

"I'm glad you're safe and sound, Grandpa, but what about mom and dad? Didn't they come with you? Where are they?"

"Oh, we got separated when we came to this world," he said, like it was no big deal.

Ruri leaned in, raising her voice. "What do you mean?! You don't know where they are?!"

"I'm not sure why myself, but according to the spirits, as they were coming here, some kind of outside power shone, space distorted, and Riccia and Kohaku got dragged off. They're *somewhere* here in this world, so relax."

"How do you expect me to relax?! And why are you so nonchalant?! Those two are practically missing!"

Though his daughter and her husband had gone missing, you couldn't tell from his calm demeanor. It almost seemed as if Ruri was the odd one here for yelling.

"Kotaro, can you search for them right away?"

"*Mm-hmm. It'll take a little longer since I don't know where in the world they are, but I can do it.*"

"That's fine by me, so please, if you could."

"*Right away.*" Not even Kotaro could search the entire world instantly, but she had no other choice but to rely on him.

"I hope they're safe..." Ruri said, worried about her parent's safety.

Anger started to set in. She was angry at her grandfather for not telling her something so important, especially since he could have easily done so if he'd wanted to.

"I can't believe you, Grandpa! If you knew that's what happened to them, why didn't you tell me sooner? It's been half a year! You don't know what could've happened to them in that time!"

"Calm down, Ruri," Beryl urged.

"As if I could!" Ruri snapped back, her tone getting edgier.

"Riccia is my daughter. A little something like this wouldn't do her in. I didn't raise her to be that soft."

Ruri saw his point. Considering her mother's personality, Ruri could imagine she was *enjoying* the situation.

"The real problem is Kohaku," Beryl said, mentioning Ruri's father. He was a straitlaced, high-strung man who was always being tossed and turned by Riccia's off-the-wall antics.

"Well, I think he'll be fine since Riccia is with him, but I worry if she's putting him through the wringer."

"Dad's stomach must be killing him by now," Ruri stated.

Not only were they in unfamiliar territory, but her father was much more delicate than her mother. Ruri worried about whether he could survive—survive her mother, that is.

"In any case, come to the castle, Grandpa. I want to introduce you to the Dragon King."

"Ooh, your hubby, huh? Been achin' to meet him."

"He's not my 'hubby'!" Ruri exclaimed. "Who even told you that?!"

Ruri had no idea where he'd learned that or how he could have picked it up. Chelsie was the only person she could think of, but Ruri hadn't even told her that she'd received Jade's dragonheart. She had planned on having a nice long discussion with her about that today.

"The old-timers there sent over a letter."

"Agate-san…!"

Ruri had almost forgotten about him. Had he really been going around telling people indiscriminately like that? She could understand that he was happy that Jade was finally in the mood for romance, but Ruri still hadn't accepted his feelings, so she wished he wouldn't report her every little move. Fortunately, the news hadn't spread to the capital, but it was only a matter of time. She wanted to tell them to have some self-control. Gradually being forced into marriage seemed like a real possibility at this rate—a possibility that was giving her a headache.

"Just so you know, that's not certain yet. Jade-sama and I aren't in that sort of relationship."

"Darn, really?" Beryl said, sounding disappointed.

"At any rate, I want you to meet Jade-sama. I'd like for mom and dad to meet him as well, but they're missing. I need to report that to Jade-sama too."

"Yes, you should report that to His Majesty," said Chelsie.

Ruri nodded. "Indeed. So, Chelsie-san, would you come with me to the capital?"

"You want me to come too?" Chelsie asked.

"I built a hot spring in the capital and I want you to take a dip in it."

"Hot spring, eh?" Chelsie said, not seeming very interested. There was the bathhouse that Ruri had built in the yard, but it was unlikely that Chelsie had used it at all. "Well, hot spring aside, I suppose I'll take a trip to the capital. Master Quartz has returned, right?"

"Yes, he has."

"I'd love to say my hellos to the man. Plus, the tournament to decide the king is around the corner, so I suppose I'll stay for a bit."

Ruri practically jumped for joy. She was happy to hear Chelsie could stay for an extended period of time, no doubt feeling similar to how Jade felt when Quartz came back to the kingdom.

Beryl added, "Oho, a hot spring?"

"Oh? There's a hot spring in the Nation of the Dragon King too, is there?" Andal asked.

Both old men were more interested in the hot spring than Chelsie. Andal was also interested in meeting Quartz and seeing the tournament, so he decided to accompany her.

12 Missing

Beryl and Andal rode on Chelsie in her dragon form, heading toward the royal capital. The plan had been to relax at Chelsie's house for a little while longer, but once Ruri had heard that her parents had gone missing, she knew there was no time to rest idly. Kotaro had been disappointed that his time with Ruri had been stolen from him, but they needed to report to Jade, so he rushed along.

When Ruri arrived at the castle, she made a straight line for the royal office and rushed inside, forgetting to even knock beforehand.

"Master Jade, may I have a word?!"

"Ruri? You're back earlier than I thought. Finished with your visit already?" Jade asked, confused.

Claus, who was present as well, blinked in surprise as Chelsie entered the room after Ruri. Once he caught sight of Andal following after Chelsie, his surprise turned into full-blown shock.

"Father?!"

"Heya there, Claus. How've you been?"

"What in blazes are you doing here?!"

"Dropped by to see Chelsie for old time's sake, one thing led to another, and here I am."

Not even Claus could hold back his amazement at the impromptu and overdue reunion with his father, Andal.

Jade had expected Chelsea to come, but he didn't expect to see the previous Beast King. His surprise was apparent.

"Well, I never expected you to be here, Andal," commented Jade.

"Ooh, Jade, been a spell, hasn't it?"

"Yes, you seem to be doing well."

"Still kicking," Andal added with a laugh.

"I won't ask what you've been up to, but you might want to pay Arman a visit every once in a while."

"No thanks. I have an inkling that if I *do* go, he's gonna greet me with a fist to the face. Well, not that I'd ever let the scamp land a free punch on me anyway. Ha ha!"

"What goes around comes around," Jade uttered with an exasperated sigh.

The previous Beast King, Andal, had disappeared without properly handing over the throne, which had plunged the nation into a huge civil war over the succession. While it was unclear what Andal had been thinking when he did that, Arman, the current Beast King, undoubtedly had mixed feelings about the root of this evil.

"By the way, who is that behind you?" Jade asked, his attention finally turning to the last person to enter the room.

Ruri grabbed Beryl's arm and brought him in front of Jade. "This would be my grandpa."

"Your grandfather? I see. So, you've come to this world."

"Yup. I'm Ruri's grandfather, Beryl."

"I'm the king of this nation, Jade."

They both reached out and exchanged a handshake.

Beryl stared long and hard at Jade's face before breaking out into a smile. "So, you're Ruri's husband, are ya? Damn, Ruri. He's a looker. You nabbed yourself quite the handsome man. He's got a face that's Riccia's type, so I'm sure she'll be giddy when she finds out."

Beryl was not the least bit intimidated even in the presence of a king. His crass behavior actually bothered Ruri more than anyone else in the room. She'd told him that he had things wrong, but in Beryl's mind, he had already identified Jade as her husband.

"You're impossible, Grandpa! Jade-sama, I'm sorry about that."

"It's all right," Jade said. "He seems to be quite the lively gentleman, similar to you. But why is he with Chelsie and the others? Did you meet them on the way here?"

"My blockheaded grandfather apparently came here half a year ago. During that time, he and the previous Beast King hit it off and went journeying around the world. Even though I've been *anxious* about *when* he'd get here."

"Well, it's a good thing he did make it here safely, isn't it? So, is it just Lord Beryl here? Where are your parents?"

Ruri's expression suddenly turned gloomy. "Well, it seems that there was a problem when they came to this world, and we don't know where they went."

"What do you mean?" Jade asked.

Ruri told Jade what Beryl had told her, but since Beryl didn't really know what happened himself, the cause was still a mystery. Even the spirits around Beryl were clueless.

"*Space went all wavy!*"

"*Riccia got yanked through!*"

"Dragged through a distortion in space, were they?" Jade mused.

"What could it be?" Ruri asked.

Jade had no idea. The only ones capable of moving between worlds were the spirits.

As they all pondered over what could have happened, Kotaro added his own conjecture.

"*I can think of one thing,*" Kotaro began as his face turned grim, "*and that is the magic that summoned you to this world, Ruri. If summoning magic was invoked while they came over, there is a chance that is what pulled them away.*"

"You don't think something's happening in Nadasha again, do you?" Ruri asked. But that couldn't be since they'd destroyed all of the documents pertaining to summoning to prevent something like that from happening.

"*No, I also thought that and checked Nadasha first, but there was nothing there. Not even a trace of people being summoned.*"

"So you're saying that someplace *other* than Nadasha summoned them?"

"*I'll need some more time to investigate further,*" Kotaro said. Not even *he* could do everything at once; he wasn't omnipotent.

Ruri knew that, but she was still impatient. Even as she spoke, she couldn't help but worry about her parents.

"Ah, quit your worrying," said Beryl. "Those two will be just fine. You're worrying too much, Ruri."

In contrast to Ruri, Beryl kept a positive attitude—a very *irksome,* positive attitude.

"Why are you being so optimistic, Grandpa?!" she asked, wanting to know where this confidence of his was coming from.

"If we can't find 'em, we can't find 'em, right? Panicking won't make them pop up. You need to have a broader mind. You must train your spirit to go undaunted!"

"Your grandfather is, how do I put this, quite the easygoing character," said Jade.

"That's certainly *one* way of putting it. But you don't have to mince words, Jade-sama. My grandpa is a total *meathead.*"

Ruri let out a deep sigh. Though she couldn't be as calm as Beryl, she knew that talking wouldn't produce anything, so she decided to wait for Kotaro to finish his search.

A few days later, Kotaro brought Ruri the results of his search. Ruri kept her excitement and anxiety in check as she waited for what he had to say.

"I couldn't find them. I used the winds to search high and low, but your parents were nowhere to be found."

"No way!"

"I had Earth help me just in case, but none of us could find them."

"So if you and Chi can't find them, does that mean they aren't in this world?"

Kotaro was the Spirit of Wind. Wherever there was air, he had free passage to. However, they were somewhere the wind couldn't reach. Not even Chi, the Spirit of Earth, could turn up anything.

A place with neither wind nor ground didn't seem likely to exist in this world.

Rin fluttered over to Ruri's cheek, nuzzling against it. *"Ruri, just calm down. He isn't done speaking yet."*

"Rin…"

"There's no way that Earth and I would come up empty. That is, given one exception—Spirit Slayer magic. Our powers have problems reaching places where it's housed."

Before Ruri could ask where someplace like that would be, Jade stepped in with a grim face and an even grimmer tone. "So…Yadacain?"

Kotaro nodded. *"No other place in the world would be using Spirit Slayer except there. If they landed there, then it makes sense why I can't find them."*

"Then again," Rin added, *"I could see this happening if that spirit was involved too."*

Rin's words caught Ruri's attention. "Who is 'that spirit'?"

"*Our brethren, the Spirit of Light. Light's barriers make it so that no other spirit's powers can pass through. Not even Kotaro would be able to tell if Light was hiding them. But I can't think of any reason why Light would hide a couple of people from another world, so I'd say the most likely candidate here is Yadacain instead.*"

Yadacain was a nation where witches dwelled and spirits didn't. Because of their use of Spirit Slayer, it was known as a place abandoned by the spirits.

"*That land is a mystery in more ways than one. Plus, it wouldn't be surprising that a witch would know about summoning magic. After all, the priests of Nadasha were capable of doing it.*"

Yadacain was the birthplace of Spirit Slayer magic, and the Nadashians had used Spirit Slayer for their summonings. It would make sense that Yadacain had somehow passed it on to the Nadashian priest.

"If I recall, Joshua is on the way there right now, isn't he, Jade-sama?" asked Ruri.

"Yes, he might have gained a lead by now. As much as I'd like to get in touch with him, that land inhibits any contact, so we'll just have to wait for his regular correspondence," Jade explained. Even *his* hands were tied in this situation.

"Aaah, of all the places to wind up, why *thereeee*?!" Ruri howled, clutching her head. However, it wasn't set in stone that they were in Yadacain; it was just highly likely that they were.

Jade placed his hand on his chin. "Yadacain is a closed nation. I think any outsider just showing up would raise some flags, but if the people of Yadacain did conduct a summoning, it must've been done with a purpose. That being said, I'm not sure what that purpose would even be."

"Well, I hope they're both all right," said Ruri.

If they were a closed nation, then it wasn't as though they were looking for someone to spearhead their war efforts like Nadasha had been. Still, no one knew what else their goal could be.

"I'll send some operatives other than Joshua there. Just have faith and wait, Ruri. I assure you, it'll be okay," Jade said, petting her head in a consoling manner.

She gave a small nod in response. Right now, she could only believe in what her grandfather had told her—along with his mysterious sense of confidence.

13 Undercover

As he stared at the swaying waves, Joshua sighed, wondering why he was here in the first place.

"Man, why does everything always fall to me? Give me a *break*, for crying out loud."

Just when he'd thought he could finally rest after returning from the Nation of the Beast King, he had been hit with an unexpected order. Not only that, but he was tasked to go to Yadacain—the number one place intelligence operatives wanted to avoid.

Yadacain's self-isolation made it difficult to conduct any sort of covert operations there. If it weren't an island, one could at least gather some intel from the surrounding areas, but there was no such luck. With no idea of how life was conducted in their land, any operative would have trouble carrying out their mission. One unwise move would instantly tip off the people, leaving things dead in the water.

Joshua had most likely been chosen because of his quick wits and stealthy movements, but he was still upset that this had happened the second he got back to the kingdom. After such a long trip away, he had lain down on his bed with dreams of sleeping in until noon. Once he'd received word to come to the castle early in the morning, he'd seriously considered just going on the run.

Jade had given him orders to go to Yadacain, and he wouldn't listen to anything Joshua had to say. Joshua tried all of the smooth-talking excuses in his arsenal to get out of it, but in the end, he'd had no choice but to suck up his tears. After all, Jade told him these were "king's orders."

Even Joshua understood it was necessary to investigate if a witch had been involved with the incident in the Nation of the Beast King. Nevertheless, he still spewed complaint after complaint, asking why it couldn't have been someone else tasked with this job.

As they looked out on the ocean, Joshua's operative colleague consolingly patted him on the shoulder. Since Joshua couldn't very well conduct covert operations in Yadacain all by himself, two other agents were accompanying him.

It was honestly difficult to predict when this mission would be over, but the very thought had made Joshua so sad that he'd decided not to think about it altogether and to instead focus on getting this over with. He'd boarded a small boat bound for Yadacain and shouted his determination toward the boundless stretch of sea before him.

"Mark my words," Joshua had said, "I'm going to get some rest once this is over. I don't care who says what; it's happening. No one's gonna get in my way!"

"Sure thing. Good luck on that," answered one of his colleagues.

Joshua had been powering the boat by using wind magic in order to travel as quickly as possible, but at a certain point, the wind stopped. No, the naturally generated wind hadn't stopped; the wind Joshua was generating had stopped. He tried using other magic as a test, but nothing worked.

"So, we're in their territory, huh?" he mumbled.

The area around Yadacain was a dead zone due to the Spirit Slayer magic crafted by the witches. Seeing as how his magic was now useless, it meant they were in Yadacain territory. There would be no more magic from here on out. They would have to rely on their dragonkin physical strength.

After a while of slowly floating toward their destination, they finally saw land ahead of them. That was Yadacain. Although he should have been steeling himself, Joshua was practically shaking in excitement as he declared, "Let's wrap this puppy up and get to vacation! Look out, Yadacain, 'cause here I come! I'm gonna expose every single one of your secrets! Ha ha!"

"Jeez, think he's been so busy that his personality changed?" asked the one operative.

"No, I think that's just the desperation talking," answered the other.

They decided to wait until night to go ashore. Under the shroud of darkness, they landed and pulled the boat up on the bank. But they couldn't leave it there like that or they'd be discovered. Joshua tried opening up his pocket space and found that it opened like normal.

"Looks like we can use our pocket spaces."

They had already confirmed in Nadasha that supreme-level spirits could still use their powers even with Spirit Slayer magic active. The one who governed time and space, the Spirit of Time, Lydia, was a supreme-level spirit herself, which meant her magic still worked.

They stored the boat in Joshua's pocket space and waited for daybreak to begin moving. They knew the lay of the land to a certain extent already, having studied the reports from a different operative who'd visited Yadacain in the past. They headed for what would be the "royal capital," or at least that's what they would have called it in the Nation of the Dragon King.

Yadacain was not very big. It was entirely overgrown with trees, but the center of the island had been developed so that the populace could live there. There were other villages scattered around, but Joshua and his cohorts had their sights set on the witches' stronghold. They started their search in the town that housed the castle, where the witch ruling as king resided.

The royal capital of Yadacain was smaller than the Nation of the Dragon King's capital, both in scale and in populace, but the comparison wasn't fair. There were small villages more prosperous than this one in the Nation of the Dragon King. However, this extremely small town had a unique atmosphere. The houses were wooden with triangular roofs, and despite being rather close to the Nation of the Dragon King, the culture felt entirely different.

The moment Joshua and his crew arrived in town, they felt the heat of the townspeople's suspicious glares. Their party looked like regular people, so as long as they didn't transform into dragons, no one would recognize them as dragonkin. Demi-humans might have been able to perceive a dragonkin's particular, intimidating aura, but the research told them that only humans lived in this nation, which meant they could avoid detection. And since they couldn't use their magic right now, their mana wouldn't be noticeable either.

This nation had been founded by witches. Witches could use magic called "sorcery" without the aid of spirits. Because of this, they had been persecuted, and had fled with their tribesmen to seek sanctuary. For reasons unknown, no demi-humans had been living among them. That was why there were only humans living here.

Though Joshua and the others looked no different from a normal human being, their clothes differed from the residents of this land. They were clearly outsiders. Also, this town wasn't even a quarter of the size of the Nation of the Dragon King's capital, so most of the townspeople probably knew each other by face. Then, out of nowhere, a pack of strangers had walked into town. It only made sense that the people would be cautious given their land's lack of foreign diplomacy.

After Joshua and the others had walked around the town for a while, a group of people with weapons—presumably soldiers—approached them. Joshua's group subtly smirked; they had been wondering when their welcome party would come.

"Who are you people?!"

"You're from a foreign land. What are you here for?!"

The soldiers threatened them with their swords pointed. Joshua and his crew pretended to be innocent newcomers who were afraid of their weapons.

"We are but simple travelers," Joshua explained, reciting the lines he'd mentally rehearsed beforehand. He was acting as helpless and confused as possible. "We met upon a whale during our journey, which destroyed our ship and washed us ashore on this island. Although we managed to survive, our boat is damaged beyond repair, so we were wandering around lost until we stumbled upon this town."

The soldiers exchanged glances. They were slightly less cautious now, but they still kept their swords drawn.

"Dreadfully sorry to ask, but where might we be?" Joshua asked, of course knowing where they were.

"This is Yadacain," one of the soldiers answered.

"Yadacain? My word, I never thought we'd end up in Yadacain!" Joshua cried, his head pointed toward the sky as if he were screaming his dismay at the heavens. Joshua's two colleagues thought he was overdoing it a smidgen, but Joshua continued, undeterred. "We are in such luck that we washed ashore somewhere with people. But as much as I'd like to repair our boat and leave the island, all of our belongings were unfortunately washed away—we have nothing but the clothes on our backs."

"I see. That sounds pretty rough."

"We would like to earn some money to fix the ship, so could we trouble you to introduce us to some form of employment?"

Joshua's performance seemed to be convincing enough, because the soldiers bought his story. They looked at each other and began to discuss what to do about the island's rare and unexpected guests. After a while, they said they would talk it over with their superiors and told the three of them to follow them. Joshua and the other two dragonkin complied.

They traveled deeper into the heart of the town where the Yadacain castle stood. This was Joshua and his crew's final destination. However, they hadn't expected to be allowed inside so soon, so they entered the castle with growing tension. Even so, they had no intention of making a move at the moment. The soldiers were wary of their heretic group. They needed to loosen their guard first. A single screw-up would make the soldiers even more cautious, which would spell failure for their operation. For today, they would follow the soldiers' orders and behave themselves.

The soldiers led Joshua and his crew to their superior, who proceeded to ask them a list of questions—place of origin, purpose of travel, so on and so forth. It seemed that any outsiders were interrogated once they entered the castle. But the three of them had already hashed out their stories beforehand, so there were no discrepancies.

The superior bought their stories, albeit warily. Joshua and his crew were allowed to rent a vacant house, establish a base for themselves, and acquire jobs. After that, they kept from making any moves for a while and proceeded with the jobs they had been provided with.

"Woo, it's payday! Oh yeah!" Joshua exclaimed.

"You sure have gotten used to life here, haven't you?"

"Gonna just ditch going home and keep living here instead? Aha ha!"

Joshua and the others knocked their mugs, filled to the brim with alcohol, together and toasted. They appeared to be fully engrossed in their merrymaking, but their minds were focused on a presence outside. Someone was outside the house, looking inside. Even though the presence had remained hidden, Joshua and the others had detected them with their superior senses. It was probably someone from Yadacain. They were monitoring them—the foreign intruders.

Thanks to that, Joshua and the others couldn't carry out their plan. *Tap, tap, tap, tap.* They all started tapping on the table—a sound-based communication method used among intelligence operatives.

(*Those guys are still here, though,*) tapped the one operative.

(*Yeesh, someone's got time on their hands. When are they gonna drop the surveillance?*) tapped the other.

Joshua tapped, (*I swear, I can't wait to go home! The food here tastes like crap.*)

How long did they have to keep up this charade of a life? Joshua wanted to go back home so bad, but that wasn't an option. He had expected it to take a long time, but he hadn't thought he'd go *this* long without making a single move. The people of Yadacain were more cautious than they'd expected.

Joshua let out a weary sigh. His two colleagues shot him looks of sympathy.

After some more time had passed, Yadacain finally lifted the surveillance. That didn't necessarily mean they could take action right away, though. First they had to gather intel. Luckily, the townspeople had accepted Joshua and his companions as residents and were beginning to loosen up around them.

The purpose of their visit here was to find out if the witches had been involved in the Church of God's Light incident. To do that, they needed to learn about the witches' abilities. It was a given that they could use Spirit Slayer magic, but the real question lay in that method of resurrecting the dead. It was uncertain whether a witch of Yadacain had taught that to the church.

"This country is ruled by a witch, isn't it? What's the king like?" Joshua asked the housewife who lived next door. She would occasionally bring them food.

"I don't know. The witches are in charge of this land, and we commoners don't know who currently resides at the top," she explained.

"Is that a fact?" asked Joshua.

"It's said that the witch with the strongest sorcery at that time will stand as the king. But they don't ever show their face, so only the people who work at the castle know what they look like."

If the king was a mystery even to the citizens, then investigating them was going to be annoying.

"By the way, what can this 'sorcery' do? I'm kind of interested."

"Not sure. Only the witches are capable of it, so I have no clue. If you want to ask, ask a witch themselves. Well, not that you'd be able to meet them anyway. I was born and raised here and not even *I* have ever even met one."

"Huh. No kidding?"

Joshua asked some other people the same thing, but he learned nothing significant. However, after some time and some additional frustration, he finally caught a break.

"Is that for real?!" Joshua exclaimed as the neighborhood delinquent kids told him some information. The kids found it easy to cozy up to Joshua, not only because of his friendly nature but because he would always reward them for their troubles.

What he gained from the kids was a way into the castle, a secret passageway that only the children knew about.

"So, where is it?" Joshua asked.

The children grinned deviously and held out their hands, demanding compensation.

"Yeesh, you kids sure are shrewd. Here."

Once he gave the children a small tip, they smiled happily and told him the secret location.

Joshua finished up work and went back to their house. He leaned in a chair and let out a loud sigh, like a father just off from his day shift. As he did, one of his colleagues smiled in delight. After he carefully scoped out the area around the window, he closed the curtain and spread a sheet of paper on the table in front of Joshua. *Tap, tap.* Then he began speaking in the intelligence operative code.

(*Look, I've done it. I got the schematics of the castle.*)

Joshua's eyes bugged out and he leaned forward, digging his eyes into the paper. (*Seriously?! This isn't some fake, right?*)

(*Nah, it's absolutely real!*) replied his fellow operative with his head held high and proud. (*With this, we can break into the castle and check it out.*)

However, Joshua frowned. He knew it wouldn't be that easy. He tapped, (*No, not as long as we don't have any idea how many guards they have posted.*)

The other operative flared his nostrils, drawing the two's attention. He then slammed yet another sheet of paper down on the table.

(*Here's a diagram of where the troops are stationed and their patrol times.*)

(*Holy crap, seriously?*) tapped Joshua.

(*Hot damn, you're a genius!*) the other operative tapped.

(*Actually, how did you guys even get all this stuff?!*)

His colleague clicked his tongue aloud and wagged his finger. (*Heh, heh, heh. That's top secret, my friend.*)

His cocky display irritated Joshua a tad, but he couldn't really complain since he himself hadn't done anything. But that was when he noticed something. Upon closer inspection of the plans…

(*Wait, this info is filled with friggin' holes!*) Joshua tapped, slamming the paper down on the table in anger. The info they'd brought was something he really wanted, but the schematics of the castle were oversimplified and full of unexplained areas. The soldier layout and patrol times were also extremely minimal.

(*Hey, lay off of us. You should be thanking us that we were able to nab this much intel!*)

(*Hell yeah. We worked our tails off for this!*)

Joshua sighed and tapped, (*Okay, sure, hard work and all, but you can't get any details off of these.*)

The operative patted Joshua on the shoulder. (*Well, we'll just have to break in and find out. Meaning it's your job to break into the castle.*)

(*Pardon?! Why me?!*) Joshua tapped, freaking out.

(*Isn't it obvious? Because you haven't* done *anything.*)

(*Yup, yup. It's time for you to get to work.*)

(*Damn it! Listen, I've put in work too. Why, I got info about a secret passage into the castle from the delinquent kids, you know!*)

(*Then that's even more reason for you to go.*)

(*Yeah, get out there. I'll make sure to collect your ashes.*)

Joshua carried out his operations on moonless nights. He would always enter the castle under the shroud of darkness.

His objective was to determine if the witches had any involvement with the Church of God's Light. In order to find out for sure, he needed to examine the area around the witches. The problem was that he had no way of knowing who was a witch. He had no choice but to check every room from top to bottom for the time being. However, he was dumbfounded by the schematics of this large castle, even though it was only a fraction of the size of the one back home.

Basically, he would move at night when there were fewer people and hide out during the day. He had been doing this for a few days now. There had been many occasions where he had almost been discovered, but he'd managed to avoid detection and stealthily move through the castle while comparing his cohorts' intel.

So far, Joshua hadn't found a single thing that seemed off. The only place he hadn't checked was the king's area—the area most heavily guarded. It was reasonable to think that the most promising area would be where the king, said to be the strongest of all the witches, resided. But there would likely be other witches around them. It was a sizable risk going near there. After all, Joshua couldn't use magic, but his targets could.

Joshua had only operated at night so far, but it seemed he would also need to search during the day if he wanted to gain any more intel. Normally, he would have pretended to be a castle worker by swiping and wearing one of their uniforms, but there weren't that many workers in this castle. And since most of them were familiar with each other, he'd be found out if he tried infiltrating that way. If he had been able to use wind magic, he could have obtained information while staying put, but that was off the table too. The only way he was getting anything was with old-fashioned espionage, a process that demanded a lot of time.

And so, after many hours of nerve-racking infiltration—while whining about wanting to go home—Joshua managed to ascertain that the king left their duties to the other witches and hid themselves during the day. They would confine themselves to a certain room and do *something* there, something that only their aides seemed to know.

Joshua waited until nightfall to break into the room. It was locked, but opening it wasn't too difficult. He picked the lock in a matter of seconds.

There was nothing out of the ordinary inside. In fact, if one were pressed to note something, it would be that there was *literally* nothing in there. What had the king been doing in this room the entire day? Joshua immediately picked up on something, however. There was an oddly strong wind blowing from underneath him.

(*These things always have some kind of mechanism somewhere…*) Joshua thought as he carefully patted down the walls and floors. He must have triggered something, because a part of the wall caved in with a click. The floor moved to reveal a staircase leading to an underground area.

Joshua grinned and slowly made his way down the dark set of stairs. He climbed all the way down and walked the passage below until he saw the floor above move again and close shut. He was confident there was a switch on this side as well, so he didn't panic and instead proceeded down the path as intended. He eventually reached a single room at the end.

The dark room didn't have any source of light, so Joshua had to provide some light of his own. But since he couldn't use magic, he lit the lamp he'd brought out from his pocket space with a match. Not using magic was inconvenient to no end.

The flickering flame of the lamp soon shed light over the room— and that was when it happened.

"*Hngaaaah!*"

Joshua jumped with a start. He looked in the direction of the scream to find several people locked in a cage. Their bodies were skin and bone, their eyes sunken and lifeless, and their flesh dry and wrinkled. Their appearance was sadly familiar to him.

"Damn, don't scare me like that. Hey, wait, ain't these the zombies from the Nation of the Beast King?" They seemed just as incapable of cognitive thought and bellowed just as incomprehensibly as the zombies from back then. "If these things are here, then that means the witches of this nation *were* involved with the Church of God's Light after all?"

Joshua searched around, shining his lamp in all directions. He then found a magic circle and vials filled with blood, just like in the Church of God's Light's hideout.

"Is this dragonkin blood? No, I mean, how would the witches of Yadacain even get their hands on dragonkin blood?" He looked through the mess of papers atop the room's table. "Resurrecting the dead with dragon blood? Summoning from another world?" The results of those experiments were written down—none of them successful.

(*Well, looks like we've caught them red-handed. Also, I'm pretty sure this other world summoning stuff is the same magic Nadasha used to summon Ruri. Those guys used Spirit Slayer as well, come to think of it. Were they connected with the witches of Yadacain too?*)

Joshua was about to stuff some of these documents into his pocket space when he heard the footsteps of someone walking the hall from outside.

(*Crap! No one's supposed to be here at this hour!*) Joshua thought. His investigation from the past few days had shown that no one visited this room at this time of day.

Joshua scrambled, ducking behind whatever cover he could find. He was in luck; the room was so cluttered with things that he had plenty of places to hide.

A few moments later, the door slowly opened and a couple— a man and a woman—walked in. Joshua realized that the woman was a witch and the king of Yadacain. He remembered her face since he'd caught a glimpse of her talking with her aides during his search. Joshua wasn't familiar with the man with her, but he always seemed to be near the king, conducting business with her. He looked like an ordinary man, but something struck Joshua as odd. He listened in to their conversation, being careful not to be spotted.

"It looks like you don't have much blood left, beloved one."

"I know! But this is all the blood they left behind. I can't do my research at this rate. I will not allow that to happen. Not until I bring them back to life," the woman said, biting her nails in frustration. "I have to get dragon blood somehow."

"Yes, but this isn't just something you can obtain easily. You gained this blood because that individual provided it."

(*That individual? Who are they talking about?*) Joshua wondered. Someone gave them the blood. A collaborator?

"If we don't have the blood, then why don't we just go out and get it?" the king asked.

"Beloved one, that would mean—"

"We will send an army to the Nation of the Dragon King. We'll capture a dragonkin and take their blood."

"That would start a war with the Nation of the Dragon King."

"It matters not. We'll bring back as many dragonkin as we can," she said, proposing war like it was absolutely nothing.

Did she really think she could win a fight against dragonkin? Or was she saying that her experiments were worth the risk?

"Will Yadacain's army be able to capture dragonkin, I wonder," said the man.

"I'll unleash the kraken. If we use Spirit Slayer, then we'll be able to capture at least one or two dragonkin, no matter how strong they are. If that doesn't work, you'll lend your powers."

(*Whoa, whoa. Are you for real here? I'd better contact His Majesty as soon as possible.*) Joshua thought.

The man placed his hand on the woman's shoulder, his face tense. "Beloved one…" He hesitated, seemingly struggling to find the right words. "Why don't you stop already? Even if you continue this research, wasn't bringing them back a failure?"

The woman glared at him and replied, "Don't be ridiculous. Do you know just *how much* I've sacrificed for this? The research shall succeed! It will just take some more time."

"But it was impossible, nonetheless, wasn't it? So many years have passed since then, but your research has borne no fruit.

The dead simply keep amassing. Well, that doesn't really matter, but don't you think they'd want you to give up and live a peaceful life, for their sake? I believe that would be the happiest solution for both you *and* them."

"That's not true! I will get them back! I swear upon it!" she declared, her words backed by a bitter sort of hope.

Based on their conversation, it was safe to assume that there was someone she wanted to bring back to life and that the zombies in the cage were the failed results of that research. That still didn't explain the connection with the Church of God's Light, though. Joshua wanted to learn the answer, but his priority now was to inform the king that Yadacain might try to invade.

(*Guess it's time for me to take my exit, and fast.*)

Just as Joshua finished his thought, his elbow bumped into a statue. He realized his mistake and reached out—too late. The statue shattered on the floor with a violent crash.

"What was that?" the woman asked.

"It seems that we have a rat," said the man.

(*Oh crap!*)

The two of them had started to walk in Joshua's direction.

14 Arrangements under Ruri's Nose

Ruri was frustrated that her parents were still missing, and she was growing impatient. She really wanted to go to Yadacain right now and search for them, but she knew that Jade would never give her permission to go off to some completely unknown nation like that. The devil in her mind whispered to her, prodding her to simply go in secret, but Jade had had enough common sense to explicitly warn her against that. Simply waiting kept her on edge, however, and she felt the urge to flee the castle at any moment.

Out of concern for Ruri—or perhaps for their own benefit—Agate and the other elders were attending to her, keeping her busy. They started off by taking her body measurements. As she sat in Jade's lap, antsy and awaiting news of her parents' location, she was suddenly hauled off by the scruff of the neck. She was taken to a room where a group of waiting women stripped her off her clothes. Then, as she stood in clueless shock, they started taking her measurements. Once the women finished redressing her, she was taken to another room where a huge assortment of fabric and dresses lined the walls.

"Now, Ruri, which is your favorite fabric?" Agate asked.

"Uh, that aside, would you mind telling me what all this is about?" Ruri asked.

"Why, it's for the dress you'll wear at your wedding, of course. How many wardrobe changes will she require for the ceremony? Five, right?" The other elders nodded.

"Five…" she repeated. Were they telling her that she needed to pick at least *six* outfits? She wasn't even sure why things had turned out this way to begin with. Ruri hadn't said one word about marrying Jade yet, so why were the elder vassals going ahead with her wedding arrangements?

"Um, just so you know, I never said *anything* about getting married. You shouldn't be going ahead with wedding arrangements! I haven't even answered Jade-sama yet."

"Nonsense, Ruri!" Agate replied. "If we wait until *after* you answer, it'd be too late."

"Hear, hear. Preparations for the wedding take time, after all. We must prepare everything as *absolutely* early as possible," added an elder.

"Um, that's all well and good if I accept Jade-sama's feelings, but what if I were to turn him down?" Ruri asked, knowing that a refusal would toss any marriage talk right out the window.

The elders were flabbergasted.

"Egads! Ruri, are you planning on turning him down?!"

"You mustn't do that! We shall not allow such blasphemy!"

"What, pray tell, is wrong with His Majesty?! There is no finer specimen of a man than His Majesty! There is also no one who cares for you more than he does!"

"Relent and jump into His Majesty's waiting arms!"

"Hurry and give him your response, now!"

The flock of elders squawked over each other, none of them understanding Ruri's young, conflicted heart. Even if she were to plead her case, it was doubtful that they would care.

Ruri let out a heavy sigh. "Aah, yes, yes. I understand. Even so, I think just *one* wardrobe change during the ceremony will be enough. Where I'm from, we typically only do that once—maybe *twice* at most."

"Preposterous! That surely isn't enough! This is His Majesty's long-awaited wedding ceremony! It must be a grand affair!"

"Okay, but still, five is *way* too many!" If she kept on changing outfits, she would undoubtedly end up an exhausted mess by the second half of the ceremony.

"Oh, how trite! That simply will not do!"

"Hear, hear! You will have to go through *at least* three changes for us!"

"Uh, whose wedding is this? This isn't for you and the other elders, is it, Agate-san?"

"Poppycock, Ruri. Do you realize how much we've done in our search for His Majesty's future bride? This is not only His Majesty's wedding, but also the fruit of our tears and hard work!"

"Oh how long we have dreamed of this day! Hearing you be so insensitive to our cause makes us weep!"

"I assure you the tears will never stop if you exclude us."

Ruri alone couldn't hope to stand up to the pressure the elder vassals projected. They were riding a wave of eager anticipation toward this wedding—more so than Ruri herself. They left Ruri no room to interject despite it technically being her wedding. They would at least listen to her dress requests, but judging by their behavior, they weren't willing to compromise on the three changes during the ceremony.

"Okay, okay. I understand. But no matter what you all say, I am *not* backing down on the dress being white, okay?" Ruri said in resignation, reaching out to the fabric.

"You said that white dresses are associated with weddings in your world, yes? Well then, how about a fabric along these lines for your wardrobe change?"

Ruri began to examine the fabrics, prompting Agate and the others to joyfully select their own individual picks for her to choose from.

"This fabric with a lace dress would be nice, wouldn't it?" suggested one.

"No, no. For that fabric, instead of lace, it must be matching embroidery with His Majesty," said another.

Yet another asked, "What other color of dress aside from white would you like?"

The wrinkly old men conversed among each other like a gaggle of chatty young women. It was very clear that they were far more into this than Ruri, their supposed bride-to-be. Ruri simply did as she was told, pressing the fabrics and dresses up against her body to see how they looked.

If Euclase were present, they would be squealing with excitement along with the old men, but they were unfortunately busy preparing for the forthcoming tournament. That made Ruri wonder if the elder vassals didn't need to be working themselves. They were, for all intents and purposes, vassals to the king, meaning they should have tons to do. Was the reason Jade and the other aides were so busy because of the strain caused by the elders not working? What did they plan to do if Jade lost the upcoming tournament and ceased to be king? Any need for a grand wedding would be entirely lost. Then again, their confidence likely stemmed from the fact that no one expected Jade to lose.

"Hmm, dress selection is important, but you'll need some jewelry to go with it."

"Right, and you'll also need jewelry for the wardrobe changes as well."

"Once we decide on the color of the fabric, we'll have to craft something to match it."

Ruri sensed that Agate and the others were getting out of control and interjected, "Wait, are you going to make jewelry for *each dress*? I'll just use one set for all of them."

"Balderdash, we must pay attention to every detail."

"Aye, there will be no cut corners on our watch!"

"But the money..." Ruri started.

Agate and the others were *very* particular about every facet of the wedding, including the clothes, so the costs were sure to add up. Add multiple matching jewelry sets on top of that and the total would be enough to turn anyone pale.

"If you're concerned about the costs, then you needn't be, Ruri. Due to His Majesty and your own rather reserved lifestyles despite being in the highest positions in the land, we have quite the excess left in the budget. We have plenty allotted for the both of you."

"I must say, while I applaud refraining from frivolously spending taxpayer money, the money won't circulate back to the taxpayers if you simply let it accumulate. Why, using it will give birth to jobs and new expenditures."

"Yes... I apologize for that." That all made sense to Ruri, but she still found it hard to use money she hadn't earned on her own. No matter how many blessings she brought to the land due to her status as a Beloved, she didn't feel like she'd done anything.

"We will use the abundant funds to the fullest and make sure to throw a wedding that will go down in this great land's history!" Agate declared.

"*Yeaaaah!*" the elders hollered in unison.

Ruri honestly couldn't keep up with their enthusiasm. She wasn't sure what a wedding to go down in history would even entail. A nice, normal wedding would do for her—emphasis on *normal*. However, the pack of elderly men, all fired up and willing to stake their lives on the arrangements, wouldn't hear any of that. She desperately hoped for someone who could stop them, but she unfortunately didn't see that happening.

Ruri couldn't help but fear what kind of wedding they would make this into. After all, she hadn't even said that she *would* marry yet...

Ruri felt tired and limp after finally escaping the elder's clutches. In the end, their opinions and requests were so at odds with one another that they couldn't even settle on fabric for the dress. The heated dispute had gotten so out of hand that Ruri had been able to sneak out. She was sure that this would happen all over again, though, if she became Jade's mate. The thought of this repeating itself was disheartening, to say the least.

How was she supposed to cure this mental and physical fatigue? While she could laze about on Jade's lap, Jade had been trying to actively woo her as of late, so she didn't want to be alone with him too often. It wasn't because she didn't like it, but it sent her pulse so high that her heart couldn't take it.

She decided to take a dip in the hot spring. She'd introduced Chelsie to the spring as soon as they'd arrived in the Nation of the Dragon King, but somewhat as expected, Chelsie had been less than impressed. She'd said she couldn't comprehend why one would waste time bathing in a hot spring when cleaning yourself with magic was easier and faster.

Hot springs weren't only for cleaning oneself, however. They also had the power to heal weary minds and bodies. She'd tried desperately to explain this to Chelsie, but it hadn't resonated with her. The other dragonkin had reacted in a similar way, with a few exceptions. Jade hadn't objected because Ruri had a vested interest in it, but he wasn't actively involving himself either. The only people who had shown positive reactions were women interested in beauty care and Quartz.

Of course, Ruri had known that would be the result. The fact that the bathhouse she built in Chelsie's yard had gone unused was all the proof she needed. Even so, it broke her heart to see Chelsie so flatly disregard the hot spring she'd toiled to create. However, as an odd consolation, her grandfather, Beryl, had loved the hot spring. He went every day and made friends with a few of the regulars.

Beryl had also hit it off with Chi since he meshed with Chi's open-minded personality. So much so that Chi had canceled his contract with Ruri and made a new one with Beryl, saying, "*This guy seems more interesting!*" It was a typical Chi move—not an ounce of hesitation, guided purely by mood and instinct. As a result, he now followed Beryl around.

Beryl had made friends with the other dragonkin soldiers as well. As soon as Ruri showed him the training grounds, he'd excitedly declared, "Ooh, me too!" He then began challenging the training soldiers, and Ruri rushed to try and stop him. There was no way he could fight with the battle-crazed dragonkin. There was a reason why their training grounds were separate from the other soldiers, and it was because they couldn't keep up with their strength.

However, Beryl had put his superhuman physical abilities on display. Perhaps it was because of his strong mana, or because his mana was strengthening his body, but he came close to matching the dragonkin soldiers in bare-handed combat. The soldiers were initially surprised, but they soon cheered and let out a chorus of "me next" as they lined up to square off against him. He'd brilliantly shattered the common belief that a human couldn't go one-on-one with a dragonkin for even five minutes.

When Beryl had told Ruri about him charging through a hail of bullets while deflecting them during his soldier days, she'd always wondered if such a human could even exist. But it looked like his tales weren't so tall after all. Now, training with the soldiers every morning was part of his daily routine.

"I wonder what I should do..." Ruri muttered, trying to come up with something to ease her fatigue.

"*Do what?*" asked a spirit.

"*What's the matter, Ruri?*" asked another.

All of the spirits floating around her cocked their heads in confusion. Just seeing their deviously cute behavior was enough to comfort her heart.

"I don't know whether to go see Jade or to go to the hot spring."

"*In that case, let's go sunbathe in the garden!*"

"*Yeah, let's!*"

"Sunbathe, huh? I guess I have been so busy as of late that I haven't had any time to do that. I should invite Kotaro and Rin too."

"*The two of them are already in the garden.*"

Neither Kotaro nor Rin were by Ruri's side at the moment. Kotaro still had a barrier in place around her, so she wouldn't be in danger, but Kotaro and Rin had probably gone to the garden because they'd wanted a quiet place to concentrate. Both of them had been searching for ways to see inside of Yadacain in hopes of finding

Ruri's parents. Since Yadacain was an island nation, Rin, the Spirit of Water, had attempted to peek in from the sea, but the Spirit Slayer had disturbed her vision.

Both Kotaro and Rin had been trying their best to make sure Ruri rested easy, but she felt sorry that they were working around the clock. "Those two need a break themselves," Ruri said, making her way to the garden.

Along the way, she spotted Chelsie, Quartz, and Andal all having tea on the terrace. Quartz and Andal had both been kings at one time, so they were already familiar with each other. Chelsie had also served as one of Quartz's aides for a time. It had been quite a long time since she'd retired, when Claus became a full-fledged aid, but she was still surprised by Quartz and Andal's unexpected connection.

Chelsie's face looked content and mellow as she conversed with her old acquaintances. She seemed to be enjoying herself, so Ruri quietly walked past so as to not disturb them.

When she arrived in the garden, she found Kotaro furrowing his brow.

"Hey, Kotaro, are you still looking for mom and dad?"

"Oh, it's you, Ruri. Yes, I'm trying my best to look for them, but I'm sorry," Kotaro said dejectedly, his tail drooping.

"You don't have to apologize. Thank you," Ruri replied, petting his head in reassurance.

It seemed that Rin hadn't had any luck either, which was trying her patience. *"Ugh, blast this cheeky magic. How utterly frustrating!"*

"It'd be quicker if I just went there directly, to be honest," Kotaro commented.

Indeed. Kotaro had proposed going to the island directly since it was blocked from his vision, but Jade had suggested he not. If a large wolf like Kotaro moved around Yadacain, he would naturally stick out like a sore thumb. And if it turned into a commotion, it would interfere with Joshua's undercover reconnaissance. Jade wouldn't allow that to expose Joshua's team to any potential danger.

Ruri didn't want to put Joshua and his men in danger either, so she'd decided to wait for their contact instead. However, they hadn't responded back at all. She knew it was hard to establish correspondence on an isolated island in the middle of the sea, but even the team's regularly scheduled correspondence was late. That made her doubly worried—not just for her parents' safety, but for Joshua's as well.

Ruri let out a big sigh. "Hurry up and contact us, Joshua," she muttered aloud. She put on her bracelet, turned into a cat, jumped onto Kotaro, and used his fluffy body as a bed while she stared at the clouds in the sky.

The Tournament

The battle to determine the king of the nation was finally underway. The town of the royal capital was abuzz with excitement. After all, this event only took place once every thirty years. The main street leading from the castle to the coliseum in the center of town, where the tournament would be held, had been decorated and filled with stalls of all kinds.

Since this was an event to decide the king of a superpower nation, many guests from all over the world had come to see the results. Some of their faces were very familiar to Ruri; Arman and Celestine had traveled all the way from the Nation of the Beast King.

"Hey, how's it going?" Arman greeted.

"Hello, I'm doing just fine," Ruri replied, "and I wound up making the hot spring I mentioned before."

"Well, that's great news! I think I'll go take a dip later, then."

As Ruri and Arman engaged in a peaceful chat, Celestine stepped forward and looked at Ruri as if she had something to say. She glared daggers at Ruri, and Ruri braced herself.

"Word has it you're making wedding arrangements. I'm curious as to *when* that happened," said Celestine.

"How do you know that?" Ruri uttered, wondering who could have told her.

"Master Jade's aide took the effort to send me quite the detailed letter about it."

"Argh! *Agate-saaan!*"

All of the aides knew that Celestine was madly in love with Jade, so there had been no need to make what was essentially a declaration of war against her. Why had they told her? Ruri wished that Agate had considered the potential damage before pulling a stunt like this.

"No, you see, I still haven't given him my answer. Agate-san and the others are moving things along on their own…"

"You know good and well you could say no if you wanted!"

"Um, well, yeah," Ruri stammered, unable to deny that fact.

Ruri didn't necessarily hate what was going on, and she wasn't going to put any serious effort into stopping the elders' rampage. Though things were developing at a bewildering pace, she hadn't said "no" to any of it.

Celestine suddenly pinched and pulled at Ruri's cheeks.

"Eowch!" Ruri said, her enunciation slightly slurred.

"You're saying you're trying to steal Master Jade from me. I'm letting you off easy, so take it in stride."

"That's unfair…"

"*Unfair*? That should be my line! You coming in as some late contender to steal Master Jade away from me is the definition of *unfair*!" Celestine cried, squeezing Ruri's cheeks even harder.

"Eowch! Ewoch!"

Celestine finally let go, and Ruri rubbed her afflicted cheeks in relief.

"But I'm left with no other option now that things have turned out this way," Celestine said. It had almost sounded like she was giving up on Jade, but that wasn't the case. "I will try my best to annul the marriage before the ceremony is ever held!"

"Oh…okay…"

Now that Jade had given Ruri his dragonheart, it wouldn't matter what Celestine did at this juncture. Also, the elders and, more importantly, Jade, were trying everything in their power to convince Ruri to say yes. But even if Ruri were to tell Celestine that, Celestine would get angry, so Ruri instead kept it to herself.

"Okay, you two keep playing nice. I'll be back. Got a *certain someone* that needs a little *killing*," Arman suddenly spat out and walked off.

"Certain someone?" Ruri repeated.

"He must mean the previous Beast King," Celestine clarified. "He *is* here, is he not?"

"Oh, yes, he is, but are you sure we shouldn't stop him? He said he's going to *kill* him." Ruri saw that Arman's face was stone cold, and he looked dead set on making *someone* deceased.

"I don't see the problem. I'm sure Master Arman comprehends where he is right now, after all," Celestine explained.

"I assume they don't get along?" Ruri asked.

"I've personally never met him, but the previous Beast King was apparently quite the wild and unpredictable character. He left Master Arman with a fair share of quandaries. Although he may not look it, Master Arman is very much a man of reason. He took on all of the problems that his predecessor had left behind, so he must be aching to give the man a piece of his mind."

"Huh, you don't say…" Ruri marveled, figuring there were some things she couldn't understand since she had no idea what happened back in those days.

"All that aside, I would appreciate it if you would tell me more about this hot spring you built."

Celestine changed subjects, now interested in the new hot spring. They continued to walk, and Ruri proceeded to tell her about how she built a hot spring with the spirit's help, hired a man from the Nation of the Beast King to design the facilities, and employed the children from the slums to help operate it.

Before long, they reached the private booth that had been prepared for guests of honor in the coliseum. Although it was an open-entry tournament and people were flooding into the spectator stands, there was no way key figures such as Ruri and Celestine could sit with the general public. Guests of honor had separate, private seats sectioned off for them.

As Celestine listened to Ruri's hot spring story, she found herself intrigued by the otherworldly activities that Ruri was describing. The Nation of the Beast King was also lacking in forms of entertainment. She was excited to hear about what other attractions there were.

"But, you see, unlike the people from the Nation of the Beast King, the people here hardly have any interest in hot springs. I have a feeling we'd gain more female customers if I added massages, like the ones I had in the Nation of the Beast King, but there's no one over here that can teach me how to do them."

Ruri reminisced about those delightful massages. She really did want to put them into practice in the Nation of the Dragon King as well. However, since she didn't know the first thing about the technique, she couldn't teach anyone how to do it, which had made her abandon the idea altogether.

"In that case, shall I show you the technique from the Nation of the Beast King?" Celestine offered.

Ruri was caught off guard by the admittedly tantalizing proposal. Her eyes looked hesitant, but they also sparkled with renewed hope.

"Wait, could you do that?" Ruri asked.

"Yes, in exchange for the otherworldly attractions you've made, that is."

"If that's all, then it'd be my pleasure!"

"So we have ourselves a deal."

"Woohoo!"

If Celestine taught her the secret arts of their massages, then she could receive the same treatment she'd had in the Nation of the Beast King every day without needing to go there.

As the excitement overtook her, Arman returned from his visit with Andal. "Looks like the crowd is getting fired up," he said.

"Welcome back," greeted Ruri.

"Yes, welcome back. Did your talk with your predecessor go well?" Celestine asked.

Arman sat back in his chair in a huff and clicked his tongue, saying, "I don't care about that *bastard*."

There were marks all over Arman's face and arms that looked like leftovers from a fight. Either he had challenged Andal and lost or someone had stopped him the hard way. Otherwise, if he had won, he wouldn't be in such a bad mood now.

Quartz and Agate both entered the booth.

"It's about to start," Quartz said.

He was right. A few moments later, fireworks went off, signaling the start of the tournament. The spectators erupted into cheers. Jade then appeared in the middle of the coliseum, and the crowd roared even louder. Seeing the Dragon King, a figure they rarely saw, made their excitement swell. But as soon as Jade raised his hand, the roaring crowd petered out into silence.

Seeing Jade command such awe from the crowd, Ruri clapped her hands and said, "Ooh, Jade-sama looks so kingly!"

"Uh, that's because he is a king," Quartz quipped, although it went in one ear and out the other as Ruri stared at Jade.

Jade began his opening speech. He was some distance away, but despite that, Ruri heard him all the way up in their booth.

"Huh? I can hear his voice?" she muttered. His voice was reaching the back of the wide coliseum clearly. She couldn't figure out how he was doing that without a loudspeaker.

"He's using wind magic to carry his voice," Quartz explained.

"Oh, that makes sense." It was a perfectly acceptable answer in a world with magic. There seemed to be no need for machines or anything of the sort here.

"And I hereby swear that I will fight honorably and justly in the name of all dragonkin," said Jade, finishing his speech.

With that, the tournament finally began. The matches were one-on-one. A competitor won by making their opponent admit defeat, or sometimes by referee decision. The rules were rather *loose*. They simply stated that anything was allowed so long as you didn't besmirch the good name of the dragonkin. That was a tad unsettling, but the matches went on regardless.

The first one out on the field was a soldier that Ruri was familiar with. He looked a little nervous because it was his first time entering, but that feeling seemingly vanished as soon as the signal sounded to begin. His face looked violent as he clashed swords with his opponent. Every new strike would cause some of the spectators to gasp and others to shout. While it didn't seem like the crowd could keep up that level of enthusiasm, they only grew more heated with each passing match.

Since this was her first time attending, Ruri felt a little at odds with the crowd. But that wasn't the only reason she couldn't concentrate on the matches. She had completely forgotten what dragonkin training at the castle usually looked like.

At the training grounds, puncturing a hole in someone's stomach due to lack of restraint was an everyday occurrence; gruesome bloodbaths unfolded on a daily basis. And that was just from *training*. Now that they were pitted in actual combat to become king, they were fighting one another with even *more* spirit and motivation.

The battles continued to unfold. Blood sprayed into the air, and the matches resembled more slaughter than sport. Vivid scenes of carnage unfit for the squeamish transpired before Ruri, scenes so graphic and gory that a PG rating didn't cut it—they needed an R rating. But as she looked out into the crowd, thinking that children shouldn't be exposed to this, she noticed that there were quite a number of children in attendance. She felt this would be terrible for their emotional development, but they were cheering with the best of them.

"Urgh, I can't stand to watch this…" Ruri said, not a fan of horror or splatterhouse in the slightest. She slowly looked away and met eyes with Celestine, who was also avoiding looking directly at the action. "Are you all right, Celestine-san?"

"I've heard the stories of this competition, but this seems to be a tad *too* extreme for my tastes," Celestine replied, looking somewhat pale—understandably so.

"I'd say this is hard to watch for ladies, yes," Ruri observed. "Then again, the women and children in attendance don't seem to be bothered by it much."

"I would assume that people who can't handle this wouldn't come in the first place," Celestine replied. It was either that or they were in such a festive mood after a long stint of nothing that they couldn't care less about the details.

That was when the loudest cry of the day resounded. Ruri turned her attention back to the venue to see Finn coming out.

"Oh, it's Finn-san!" Finn was the second favorite out of all the competitors, according to the betting scale. As soon as he made his entrance, a huge wave of cheers erupted as if everyone was awaiting his appearance.

Ruri's eyes caught a glimpse of someone at the very front of the crowd waving a huge flag and roaring louder than anyone else in the arena—that someone being Ewan.

"Ewan…" she muttered.

Dragonkin soldiers not competing were supposed to be either guarding guests from other nations or guarding the tournament venue, but Ewan had prioritized cheering on Finn. He had put in his request for time off without a second thought and was now supporting his brother with all his might. Ruri was surprised to see that his request had been approved with it being so busy.

Finn performed to his reputation of being second to Jade in skill. His opponent didn't stand a chance, and Finn landed a quick and easy victory. It was a display of strength distinguished from all the rest.

"Brotheeeeer!" Ewan cried, ecstatic despite it only being his first match. He was acting as if Finn had already taken the tournament.

It was clear that Ewan was happy about his beloved big brother winning, but Ruri thought it would do him good to learn to keep his wits like Finn. Unlike Ewan, Finn was cool and composed from beginning to end. His expression always showed that he was more focused on the goal ahead, not the goal in front of him. Jade was the same way.

Chapter 15: The Tournament

As Finn exited the arena and Jade entered, their eyes met for a brief yet tense second. Then Jade fully stepped into the arena, and the audience rained down a chorus of shouts louder than any before.

With speed rivaling Finn's, Jade felled his opponent with only the sword in his hand. It hadn't been a bloodbath like the other fights. Instead, Jade had struck his opponent with a beautiful array of swordplay moves that his opponent hadn't been able to withstand, culminating in their defeat.

Jade and Finn stood above the rest. They deserved every bit of their high betting odds to win the tournament.

"Whoa…" Ruri marveled. She'd never seen Jade fight before. She'd known he was strong since he was Dragon King, but it was entirely different seeing him in action. Her amazement overshadowed her joy for his victory as she stared at him.

Quartz, sitting by her side, noticed this and chuckled. "Your face says that you've fallen in love all over again, Ruri."

"I-I wouldn't say that… No, I mean, maybe I would, but…" Ruri stammered. He had hit the nail on the head, but she was embarrassed her expression had been so transparent that people could point it out. Ruri wasn't the only one feeling that way though. Celestine was also blushing at Jade's valiant form.

The Champion

The tournament proceeded in fine fashion, and Jade and Finn won their way through the bracket easier than expected. Every opponent was a skilled competitor, but to be entirely honest, it seemed that only a handful of them had entered with serious designs to take the throne. Jade and Finn simply stood out above all the rest. Everyone was steadfast in their predictions that one of them would take the tournament.

That extended to the entrants as well. Most of them were either combat junkies who'd just wanted to fight or people who'd wanted to test their might. Nevertheless, the higher in the bracket Jade and Finn climbed, the more tough fighters they met. And as strong as the two of them were, even they weren't able to beat these opponents so easily. Their opposition fought back, leaving wound after wound on their bodies.

Every time an opponent struck Finn, Ewan would fly into a massive uproar. But Ruri's mounting concerns about Jade's safety made her scream just as loud as Ewan. However, to a dragonkin, those were nothing more than flesh wounds.

The only thing that Ruri could do was pray from afar, but Quartz and Agate were extremely nonplussed, most likely because they were confident that Jade was in no danger of losing.

"Hmm, hmm, hmmmm, hmmm!" Ruri hummed in joy. She was happy to see so much of Jade's dashing performance throughout the competition.

"You seem to be in a good mood, Ruri," Agate commented, charmed by her high-spirited display.

"Of course," Ruri replied. "Jade is climbing higher and higher in the tournament, after all. I'm happy to see it."

"Well, His Majesty can't put on an unbecoming show while his beloved mate cheers him on from the crowd," Agate said with a smile beaming across his face.

Ruri could more or less tell what was on Agate's mind as he looked at her with that big grin. He was pleased as punch that the two were showing signs of romantic affection.

"That aside, is that song you're humming from your land, Ruri?" Agate asked. "It's quite the beautiful melody."

"It is, isn't it? But I'm not sure *what* land it's from, if any," Ruri admitted. Since the song she was humming came from the ghost in the pocket space, there was no way she could have known its origin.

"Err, I don't follow," Agate replied.

Suddenly, Ruri looked at Quartz, who wore a look of shock, like he couldn't believe his own eyes.

"Quartz-sama?" she asked.

Quartz came back to his senses upon hearing his name, but his face was still pale and tense.

"What's the matter, Quartz-sama?"

"No, it's nothing. Nothing…at all…"

It certainly didn't *look* like nothing, but Quartz didn't seem like he was willing to elaborate further. Then he fell silent, almost contemplative.

Ruri was curious about what had startled him, but she decided to concentrate on rooting for Jade instead.

Despite some difficulties along the way, Jade and Finn had made it to the finals, as most expected. All that was left was their match. To the victor went the title of Dragon King.

"I-I'm starting to get nervous," Ruri admitted. Her heart throbbed like mad even though she was just a spectator. She took a deep breath to calm her nerves.

Ruri was close with both of them, so she wasn't sure who to cheer for. As Jade's mate, the right thing to do would be to cheer for Jade, but Finn was like an older brother to her. She wanted to cheer for Finn, but if Jade ever found out that she had, he would probably get upset. Maybe rooting for Jade was the best call here…

As those thoughts ran through her mind, the signal for the start of the match sounded. But neither competitor took a single step forward. Instead, they stared at one another, their swords drawn and poised. Despite this, no crude jeers to hurry up came from the crowd. The tension wrapped around the entire coliseum. Not a single person in attendance could make a peep.

Then, out of nowhere, their swords fell and clashed with a loud *shiiiing*. Everyone realized that they'd been so entranced by the sudden development that they'd forgotten to breathe. They all slowly exhaled in unison. Then an explosion of roars filled the coliseum, each one directed toward their competitor of choice.

Ruri got caught up in the voices of the arena and cheered as well, but most of all she was hoping that neither got hurt. But despite her hope, it was highly unlikely that a fight between two skilled combatants would yield no injuries. Bit by bit, their swords slashed new wounds into each other.

They were pretty evenly matched in strength. But while it seemed that way for a while, Jade soon started to push Finn back ever so slightly.

"Brother, hang in thereeeee!" Ewan exclaimed.

Finn's expression, which had been the picture of sturdy serenity this entire time, finally started to crack as a distressed grimace flashed across his face. Then Finn staggered, if only for a second. But that small gap was more than enough for Jade to pour on the pressure even more.

Finn tried to regain his balance as he fended off Jade's fierce offense. Jade, however, used his magic to knock the sword right from Finn's hands and pointed the tip of his own sword toward Finn.

"I'm bested," Finn said.

Applause and shouts shot throughout the arena. Ruri and Celestine both clasped hands and rejoiced.

"He did it!" Ruri exclaimed.

"That he did," Celestine agreed.

Ruri felt sorry for Finn, but she had ended up cheering for Jade halfway through the match.

Finn had a right to feel frustrated, but although he'd lost, his expression looked more refreshed than anything. "It seems I am defeated," he said with a wry grin as he took Jade's hand.

"It got pretty close halfway through, though. I just managed to win."

"You haven't been exercising much due to your official duties, so I thought I stood a chance."

"I've been keeping myself up in private. And since Ruri is watching this time around, that's even more reason why I couldn't be bested."

"I shall train myself even harder for the next time," Finn replied.

"Well, just know that I'm not going to rest on my laurels just because I won."

Jade and Finn congratulated each other with calm smiles. In contrast, tears streamed down Ewan's cheeks as he grieved for his brother's loss. Finn had accepted the results of a hard-fought battle in stride, but it looked like Ewan was going to be stuck in a gloomy rut for quite some time.

With the finals concluded, everyone thought that the tournament was over with and that Jade would retain his title of Dragon King. Yet Jade stayed where he was and shouted to the stands, "Master Quartz!" Many of the people who were ready to leave, thinking that the festivities were over, stopped what they were doing and curiously listened in.

Quartz, not having been informed of this sudden turn of events, looked over to Agate as if asking for an answer. Agate looked just as clueless, though, and shook his head in surprise.

Jade looked at Quartz and yelled, "Master Quartz! I request you spar with me! I may have become king after you, but I cannot consider myself the true Dragon King. Only the strongest becomes the Dragon King. I've never sparred with you even once, Master Quartz. I wish to defeat you and proclaim the title of Dragon King with pride. Would you do the honor of granting my most indulgent request?"

Quartz had given up being king in order to search for his mate. As a result, Jade had become the next king without a bout to decide it. Normally, whoever defeated the previous king would become the next king, but Jade must have felt apprehensive about foregoing that stipulation.

Quartz smiled, undaunted. He then jumped down from their private booth and descended upon the arena, directly facing Jade.

"Do you really intend to fight me?" asked Quartz.

"Yes, it would be an honor," replied Jade.

"Fine, then. If you insist, Jade, let's do battle." Quartz unsheathed and readied his sword.

Seeing this, Ruri flew into a panic. "Agate-san! Is this all right?!"

"Whether it is or isn't, there's nothing we can do. We just have to let His Majesty do as he pleases."

"But...!"

"They should have fought a long time ago, actually. One must defeat the previous king to become the new king. That was how it continued for quite some time, but Master Quartz's departure was a bit of a special case. At the time, there was no shortage of people dissatisfied with the young king who hadn't even defeated his predecessor."

"Oh, was that so?" Ruri asked.

"Indeed. Now, of course, everyone acknowledges His Majesty as the Dragon King, but at the time, there were those who were overtly dissatisfied."

Ruri was shocked. "Who said that?! I'll make sure they *pay* for their slander!"

The only Dragon King that Ruri knew was Jade, so Jade *was* the Dragon King as far as she was concerned. To hear that anyone had qualms about that was inconceivable. Nevertheless, a Dragon King was chosen based on strength. It was natural for some to be unwilling to accept Jade after he became king without fighting the strongest dragonkin at the time, Quartz.

Jade must have known that as well. While he was well recognized as king now, he most likely felt inferior because of the circumstances. That was probably why he wanted to use this chance, while Quartz was back, to show that he was indeed the Dragon King—for his own benefit, above anything else.

This was quite a risk, though. It would be fine if he beat Quartz, but if he lost, it would be like saying Jade wasn't qualified to be the Dragon King. He couldn't afford to lose in front of the masses. And though it was hard to believe that Quartz would ascend the throne again even if he won, it would undoubtedly be a source of anxiety for Jade as he proceeded as the Dragon King. It also might cause even more discontent than when he'd first become king without fighting Quartz.

"Agate-san, is Quartz-sama strong? Which of them will win?" Ruri asked.

"Master Quartz was once king himself. Of course he's strong. At the time, he claimed victory against scores of powerful challengers with his overwhelming strength. He's had bouts with His Majesty before, but I haven't seen His Majesty win a single time."

"He *what*? That's terrible news!"

"That was a rather long time ago, though," Agate explained. "His Majesty has developed and has become powerful enough to win this tournament as king. As for who would win if they fought *now*? That's hard to say…"

"But what are we going to do if Jade-sama loses?!"

"Hmm… I would say His Majesty's future would look very grim."

While Ruri made a huge fuss up in the booth, Quartz and Jade had already started their fight.

"Oh no. They're doing it," she whispered when she saw them.

Unlike the cautious wait-and-see tactic that Jade had used with Finn, both he and Quartz intensely clashed swords from the very start.

"They're so fast!" Ruri gasped. She couldn't even track where their swords were swinging. They seemed to be evenly matched at first glance, but that was just in Ruri's amateur opinion. It was too early to tell who had the upper hand. All she could do was sit and watch, unable to stop them. Ruri could technically employ the spirits to break up the fight if she felt so inclined, but it wasn't her place to interfere with the match Jade had been hoping for.

The gentle Quartz may have looked more suited to be holding roses than swords, but he was reacting and dealing with Jade's attacks one after another. In addition, Jade had just finished his match with Finn. He was probably fatigued, which put him at a huge disadvantage.

Ruri's hunch was right on the mark. Jade gradually began to lose ground.

"Oh nooo! Jade-sama, stay firm! Stay firm and don't give up!"

"Ruri, settle down, will you?" Rin scolded, unable to watch Ruri acting so foolish.

Still, there was no way Ruri could settle down. "Now's not the time for that. Jade-sama, you can do it!" she yelled out.

That was when a violent *kabooom* echoed and a set of earthquake-level tremors shook the ground.

"Oohyaaaa!" Ruri screamed, covering her head and crouching down.

Shrieks came from all over the spectator stands. Jade and Quartz lowered their swords and looked around them. Not a single person could grasp the situation.

"What...was that?" asked Ruri.

The quaking soon stopped, but everyone clamored, wondering what the noise could have been. It almost sounded as if something had been demolished.

"I will go check out the situation," Agate said. "Beast King and Beloveds, I implore you all to please wait right here. Especially *you*, Ruri. Stay put."

"Why are you singling me out?" Ruri was unhappy that Agate had assumed that she would do something. She would have stayed put even without being told to do so by name.

As she waited for Agate to return, Ruri heard what sounded like cannon fire and explosions in intermittent spurts. Her worries grew.

Panic had briefly descended upon the spectators, but Jade had ordered them to stay in their seats until they received confirmation on what was happening. They were now remaining calm, in part due to the sense of security Jade had instilled. After all, this coliseum housed a host of dragonkin—the strongest breed of demi-humans around—who were ready to defend them if the situation called for it. Nevertheless, the spectators still couldn't wipe the worry off their faces.

A few moments passed, and then a single soldier could be seen running up to Jade.

After he heard the message, Jade briefly talked with Quartz. Quartz returned to the booth along with Agate soon after. Their faces looked grim. It was very clear that they hadn't come bearing good news.

"What just happened?" asked Ruri.

"A large number of suspicious ships have been spotted in the waters around the royal capital," Quartz said. "They wouldn't respond to any warnings, and when our navy tried to employ force, several kraken impeded them out of nowhere. Apparently, those ships entered port and opened fire on the capital."

"Why would they do that?" Ruri asked.

"Who they are and their purpose is unknown. Jade is going to retaliate with the dragonkin who are able to fight. We need you and the Beloved of the Nation of the Beast King to evacuate to the castle at once, Ruri. The safety of Beloveds is always top priority."

Ruri looked at Celestine, who nodded and stood up.

"Okay, I will," Ruri agreed. "But will Jade-sama be all right? Especially after all that fighting?"

"Yes, he'll be fine. He isn't that soft. Right now, the safety of all of you is more important. Now, hurry on."

In addition to Quartz, several soldiers stood outside their box, waiting to escort Ruri and the others. But just as they were about to head off for the castle with them as their security detail, Kotaro stopped in his tracks.

"Kotaro?" asked Ruri.

"*I'm going to take a look around. I feel a disturbance. Rin, take care of Ruri,*" Kotaro said.

"*You got it,*" Rin replied.

"Hey, wait! Kotaro!" Ruri shouted, but Kotaro had already run away before she could try to stop him.

"*Don't worry, Ruri. It's Kotaro. He'll be fine.*"

Ruri nodded. "Yeah. You're right." She looked back for a second, but then she quickly turned back around and made her way to the castle.

17 Suspicious Ships

After parting ways with Ruri, Kotaro headed for the port where the suspicious ships had appeared. An unpleasant sensation had rocked his body, a sensation that Rin had most likely felt as well. That was why she hadn't said anything about him leaving Ruri to go off on his own. But Kotaro needed to see what was happening. He was sure the dragonkin couldn't handle this on their own.

Kotaro had a barrier in place around Ruri, so he knew she'd be safe. Rin was also there for added insurance. Even so, he had still been a bit worried, so he'd told the lesser spirits in the capital to make their way to the castle. His reason for doing so was twofold: to give Ruri some extra protection and to protect the spirits from the disturbance he'd felt. With that taken care of, it was high time to do something about this.

The capital town was in turmoil, understandably so, due to the ships' attacks. Still, this would have been only a minor incident if the arrival of the suspicious ships had been the only commotion. Not only did they come with a multitude of normally rare krakens, but they were laying siege with cannon fire. Rubble lay on the ground in several areas, remnants of buildings destroyed in the wake of the bombardment. And people yelled from every direction—no doubt the injured who had either been pinned underneath or hit directly by debris.

Kotaro, however, simply glanced in that direction and continued to fly toward the port. He'd considered helping them, but he had something more important to do at the moment.

The port was a jumbled mess of ships, some flying the flag of the Nation of the Dragon King and some from parts unknown. There were also scores of thrashing kraken, impeding the Nation of the Dragon King's ships. They must have been tamed somehow. Kraken didn't just show up around these parts, especially in such large numbers. Due to their interference, the ships of the Nation of the Dragon King were pretty much stuck where they floated.

The krakens were massive, and just one of them could easily suck up a ship and drag it to the briny depths. The Nation of the Dragon King's navy, however, was putting up a good fight against the sea creatures, dodging their attacks and proving they were not to be trifled with. Though as powerful as the navy was, they had their hands full with their tentacled opponents and weren't able to fend off the attacks from the mystery ships in the rear.

That was when the dragonkin, led by Jade, arrived on the scene. Now in dragon form, the fleet of dragonkin took on the giant krakens. They were at last able to gain a leg up instead of remaining solely on the defensive.

As Kotaro observed the waging battle, he remembered that Ruri had wanted a kraken before.

"*Perhaps I should bring one back with me,*" Kotaro said aloud with a canine grin. He thought of how Ruri would be delighted and would hug him. "*I should ask her to make this 'takoyaki' of hers.*"

Even though Kotaro had no idea what an "octopus" or "tako" was, Ruri always made the best dishes, so this "takoyaki" was bound to be delicious, whatever it was.

While Kotaro nonchalantly mulled over his dinner plans, a fierce clash unfolded below. Jade was moving around, giving orders to his soldiers. Just then, there was a loud *kabooom* and the mystery ships unleashed a hail of cannonballs toward the capital. Without a second to lose, Jade ordered his men to stop the attack. Several soldiers unleashed their magic into the air. The cannonballs made contact with their magical veil, which normally would have stopped them, but for some reason, they broke through the magic and whizzed toward the town at even greater speeds.

The soldiers were flabbergasted.

"What the hell?!"

"Hey, what the hell is going on?"

"No clue! Our magic isn't working!"

A second wave of shots came flying in. The dragonkin tried to stop them once again, but those cannonballs were impervious to magic.

"*I knew it,*" Kotaro said, sensing the cause of the disturbance. He descended over to Jade, who was standing there at a loss for what to do.

"Oh, it's you, Lord Kotaro."

"*It's no use. Those things are using Spirit Slayer.*"

"They're *what*?"

"*Even if you use magic against those cannonballs, they'll simply absorb the mana and increase their force.*"

"That's terrible. Then, what should we do?" Jade asked.

Wind started to rise and wrap around the port. Though not visible to the naked eye, it was clear that there was a large blockade of wind around the area.

"*I've built a wall to prevent any more damage to the town. Now you just need to destroy the main culprits—the cannons.*"

Kotaro had built a barrier large enough to cover the town of the royal capital. Even though Jade should have been used to this display of power by now—the power of a supreme-level spirit—Jade couldn't help but be surprised.

"Thank you for your help," Jade said.

Kotaro then took to the skies again. As he looked at the people from overhead, several more shots came from the cannons. But Kotaro's powers outmuscled them, ensuring that no harm came to the town.

Spirit Slayer magic was in use here again. No doubt about it, Yadacain had to be behind this. It wasn't just the cannons that were using Spirit Slayer either. He felt a disturbance from the enemy ships as well. They were probably using the siphoned mana for power. They were moving far too fast to be a regular sailing ship, and mana was flowing into their sails.

Kotaro was relieved he'd evacuated the other spirits to the castle beforehand. The Spirit Slayer would have siphoned out all their powers.

The only people capable of processing Spirit Slayer magic and using it like this were the witches who'd first created it. This fleet had to be from Yadacain, the nation founded by those witches.

Considering that the residents of Yadacain never left their island, spirits were safe so long as they never approached it. That was why the supreme-level spirits had strictly ordered the less powerful spirits to stay away, essentially abandoning the island. But if the residents were to leave their home and come into the outside world with Spirit Slayer at the ready, Kotaro would probably have to do something for the sake of the other spirits. Otherwise, there was a real possibility that the spirits would get hurt.

Kotaro considered wiping them out—nation and all.

At the moment, there were four supreme-level spirits in the Nation of the Dragon King. Rin of water, Chi of earth, Heat of fire, and himself, Kotaro of wind. Since they were supreme-level spirits, they were the strongest among all spirits. They had more than enough power to take down a nation. The other three would certainly cooperate if it were to save the spirits. Ruri's protection would be stretched thin in the meantime, but it wouldn't really matter.

If push came to shove, a supreme-level spirit had enough power to do things on their own. Heat could burn the entire island to cinders with fire. Rin could wash everything to the currents with water. There were a plethora of methods available. Whatever the case, Kotaro would need to talk it over with the other supreme-level spirits currently in the kingdom.

As Kotaro pondered all of this, the ships from the Nation of the Dragon King slipped through the opening that the krakens had made and approached the enemy ships. Dragonkin in dragon form swooped down from the sky to crush their cannons. However, the enemy ships were much faster than their own due to the Spirit Slayer magic boost, so it was hard to follow after them.

Seeing them struggle to keep up, Kotaro lent his power to the dragonkin ships. His wind gave them the push they needed, and they sped up and made contact with the fleet of enemy ships. Using bridges, they raided the ships one by one, taking out their cannons.

"That should do it."

Kotaro's powers rendered the cannons useless, and the dragonkin in dragon form slew the kraken. The Nation of the Dragon King's troops boarded the enemy ships by sky and by sea and commandeered them. The outcome was all but decided. All that was left was to wait for soldiers to completely overtake the enemy ships.

Something concerning stood out, however—a ship in the very back of the fleet of enemy ships. It looked no different from all the others, but something about it stimulated Kotaro's senses. He watched it closely to see if it would make any moves, but then he heard yells from the ships in front. Screams came not from the enemy but from the dragonkin, the group that should've had the upper hand.

"Wha?! What the hell is this?"

"H-Hey! Are you okay?!"

"I can't get out of here!"

"You gotta do something!"

A few of the dragonkin were encased in some sort of black, spherical membrane. None of them could break free despite their best efforts. Their companions on the outside tried to slash at it with their swords to free them, but the mysterious membrane deflected their weapons. Punching, kicking—they tried everything they could think of, but the sphere showed no signs of breaking.

Kotaro looked at the black sphere and squinted at it suspiciously. He realized what it was and his eyes widened in shock.

"Impossible. That can't be…!"

The black spheres floated up and carried the dragonkin still trapped inside across the water to the place that Kotaro had been observing just a moment before—the enemy ship furthest to the back. By the time Jade noticed this and gave the orders to the dragonkin in the sky, the spheres had already reached the back ship. Then that ship abandoned its fellow vessels and began to move out into the open sea.

"After it!" Jade ordered, but all the available ships were still attached to the other enemy ships. They couldn't take off right away. In addition, not only was the back ship far away, but they were using

Spirit Slayer to move their ship even faster. They were too speedy to catch up with.

The airborne dragonkin tried to pursue it, but the cannons from earlier shot at them. Since their magic was ineffective, they had no choice but to dodge them. However, their tight aerial maneuvers allowed them to navigate through the bombardment and continue chasing the ship.

The flying dragonkin were almost at the back ship when the black spheres that had captured their comrades assaulted them. The spheres practically swallowed them whole. No attack, inside or out, proved effective against them. It encased the dragonkin inside and carried them off toward the ship. There was nothing they could do now. If they pursued the ship without a plan and were captured by those spheres as well, then it would just be even more damaging. The group hovered in frustration, no other choice but to watch them sail away.

Watching from the skies, Kotaro was astonished. He hadn't been just *looking* at the spheres that took the dragonkin. He had blasted them with his wind powers, but the wind had fizzled out. There were only a handful of people who could shut down the powers of a supreme-level spirit like Kotaro.

"*Don't tell me. Those are Darkness's...*"

It was unbelievable, but at the same time, Kotaro couldn't say it was absolutely impossible.

Supreme-level spirits referred to one another as "brethren." That wasn't to say that they were particularly close, though it didn't mean they didn't get along either. Some of them were very close with one another, but that didn't apply to all supreme-level spirits.

It was safe to say that Kotaro, in particular, didn't have much interaction with other spirits. He was "hands-off" when it came to his fellow spirits' business, but his brethren never really got involved in each other's affairs either. As a result, he didn't pay much attention to what his brethren were currently up to. That power that he just saw, however…

When Kotaro had initially realized that one of his brethren might be involved, he'd frozen for a moment. Fights between spirits were taboo, but if one of his brethren was involved in this Yadacain raid, that would mean that Kotaro was locked in a fight with them. He had just been thinking about wiping Yadacain off the map earlier as well. He realized that if he had done that, his brethren likely would have stopped him.

More importantly, why did his brethren snatch away dragonkin? At this rate, war would break out between the Nation of the Dragon King and Yadacain. Kotaro, of course, would side with the dragonkin should that happen, but it meant that he'd have to oppose his brethren siding with Yadacain.

"*I can't make this decision on my own, I suppose…*" Kotaro said. He needed to consult on this matter. It was too much for him to decide on his own. He would talk to Rin and the others, and if necessary, he would employ the help of the dragonkin.

Just to be sure, Kotaro tracked down the enemy ship to see where it was heading. Sure enough, it sailed toward Yadacain—the land of witches.

18 Rescue Strategy

After returning to the castle under the protection of Quartz and the guards, Ruri headed straight to the garden of Sector One, on top of the mountain. From there, she had a sweeping view of the city and the harbor. She could see a set of unidentified ships afloat in the sea, a group of kraken, and the Nation of the Dragon King ships. She could see the ships moving, but not the people, so she couldn't tell from a glance which side had the upper hand.

As Ruri watched the battle unfold, many of the smaller spirits gathered around her. According to them, Kotaro had told them to evacuate because Spirit Slayer was present. There was only one thing that popped into Ruri's mind upon hearing this: Yadacain. Rin affirmed her suspicions, stating that it was highly likely.

The spirits weren't the only ones to assemble, however. Euclase and the main aides, who hadn't gone into battle, came to the garden as well. They were there to get updates on the situation from Rin, who was giving a play-by-play while watching the battle through Kotaro.

"*Those cannons and the ships are using Spirit Slayer. It must be Yadacain's handiwork. Only their witches could construct such things,*" Rin said.

Everyone's faces turned grim.

"I assume those suspicious ships we've seen recently are one and the same," Euclase said, referencing the ships that had been making frequent appearances near the capital as of late.

Whenever the navy tried to apprehend them, krakens would appear and impede their arrest—just like now. It was natural to assume there was a connection, just as Euclase had said.

"*It seems we have the upper hand here. Though I suppose that goes without saying since Kotaro is with them.*"

Even if the witches of Yadacain were using Spirit Slayer, they stood no chance against dragonkin with a supreme-level spirit on their side. But even though everyone already knew that to be true, it was a relief to hear it aloud. The only thing left was to remain calm and wait for the battle to reach its end—at least, that was what everyone assumed.

"*Oh. Well, that's not good...*"

"Is something the matter?" Euclase asked.

"*A few dragonkin were captured.*"

"They were *what*?! What do you mean?!" Euclase shouted. Their eyes bugged out, and they looked ready to grab Rin at any moment.

"*I can't say for sure. It seems that some sort of power captured the dragonkin and took them to a ship. And this power, it's...*" Rin trailed off.

They couldn't make out any details from their vantage point in the garden, but the one thing that Ruri and the others could see was that a lone ship among the fleet was heading out into the open sea.

As panic and frustration mounted, Jade finally made his return. His aides gathered around him, trying to get details, but Jade didn't know much more than what Ruri and the others knew.

Jade had been slightly surprised to learn that the ships probably belonged to Yadacain, but at the same time, he couldn't think of any other group who would use Spirit Slayer. Once they questioned the crew of the captured ships, they would know for sure if they were from Yadacain.

The interrogation was currently underway—a somewhat *rough* interrogation by Jade's own prediction. Several of his fellow dragonkin had been captured, so it only made sense. The biggest problem, aside from them being captured, was that they needed to get them back as soon as possible.

"Finn, assemble the troops immediately. Once we have conclusive evidence that Yadacain is behind this, I'm sending our men there posthaste," Jade stated. He was obviously willing to go to war.

"Your Majesty, I would, but what of the alliance agreement?"

Finn referred to the set of rules agreed upon by the Alliance of Four Nations. That alliance comprised four nations: the Nation of the Dragon King, the Nation of the Beast King, the Nation of the Spirit King, and the Imperial Nation. The agreement stated that the Nation of the Dragon King was not to incite war. If they were to do so, they would need a suitable reason and the consent of the other three nations.

"If we need consent, then now is the perfect time," Jade stated. Not only was the Beast King here for the tournament as a guest of honor, but so were the Spirit King and the Emperor as well. "Request a meeting at once. Time is of the essence. On the double."

"Very well, Sire," Claus, who was also present, replied before rushing out of the room.

That was when Kotaro returned, entering the room as if taking Claus's place.

"Kotaro, were you okay?" Ruri asked. She was confident that nothing had happened to him since he was a supreme-level spirit, but she'd been concerned that he hadn't come back to the castle until now.

"*I'm fine. I was trailing the ship that took the dragonkin. As suspected, it was headed to Yadacain.*"

"I see," Jade said, uttering what everyone else had dreaded to hear. The dread even started to show on their faces.

"*King*," Kotaro said, addressing Jade, "*we simply cannot let Yadacain go unpunished. If they continue to use their Spirit Slayer, then it might harm our fellow spirits as well. I want to use this opportunity to completely remove the Spirit Slayer magic from Yadacain.*"

"If that is what you've decided, then we have no objections," Jade said. "We simply wish to help save our comrades. Our interests are aligned. I cannot think of anything more reassuring than you gracing us with your cooperation. After all, we dragonkin can't use magic when they use Spirit Slayer."

"*Quite. Are you all right with this too, Rin?*"

"*Yes, well, I wouldn't have said anything if Yadacain had remained docile, but now that they're running amok on the outside, it's best to eliminate their power once and for all. After all, we'll be fine, but the other spirits might end up getting wiped out.*"

As Rin and Kotaro both discussed removing the Spirit Slayer for good, something about how they spoke disturbed Jade. He couldn't pass it off as his imagination either.

"One thing, if you don't mind? By saying you wish to 'remove the Spirit Slayer magic,' do you mean *along* with Yadacain itself?" Jade asked, hoping to quell his concerns.

The two glanced at him as if he'd asked a ridiculous question.

"*Quite naturally,*" Kotaro replied.

"*Well, of course. Destroying the whole nation would get rid of it for good.*"

Everyone's faces turned deathly pale.

"Wait a minute, both of you!" Ruri exclaimed. "Destroy the whole nation?! I don't think we need to go *that* far!"

Jade hurriedly added, "Yes, I can't really agree with that method. We may be at war, but we have no intention of destroying a nation because of it. I would like to settle this while sparing them in order to prevent any needless disputes. Eliminating the whole country is a last, *last* resort."

"*But you can't erase people's memories, can you?*" Kotaro asked. If they were to destroy just the Spirit Slayer magic, someone was bound to remember how to create it.

"We'll handle it," Jade replied.

"*Oh dear, I think it'd be easier to just erase the whole nation,*" Rin said. "*But we'll leave it in your hands if you insist. As long as you make sure that the Spirit Slayer can't be used in the future, then things will be fine.*"

It was a relief to hear them agree, but it was a wonder why spirits' methods were so radical.

"*But there's one problem, isn't there?*" Rin said cryptically after exchanging glances with Kotaro.

"That being?" Ruri asked, tilting her head.

"*And you're sure about that, right?*" Rin continued.

"*Yes, I am very sure,*" Kotaro answered.

Kotaro and Rin shared a conversation only they understood, but judging from Kotaro's stern expression, it certainly wasn't good news.

"*It's likely—no,* more than *likely that one of our brethren, the Spirit of Darkness, is aiding Yadacain,*" Rin explained.

"The Spirit of Darkness?" asked Jade.

"*It was the Spirit of Darkness who took away the dragonkin. I sensed their power, so I am sure,*" said Kotaro.

"Why would the Spirit of Darkness join forces with Yadacain?" Jade asked. Yadacain, from a spirit's perspective, were murderers of their kin who used their devilish Spirit Slayer magic. No one had any idea why a spirit would affiliate with people like that or why they would take away dragonkin in the first place.

That included Kotaro, who was just as clueless. *"I fail to understand this myself. Not unless I speak to Darkness personally."*

"So, what will you do if the Spirit of Darkness is siding with Yadacain?" Jade asked, a dour look on his face. He feared the worst.

"Would you end up fighting?" Ruri asked, worried that their difference in opinions would lead to a fight between spirits.

"No, that's not going to happen. Spirits would never fight among each other. You can rest assured of that," Rin said, much to Ruri's relief. *"However, if Darkness is going to side with them, there are two or more supreme-level spirits who can stop them. We can essentially talk it out, and if that's not possible, we'll decide by majority vote."*

Since they had four supreme-level spirits, the numbers were overwhelmingly in their favor. Nevertheless, it was hard to understand why spirits aimed for peaceful solutions through discussion when their attitudes toward everything else was so extreme that it involved either crushing, erasing, or destroying.

"That being said, we don't know why Darkness is siding with them. Nor do we have any way to predict how they'll strike," Rin added.

"Another question is who do we leave by Ruri's side," Kotaro said.

"That's right. I'd really like all four of us to go since we don't know what lies in store. But since Earth lives by his own whims, there's a chance he might just side with Darkness instead if we brought him along, so that's out."

"Yes, sounds like a surefire way to make things more complicated," Kotaro agreed, his mixed feelings painted on his face.

Ruri wasn't sure what to do either. Even though the unknown entity that was the Spirit of Darkness had sided with the enemy, Chi just might flip sides and say it was simply because it was "interesting." He might say he wanted to go to discuss things, but it was too dangerous to bring him along.

"*If anyone is going, it's Fire and me,*" Rin said. "*Kotaro, you have your barrier around Ruri, which means you staying with her is the safest option.*"

"*Yes, I agree.*"

The problem was whether Heat would actually comply. It was safe to say that he would have *no* intention of coming at all. He wasn't the type to prioritize something potentially bothersome if it had nothing to do with himself. They pondered over how to lure him in this time around.

Just then, Claus came back to inform them that a meeting with the other rulers was ready. It was surprising that he'd set things up so quickly. Perhaps the other kings had received a certain degree of information as well.

Then, almost at the same time, a new piece of information came in. The interrogation of the enemy crew had revealed that they were indeed from Yadacain. It seemed that the interrogator had done a thorough job. Ruri didn't want to know what kind of interrogation tactics he had used to get them to talk so quickly.

Though they now had confirmation, something about Yadacain's plan felt amiss. Their purpose was unclear, but they had succeeded in taking the dragonkin with them. However, leaving their other ships behind would inevitably lead to interrogation and leaked intel.

They should have expected that the Nation of the Dragon King would move to rescue their men as soon as they found out Yadacain was at fault. Were they just that confident that they stood a chance against the Nation of the Dragon King?

They probably thought that they could repel the dragonkin with the Spirit of Darkness's power, but wouldn't the Spirit of Darkness know that Kotaro and the others were in the kingdom? Spirits were said to have a unique communication method with each other, so the Spirit of Darkness should have known this even if they were in Yadacain. Why would they oppose Kotaro and the others as enemies, despite knowing they would be outnumbered?

While the designs of the Spirit of Darkness and Yadacain remained unclear, the kings held their council and decided to send troops to Yadacain to recover the captured dragonkin.

Dispatching the Troops

The troops were quickly readied to be dispatched. Many dragonkin were participating in the expedition. Dragonkin had a strong sense of camaraderie, and plenty of them were so livid about the kidnappings that they were shoving each other out of the way to offer their services. Yadacain had *completely* incurred the dragonkin's wrath.

However, the kingdom couldn't bring every available person on hand as it would thin out its domestic defenses too much. Therefore, a mass lottery had been held. While it seemed a silly thing to do for such a dire situation, this was the most peaceful solution, all things considered. Even some who weren't soldiers and who normally wouldn't participate in battle added themselves to the mix, which caused a handful of soldiers to fly into an uproar. Nevertheless, their anger toward the enemy was just as strong. And though they weren't soldiers, they were still dragonkin. It was well known that even civilian dragonkin had exceptional fighting prowess, which was why they were allowed to enter the lottery in the first place.

Preparations were proceeding at a blinding pace. The only issue left to square away was Heat. Ruri hesitantly visited him to find his entourage of women waiting on him, despite the impending war. She gave Heat a rundown of the situation and asked him for his cooperation.

In the past, she had been forced to offer some sort of woman-related prize in order to lure Heat into doing what she wanted—whether it was arranging a banquet with a hundred beauties or taking him to a night out at Knies. What kind of conditions would he force upon her this time? Ruri had a certain level of foresight and was already slightly prepared. Certainly, she could assemble a hundred women if need be. She braced herself for the absolute worst he could dish out. However…

"Very well. I will help you," Heat replied, most unexpectedly.

"Huh?" Ruri was literally stunned speechless. She couldn't believe that Heat would accept her offer with no strings attached. "You mean you'll go?" she asked, in case her ears were deceiving her.

Heat glared at her and responded, "I just told you that I would, didn't I? Are you going deaf, brat?"

"No, it's just that there's usually some kind of catch. Are you not feeling well? Should I call the doctor?" Ruri asked him. She wasn't joking either; she was absolutely serious.

"Okay, brat, just *what* do you think I am?"

She was about to say "an insatiable womanizer," but she caught herself just in the nick of time.

Unfortunately, he seemed to have guessed what she was going to say, and he humphed in dissatisfaction. "I am a spirit as well. A supreme-level one, at that. If the lesser spirits face danger, then I can't afford *not* to act. Besides, I've always hated that blasted Spirit Slayer, and this is a perfect chance. I'll get rid of it once and for all."

"*Wow, so cool!*"

"*You're giving me shivers~!*"

The little spirits praised Heat with great enthusiasm. This pleased Heat so much that he stuck out his chest with pride.

"Heh, heh. This is only natural. I am a supreme-level spirit, after all."

"I thought I would need to lure you in, so I had already contacted all the girls in the castle, but it looks like I didn't need to do that."

Heat's ears picked up on what Ruri had said, and his eyes lit up. "Well, you're certainly prepared. In that case, I'll have a banquet upon my return. Get things ready."

"So I *did* need to do that after all..."

This should have been the moment where Heat confirmed he didn't need anything in return, but Heat wasn't about to fix his womanizing ways.

Preparations had managed to proceed, but with little time to rest. If they were to rescue their dragonkin comrades, they had to use their time effectively. The soldiers' desire to rescue their kinsfolk paid off, though, as things were ready ahead of schedule. It was now time to ship out.

The naval ships all lined up in a row at the capital's port was a magnificent sight to behold. Ruri would have been excited if the situation were different, but the only thing stirring in her chest was anxiety. Since the Spirit of Darkness was involved, no one expected this to be a straightforward affair. And Jade would be joining the deployment and leading the troops on this operation. It was his intense desire to do so, but that only exacerbated Ruri's fears.

Rin and Heat were also going along, so Ruri asked both of them to take care of Jade. They couldn't just care for him alone, though. There were other soldiers going, and the two of them would have to face the Spirit of Darkness. If something were to happen to Jade, they might not be in a position to help. Besides, Jade was the Dragon King, the man who'd displayed his awesome strength for all to see in the last tournament. That being said, it wasn't enough to quell Ruri's worries.

Ruri came to the port to see Jade off. It was almost time to set sail. She said her goodbyes to him as he gave the sign to depart to the other men. She looked extremely worried and glum as she stood before him.

Jade looked at her and smiled wryly. He reached out and stroked her cheek with his thumb. "You don't have to worry. I'll just be out for a bit. I assure you, I'll be back soon."

"Please, *please* be careful out there," Ruri said.

Ruri had been born and raised in a land of peace and security. In this world, so different from her own, war and strife were commonplace. Nevertheless, it wasn't something she could get used to—especially if people she held dear were going into the thick of it. She was going to worry even if told not to.

In contrast to herself, Ruri didn't sense any kind of tension or anxiety coming from Jade, even though he was heading into battle. His face was exactly the same as always. Did experience make that big of a difference?

"It'll be fine. I'm the same person who won the tournament— the Dragon King. I'll have both Lord Rin and Lord Spirit of Fire by my side, so there's nothing to fear. If I had to worry about something, it'd be trying to contain the other dragonkin since they're so fired up."

Since they wouldn't be able to use magic due to the Spirit Slayer in Yadacain, the soldiers had a large stockpile of armaments ready. Droves of dragonkin stood around them, brandishing weapons. Their bloodthirstiness was understandable; their kinsmen had been captured. Looking out at all of them, raring to go, the future of Yadacain seemed bleak. They were liable to ground the whole nation underneath their dragonkin heels. It would take an inordinate amount of effort just to hold them all back.

Keeping any eye on his men to make sure they didn't go overboard would probably be more difficult for Jade than the battle with Yadacain itself. Jade was participating in this operation partly because they needed someone to keep them in check.

"Your Majesty, the preparations are in order," said a soldier, who had come over to address Jade.

Jade's face straightened. "Very well." He turned his attention back to Ruri. He pulled her toward his chest and braced his arms around her. The embrace was short-lived, though, as he soon released her and said, "I'll be off now. You should be fine with Lord Kotaro by your side, but considering the off chance that Yadacain might try something, you should keep a watchful eye on your surroundings."

"Yes, I understand," Ruri replied with a nod.

"Don't worry, I'll be here too," Quartz said, as he put his hand on Ruri's shoulder and gave a reassuring smile to Jade.

"Master Quartz, I leave Ruri in your capable hands."

"Right. Just leave her to me."

Jade had nothing but unwavering trust in Quartz. He was sure she would be fine with Quartz around.

Jade turned around and boarded the ship. Once everyone was aboard, the boats slowly started to sail away.

"*See you later!*" Rin said, flapping her little wings from the deck of the boat.

"Be careful, Rin! Heat-sama, take care of everyone!" Ruri called back, shouting her lungs off.

As she held onto the hope that they'd all come back home safely, Ruri watched the boats disappear into the horizon.

The Nation of the Dragon King's warships, packed with an excessive amount of soldiers, borrowed Rin's water-based powers to zip across the sea at speeds unthinkable for a sailboat. It was a race against the clock. Even as they sailed, no one knew what was befalling the dragonkin in captivity. Dragonkin had strong and sturdy bodies, which was a bit of relief, but since the reasons for their capture were unclear, none of them could imagine what those dragonkin could be facing right now.

There was also something else concerning. Joshua and the other reconnaissance agents who'd gone to Yadacain hadn't been relaying their regularly scheduled reports. Since not much time had passed between the kidnapping and their departure, it was possible that Joshua had contacted them as they were going. Nonetheless, the lack of communication was pretty concerning. They could only pray that nothing had happened to them.

They also had to consider Ruri's parents. It was entirely possible that they would find Ruri's parents in Yadacain, meaning they would need to sweep the island for them before leaving.

The ship was proceeding toward Yadacain at a brisk pace. The weather was fine, and nothing impeded their progress.

"Your Majesty! Yadacain spotted!"

Their island destination was in sight off the starboard bow. In one fell swoop, everyone on the ship was overcome with a mix of tension and excitement for the forthcoming battle.

"Prepare to land," Jade declared, ordering his armada.

Normally, magic would have stopped working by this point, but it seemed that Rin's supreme-level powers were unaffected, so they maintained their speed. However, everyone aboard the ships was hindered by the Spirit Slayer magic all the same. The soldiers tried to use their magic as a test, but it failed to activate.

Now that they couldn't rely on their magic, weapons would be essential. They all took up arms and eagerly awaited to dock. But while they were brimming with bloodlust, they still hadn't lost control of their rationale.

The crews on each ship began to worry about their speed, which hadn't dropped despite being so close to land. They scrambled to grab onto something as they quickly approached the beaches. The ships proceeded to run straight up onto the shores, practically at full speed. It almost seemed as though they would die before they got a chance to take down Yadacain, but everyone came out of the bumpy landing unscathed.

Jade and his men swiftly enacted their next course of action. Jade left a few men aboard the ships as lookouts, and the rest moved further into the island. They were somewhat familiar with the lay of the land due to Joshua's earlier reports. The report had also detailed that while normal magic was unavailable, they could still utilize their pocket spaces. This meant that they were spared having to carry their extensive load of things.

Jade led the extremely motivated dragonkin toward the castle. Their eyes were bloodshot with rage, and they looked more like invaders than rescuers. After moving through the trees past the beach, they spotted the city. The people came outside their houses to see what the commotion was, but Jade and his men had no intention of doing anything to the nonresistant townspeople. Their objective was to rescue the abducted dragonkin and to eliminate the Spirit Slayer magic.

The residents could only watch from a distance, terrified by the armed strangers of the Nation of the Dragon King. But before long, a slew of people, presumably Yadacain's soldiers, arrived and confronted them.

"Wh-Who are all of you?!" a Yadacain soldier asked. They pointed their weapons at the Nation of the Dragon King's soldiers, who also primed their weapons in return. They were seething with rage, but Jade managed to keep things from escalating.

"We are from the Nation of the Dragon King. Our kinsmen were captured by your nation's people the other day. We've only come to reclaim them. Let us have an audience with your king."

"If you think we're just going to usher you to our leader just because you tell us to, then think again!" the soldier said.

His response was predictable. There was no way the Yadacain soldiers would take a group of armed people to their king. At the same time, Jade couldn't just compliantly turn back home either.

"We'd rather you comply," Jade said, "but if you stand to oppose us, then we will make our way through *by force*!"

Jade's words acted as a sign for the Nation of the Dragon King's soldiers to start moving ahead. Although Yadacain's forces faltered, they were determined not to just freely let them pass, and they swung their weapons in defiance. However, these were soldiers of a sleepy island nation. Their only strife came from occasional drunken quarrels and marital spats—nothing close to warfare. Not only that, but they were all humans. They stood no chance against the battle-hardened dragonkin. The dragonkin might have been stripped of their magic, but they were strong enough with just their raw strength.

Just as it looked like the Yadacain soldiers would have no choice but to allow them to pass, another Yadacain soldier came up from the rear and tossed a round object at the dragonkin soldiers. Rin recognized what it was and immediately cast a wall of water around them. The orb exploded viciously over their heads. Rin shielded everyone from harm, but the Yadacain soldiers kept tossing more and more orbs at them. The dragonkin had to halt in their tracks. The upside—if you could call it that—was that their orbs weren't as strong as the ones Nadasha had used, so there was no major damage to the surrounding houses.

"*Those are the same things that Nadasha used in the past,*" Rin said, identifying them as the same items that Asahi had thrown during the war with Nadasha and that the priest had thrown while infiltrating their castle. It was a troublesome little trinket that absorbed mana from the area and exploded. "*I guess that means Nadasha* was *involved with Yadacain,*" she added.

As Rin pondered whether they should stay put until they ran out of orbs, a red-haired man stepped forward.

"Truly wretched magic," Heat said, furrowing his brow. He stretched out his arm and a surge of roaring flames assaulted the Yadacain soldiers.

The soldiers ran to get out of the way of the encircling blaze, so they couldn't throw more of the exploding orbs. And the sparks from the fire didn't just fly at the soldiers, but the surrounding houses as well, causing a huge uproar. The townspeople panicked and tried to extinguish the flames, but they spread too fast.

If Rin had felt so inclined, she could have easily used her powers to douse the flames. She wasn't so inclined, however. She didn't know why these people lived in this nation, but they lived under the blessings of Spirit Slayer magic, a magic that threatened the lives of spirits everywhere. As a spirit herself, she couldn't dream of helping them. Heat most likely felt the same way, which was why he was letting his flames run amok without any regard for the surroundings.

"Come. We're moving on. *Now,*" Heat proclaimed as he gazed icily at the Yadacain soldiers that had dispersed, leading the dragonkin forces onward. He was a one-man army, mowing down every Yadacain soldier in his path as he marched himself and the others straight up to the castle's front doors.

Jade and the others positioned themselves in front of the castle. Even more soldiers came out to threaten them, but Heat made sure that none of them tried to make a move. All they did was menacingly glare at Jade and his men.

"Let me see your king. We're going to retrieve our kinsmen."

They didn't know who had kidnapped the dragonkin or for what purpose, but this was an awful lot of men that had come to intercept them. Given that, there was no way the king was oblivious. Even if the king didn't know, Jade needed to talk to them and ask for their cooperation.

None of their adversaries showed any signs of budging. Jade had never thought they would just let them pass in the first place, but he considered employing some rather forceful measures before this stalemate persisted. Perhaps that went without saying. He wasn't sure he could hold the dragonkin back for much longer. They were geared for battle and seemed ready to charge at any moment. They were worried about their comrades. Jade didn't want to do anything too drastic, but it was a little too late now that Heat was on his rampage.

Just as Jade was about to give the order to charge, several women appeared from the back.

"Back down, all of you," said one of the women. From how the soldiers immediately obeyed, they seemed to hold relatively high positions.

Jade stepped forward, hoping to be able to have some sort of discourse.

"I am Jade, the Dragon King of the Nation of the Dragon King. You have taken our kinsmen. Don't tell me you have no clue either.

We have your soldiers captive as well. If you will return our men, we will do the same. But first, I want you to take me to your king."

The women stared back at Jade, unfazed. One of them answered, "We understand your terms. We'll take you to see the king. However, we request that you bring only a few of your representatives."

After a short pause, Jade replied, "Very well, then."

Jade went with Rin, Heat, and a few soldiers in tow. He ordered the rest of the soldiers to remain on standby and followed behind the women into the castle.

As they walked down the corridor, one of the women said, "We are terribly sorry for what happened. We have no intention of resisting, so we implore you not to attack our citizens."

"That all depends on your actions. We don't wish for any unnecessary bloodshed either. Are our people safe? Who ordered this to begin with?"

They all wore grim expressions as one of the women started to awkwardly explain. "This is the order of our ruler. We believe that your companions are still safe. They will most likely not kill them. It would hurt their objective."

"What do you mean? What is your king plotting?!" Jade asked, infuriated. The women shuddered in fear, but Jade showed no compassion. He wanted them to return his men quickly; that was all.

The women stopped, turned around, and bowed their heads vigorously.

"Not even we wanted to send troops to the Nation of the Dragon King. We are terribly sorry for that. We realize that this is wrong for us to request of you all, but please...*please* stop our ruler. They will no longer listen to our attempts at reasoning."

Jade looked at them suspiciously. "What is the meaning of this?"

"We don't know the details either. All we can say is that our king was betrothed to someone, but that person fell ill and passed away. Our ruler became weak and emaciated. Shortly thereafter, they began to dabble in some rather questionable research. They've never been the same since. They said that they were sending troops to the Nation of the Dragon King for that very purpose. We tried to stop them, but nothing we said would convince them otherwise."

The woman spoke with tears in her eyes. She didn't seem to be lying. So if what she said was true, then this incident was the king's personal decision. That was why they wanted dragonkin? For some questionable research?

"I wish to speak to them directly. Will you let me have an audience with your king?"

"Yes, please. Right this way."

The women led Jade and his crew to a large hall. Toward the very back, a throne-like chair sat atop a raised platform. Someone was sitting on it—a woman. She seemed to be slightly older than Ruri. Her face was very pale and haggard, but her eyes were strong and determined.

Behind her, a man dressed in black was leaning against her like her shadow. He was slender and appeared to be in his early twenties. His hair, eyes, and clothes were all jet black. His appearance didn't feel out of place at all, though. Black suited him quite well. It was almost as if instead of being clad in black, he was the very shade itself.

Rin and Heat both reacted upon seeing the man.

"*Darkness*," Rin stated.

"Well, it really was you after all, Darkness," Heat commented.

"It's been quite a while, Water, Fire," he replied without even a twitch of his brow. His eyes, silently staring at his brethren, were black as the darkness.

"What are you doing there?" asked Heat.

"Nothing in particular," the Spirit of Darkness replied.

"*It's absolutely not 'nothing'! You took away those dragonkin!*" said Rin.

"I was just granting my beloved one's wish."

"*'Just'? You can't be…*" Rin started, about to argue his point.

That was when Heat looked over at the Yadacain king, or rather queen, sitting still on her throne and muttered, "So, she's a Beloved, is she?"

Jade turned and looked at Heat. "A Beloved?" he repeated.

"Yes, she's a Beloved, just like the brat."

Jade looked at the queen in surprise. "A Beloved just like Ruri…"

There were said to be five Beloveds in the world. One in the Nation of the Beast King, one in the Nation of the Spirit King, one in the Nation of the Dragon King, one in Cerulanda, and one in Yadacain. However, the Beloved of Yadacain had never actually been confirmed; it was always just a rumor based on the accounts of those who had washed ashore from Yadacain. Considering that Yadacain was devoid of spirits, there was no possible way to know if someone beloved by the spirits dwelled here, which was why many people had assumed it was mere hearsay. Plus, searching Yadacain was difficult when its borders were closed to begin with. No one had been able to check, even if they had wanted to, and certainly no one expected the Beloved to be the queen of Yadacain.

Jade, on the other hand, couldn't care less if the queen was a Beloved. That wasn't why he was here. He took a step forward and said, "Oh *King* of Yadacain, you took my kinsmen, and I want you to give them back."

But the queen simply replied, "I can't do that. They are essential. For both my sake and *that person's*."

"I don't care *what* it is you're trying to do. It has nothing to do with any of us. Give back my people now, or we take them back by force."

The queen, who looked pale enough to collapse at any moment, threw a sharp glare at Jade. "I cannot allow you to do that. I need your dragonkin blood. You taking them back would hinder my plans."

"Your plans do not concern us. I will turn over every stone in this castle to find them if I have to."

"You shall not! I will not allow it!" the queen cried. Part of the ceiling quickly dropped down, revealing that it was swarming with the same zombies that the Church of God's Light had created back in the Nation of the Beast King—except these held weapons in their hands. They were similar to the zombies from back then, but they weren't quite the same. Those zombies only reacted to blood, but these set their sights on Jade and his men regardless.

"Hngaaaah!" screamed the zombies as they came charging their way.

Jade unleashed his blade. While his sword technique was befitting his title of Dragon King, there were just so many of them.

Jade clicked his tongue at the overwhelming number of zombies and proceeded to slash through them. This was Jade's personal battlefield. While there were a few other soldiers with him, Jade was moving at such a tremendous speed that they would only get in the way, so they held back. It didn't take long before all of the zombies hit the ground, a sight that reminded the troops that their king was indeed incredible.

"Seize him! I'll use him as fodder as well!" the queen commanded.

The Spirit of Darkness's pitch-black eyes locked on to Jade, and the same black sphere that had captured the dragonkin before came flying toward Jade. Jade's singular focus on the queen made him slow to react. He seemed to be as good as caught, but one of Jade's soldiers pushed him out of the way and became trapped in the spherical prison instead. Jade watched in shock, but he quickly came back to his senses and shot a piercing glare at the queen.

The sphere came flying at Jade once again, but he dodged its advances and tossed a dagger toward the queen. Of course, before it could reach the queen, the Spirit of Darkness swatted it out of the air, but Jade had done that knowing Darkness would stop it. With his focus on the queen, the Spirit of Darkness's attack let up.

"What the hell are you trying to do?! Why are you targeting dragonkin?! Does this have to do with your dead fiancé?!" Jade yelled. The queen had supposedly changed after the person she was betrothed to had died.

The queen's eyes wavered hesitantly. "I…just want to get them back. I just want to be with my beloved! What's so wrong with that?!" she shouted, clutching her head in a deranged manner.

The Spirit of Darkness then took her into his embrace. His eyes were tinged with sadness, unlike before.

Rin and Heat stood in front of the Spirit of Darkness.

"*Darkness, I don't know your reasons, but you'll be crossing the line if you use Spirit Slayer magic any longer,*" Rin said. Her hair would have been standing on end if she'd had any. "*We have decided to eliminate Spirit Slayer—to keep the other spirits safe. You will not get in our way.*"

"So, what will you do?" Heat asked to confirm his intentions. He didn't need to hear his response, however. As a fellow spirit, he already knew the answer. Spirits did not fight one another.

The Spirit of Darkness was by himself against two other spirits of the same class. He had no chance of winning, even considering the numbers.

The Spirit of Darkness didn't oppose and sorrowfully looked down at the queen.

"What are you doing? We must deal with these cretins!" she protested.

But the Spirit of Darkness remained still, staring at her and nothing more. "I'm sorry, beloved one. It seems that I can no longer help you." The spheres cracked, and the captured dragonkin soldier was released.

"Are you...betraying me? Are *you* going to leave me as well?" she muttered in disbelief.

"I'm not leaving you. I'll always be with you. But this is the end. That one isn't coming back. You will just have to accept that," he replied.

The queen looked absolutely floored, as if the words that had come from his mouth sounded unreal. Her voice quivered. "What are you talking about? Are you saying that everything I've done so far was for naught? You've been helping me, haven't you? They will come back. Soon enough. I just need to make a little more progress in my research and I can get them back! Isn't that right?!"

"The dead can't be brought back to life," Heat said, telling her the cold, hard reality of it. "No matter the means, not even with a spirit's power. It's *impossible.*"

While Jade couldn't piece together all the threads of her story, he was able to predict that the queen had someone that she wanted to bring back to life and that was the reason why she was conducting her research. He remembered how the Church of God's Light had brought back the dead. Did that mean that the queen had conducted that magic—that research? The spirits were confident that it was an impossible feat. So why hadn't the Spirit of Darkness made that clear to her?

"That's not true! I've actually managed to bring the dead back to life!" the queen argued.

"Are you talking about those corpses?" Heat asked. "Those are simply animated vessels. Soulless puppets. Saying that they're 'alive' is a misnomer."

"Which is why I am doing research! With just a little more time, returning the person I love back to how they were when alive will be—"

"Useless. You can't bring someone back to life unless you bring back their soul. And a soul that's left its body can never return. They're probably floating around the circle of reincarnation by now. In fact, I'd venture to say that they've already been reborn as someone else. What you're doing is utterly pointless," Heat said, telling her the reality of the situation as bluntly as possible.

The queen started to get agitated. "No. No, no. That can't be. It simply can't…"

That was when Jade's sensitive dragonkin nose caught a whiff of a peculiar smell. "I smell something burnt. It almost smells like something is on fire."

They heard a large commotion coming from outside. Then, with a loud clatter, the women who had escorted Jade's group barged in.

"Your Majesty, we need to evacuate immediately!" said one of the women. "The room you always seclude yourself in has caught fire!"

The queen stood so fast it rattled her throne. Her pale face turned even paler and she started running.

"Ah, Your Majesty, where are you off to?!" the woman cried.

Jade and his men pursued the fleeing queen.

As soon as she'd left the room, the queen ran down the corridor at top speed. The closer she got to where she was heading, the stronger the smell of smoke became. Then she finally came upon the room, engulfed in furious flames, and stopped in front of it.

She tried to enter the burning room in a panic, but this was absolutely not the right time to enter. The Spirit of Darkness grabbed her from behind.

"Unhand me! All of my research is inside there!"

"You can't, beloved one. The fire is burning too greatly; you must abandon what is inside."

"I won't! Unhand me! Let me go!" the queen screamed, thrashing like a spoiled child while the Spirit of Darkness clutched both of her arms from underneath.

The castle attendants were running all over the place, trying to extinguish the flames, but the fire couldn't be contained.

Jade suddenly saw something move out of the corner of his eye—a person on the other side of the corridor moving as if to avoid detection. Upon closer examination, he recognized the face and exclaimed, "Joshua?!"

Noticing Jade from his call, Joshua stopped in his tracks, looking surprised. "Whoa, Your Majesty?!" he exclaimed.

He was followed by a few others whom Jade also recognized. They were the reconnaissance agents that had come with Joshua and also the dragonkin captured by the Spirit of Darkness.

"What are you doing, Sire?" Joshua asked in an awfully lighthearted tone. Despite the situation, he wasn't feeling the stress at all.

"That's my line. What are you doing over there? You didn't give your regular reports, and you've got the kidnapped soldiers with you."

"Well, y'see, I infiltrated the castle, but I screwed up and ended up getting caught," Joshua reported with a jovial grin. "Then, much to my surprise, they brought some other folks from back home here. I managed to bust out of jail with the help of my partners. I set fire to the laboratory in order to provide a distraction till we could make our escape. You caught us right in the middle of said escape."

Jade sighed deeply. "So this commotion is your handiwork, eh?"

Jade had been worried sick, but Joshua was as casual as could be. Plus, it seemed they didn't even need to come rescue Joshua seeing as how he was escaping on his own.

"Well, I'm just glad you're all right," Jade said.

"Oh, did you, by any chance, come to rescue me? Thank you very much, nonetheless," Joshua replied.

Jade was also relieved to see that the kidnapped dragonkin were safe and uninjured. When he expressed as much, they all thanked him in unison.

Although Jade hadn't *needed* to come to their rescue, he still had things to do. Who better to talk to a ruler about the Spirit Slayer magic than a fellow ruler?

Jade looked over at the queen. She had been flailing about trying to get into the blazing room, but now she sat on the floor, her spirit broken. She was slumped over as if she didn't have the willpower to even stand up. She watched in a daze as the room went up in flames before her eyes. The Spirit of Darkness rubbed her back, but the queen was too numb to care.

"I don't think she's in any condition to talk at the moment," Jade commented.

It seemed that they would need to play wait and see.

206

20 Collaborator

Gentle memories came to mind.

"Hey, dear? There's something I want you to listen to."

"What'd that be, Seraphie?"

"I wrote a song. I put a lot into writing it."

"Oh, did you now? Well, this should be a treat. Take it away."

A captivatingly soft and oh-so-gentle singing voice lived on in Quartz memory, remaining just as vivid as the day he'd heard it.

"That's a beautiful song," said Quartz.

"Of course it is. I wrote it with you in mind," Seraphie admitted.

"How flattering. Then will you sing that song only for me? Don't sing it in front of anyone else. Sing it only for me."

"That's fine by me. I'm singing for you with you in mind, so keep by my side and listen to it always."

Always by her side, for now and forever.

Unfortunately, his farewell with Seraphie had come sooner than he'd expected.

Normally, once the wedding had been held and the dragonheart had been introduced into a mate's body, it would align their lifespan to a dragonkin. That was how it was supposed to work, but Seraphie was stricken with an illness—an incurable disease that neither dragonheart nor dragon's blood could cure.

Rocked with sickness, even though she had accepted the dragonheart and gained a long lifespan, her body couldn't hold.

Though the dragonheart expanded her lifespan, it wouldn't cure the illness. Seraphie was going to die—a fact that was too much to bear.

Quartz lived his days in dread. He hated watching his beloved mate's body wither away. Day after day, he would check to see if she was still breathing. The experience started to whittle away at his mind.

That was when Seraphie had said something to him— a cruel declaration.

"Listen, dear? Even if I die, don't follow after me."

"You're asking the impossible, Seraphie. I can't live in a world without you. If you die, then I die with you. You said we'd be together forever, didn't you?"

"Don't. Don't you dare do that. If you do, I'll never forgive you."

"But I can't live alone. It'd be simply unbearable!"

Yes, the mere thought of living in a world without Seraphie was unthinkable.

Seraphie then smiled at Quartz. "Say, did you know? When people die, we become souls, and we are reborn into the world again."

"I know that, but why are you bringing this up?"

"If I die, I'll be reborn again. When that happens, dear...I want you to find me," Seraphie said, uttering a ridiculous wish. "I won't forget you even if I am reincarnated. And even if I do, I swear that I'll remember you. So, please, find me. A certain person told me it's not impossible. Will you grant this last wish of mine?"

"Yes, I will. If that is what you want, I'll find you in this world, no matter how long it takes."

With that cruel wish as her last words, Seraphie left this world right before Quartz's eyes.

For a while afterward, Quartz couldn't bring himself to do anything, and he barely remembered how he even passed the days. However, something happened that poured salt on Quartz's already open wounds—a grave robbing.

Quartz had laid Seraphie to rest along with a few of her favorite pieces of jewelry. Some foolish people had caught wind of that information from somewhere and had ransacked her grave. Fortunately, Seraphie's body was safe, but the jewelry she'd loved to wear while she was alive was gone.

Quartz was practically seeing red as a fierce rage swelled within him. He soon found the grave robber, beat him so badly that he was better off dead, and handed him off to his troops. He had really wanted to kill him right then and there, but Finn and Agate had stopped him before he could.

They recovered all of the jewelry the man stole—except Seraphie's treasured ring. The grave robber had had an accomplice, but he'd ended up killing them in a fight over the loot. The ring had been left behind in the pocket space of his dead partner, and now that he was dead, it couldn't be retrieved.

This shocked Quartz so much that he decided to place Seraphie's remains in his own pocket space, so as to never expose her to the public ever again.

Quartz had mentally hit rock bottom, but there was one thing that brought him back to his senses—the promise he shared with Seraphie.

(*This isn't the time to dawdle. I have to find you. I promised you I would.*)

In order to search for Seraphie, Quartz gave up his throne, his kingdom—everything to grant his beloved mate's wish. He then traveled the world in search of his one and only. He didn't know where she would be reborn, or the color of her hair, skin, or eyes. He didn't even know if she would be a human or demi-human, but he searched all over. It was like trying to find a needle in a haystack.

Everyone said it couldn't be done, but someone had told Quartz that it wasn't necessarily impossible. If it *was* possible, there was still a chance that he could see Seraphie again. Quartz clung to that sliver of miraculous hope, because if he didn't, he wouldn't be able to keep himself sane.

He searched, and searched, and searched—for years, for decades. Still, Seraphie was nowhere to be found.

(*Can I really find her? No, I will find her.*)

The fact that Quartz hadn't found Seraphie after all these years was starting to make his weak side rear its head. Would he just never find her again? Would he die without ever meeting her? The world without Seraphie was devoid of color and filled with sadness. He couldn't bear to continue living in a world where she was gone. He'd lost count of how many times he'd contemplated taking his own life.

But every time Quartz felt like giving up, he recalled Seraphie's face in her final moments. That alone motivated him. Be that as it may, he was nearing his limits. He grew weary of living without her. He was granting her last wish, but a part of him wanted to shed blood and scream his desire to just end it all.

Quartz thought he had lasted long enough. He'd spent decades in this world without Seraphie. He'd said that he came to the Nation of the Dragon King in order to see Ruri, but that wasn't his actual reason. His actual reason was…

Ruri had been restlessly pacing around in her room, unable to quell her worries about Jade.

"Calm yourself, Ruri," Chelsie said, sick of her antsy behavior.

"But Chelsie-san, they should already be in Yadacain by now. I'm worried something happened."

"I'm sure they'll contact us sooner or later, so just wait till then. You making a fuss right now isn't gonna do much of anything," Chelsie replied.

"Ungh... I know that, but *still*~!" Ruri whined.

"Why don't we have some tea?" Quartz suggested to calm Ruri's nerves. "I'll brew up a pot of my special tea to help settle you down."

"Thank you, Quartz-sama," Ruri said in honest delight.

Quartz turned his back on Ruri and headed toward the kitchen to brew the tea. He pulled out a small vial from his breast pocket, one that contained a blood-red liquid. He put a few drops of it into the cup.

"Seraphie, would you rebuke me for this? But I'm so very tired..." Quartz murmured.

No one was around to answer his question.

Meanwhile, in Yadacain, Jade was shown to a guest room.

The fire that Joshua and his men had set was fortunately not big enough to engulf the entire castle, but the room where the fire had started had been completely burned.

According to Joshua, there was a hidden room in the basement where the queen had been conducting research. But since they'd set fire to it, it was unlikely that anything inside of it had survived the blaze.

The queen, who'd been stunned that her research had gone up in smoke, had allowed the Spirit of Darkness to take her off somewhere.

Jade and his men from the Nation of the Dragon King were technically invaders, but they were being treated surprisingly well—as guests of the island nation. The invasion and abduction of dragonkin had been the queen's sole decision. Her aides hadn't had time to stop her. Yadacain's general consensus was that they didn't want to oppose the Nation of the Dragon King due to the overwhelming power they possessed as a nation.

As for Jade, his men were safe. Yadacain had no intention of launching any more attacks against the kingdom either.

The soldiers that Jade had left outside the castle had been ushered in and were currently resting. They were disappointed they hadn't been able to go on a warpath, but they were glad their comrades were safe. Granted, if they *hadn't been* safe, that warpath would have *undoubtedly* taken place.

Though everyone else in Yadacain was being hospitable, it was up in the air whether the queen would comply to be non-hostile. Jade wanted to speak to her in person, but she most likely couldn't in her condition. Instead, he listened to Joshua give his report.

"I don't know what her connection is with the Church of God's Light, but the resurrection magic was created with the queen's research," Joshua explained.

"I see," Jade replied.

"There might be connections to Nadasha as well."

"What?"

"I found this in the queen's lab," Joshua said, presenting some documents to Jade. They chronicled the results of the resurrection research, and they contained details about how to summon people from other worlds.

"So, this is the summoning Nadasha performed, huh?" asked Jade. "The one that brought Ruri to this world?"

"Yes. It seems she was conducting research into that too. When we did our investigation of Nadasha, we didn't find anything this detailed. Maybe it was the queen who created it," Joshua conjectured.

"So they had a link to Nadasha after all," Jade surmised.

"Looks like Ruri is going to be mad," quipped Joshua.

"Yes, I'd say so."

Nadasha was responsible for summoning Ruri to this world. Ruri had gotten extremely upset about that and had plotted revenge against the king and high priest, the two who'd conducted the summoning. But if she knew that it was someone else who had created it in the first place, she would let them know her wrath as well. After all, if it hadn't been for that, she wouldn't have been summoned. Jade wanted to thank them for bringing Ruri into his life, but Ruri would certainly have the opposite reaction.

"Why did she target dragonkin?" Jade asked.

"I don't know any of the details," Joshua said, "but I overheard them talking about running short on blood. The Church of God's Light's revival method utilized dragon blood as well. My guess is that they kidnapped the dragonkin because they were running out."

"But where did they get their blood supply in the first place?"

"Well, Sire, I recall she said she had a collaborator."

"The collaborator got them that blood?" Jade asked.

"I'm afraid that is about as much as I know."

Some amount of the story was starting to come to light, but there were still many things left unknown.

"It's still too early to get the story straight from the horse's mouth," Jade said. He had thought to ask the women who'd brought him here, but he figured they wouldn't be very cooperative with the queen in that state.

Joshua continued to give his other reports, and after a little while, someone opened the door without knocking and came in. It was the Spirit of Darkness.

"Would you mind if we talk?" he asked.

"Not at all. Please, take a seat," replied Jade. He politely offered the spirit a seat even though it wasn't a custom of Yadacain to do so. He then said, "I would like to speak with the queen. Is that possible?"

The Spirit of Darkness looked sad as he shook his head. "No, not for a while. I told her…I told her that she couldn't bring back the dead no matter the means. She is in severe shock and is in no condition to talk."

"So I see."

"It's all my fault," the Spirit of darkness said with deep regret. "She held on to hope while she was conducting her research. As I watched her so desperately clinging to it, I couldn't find it in myself to tell her the harsh reality of the situation. As a result, I wound up hurting her even more."

"What did you want to speak about?" Jade asked.

"You want to know how things turned out this way, I presume," the Spirit of Darkness offered.

"Indeed."

"I'll tell you, but on the condition that you not touch her. I'll make her stop the research, so just don't."

"I understand," Jade said, nodding.

The Spirit of Darkness looked surprised. "Are you sure about that?"

"I came here to rescue my men and eliminate the Spirit Slayer magic. My men have been returned safely. If she'll comply with the matter of the Spirit Slayer as well, then I have no further intention of interfering in Yadacain's affairs."

"I see. I'll help you with the Spirit Slayer as well."

"You know, if you had just done that from the start, things wouldn't have gotten so complicated," Heat quipped, sounding arrogant and smarmy. He was sitting in a chair beside Jade.

The Spirit of Darkness brushed it off with an awkward grin. "It all started with the death of her fiancé. She had withered away so badly that she couldn't even pass food down her throat. I was so worried about her, but the only thing I could do was remain by her side. Some time passed, and she suddenly had the idea to conduct magic research. I was overjoyed to see that she was finally getting past things, but I found out that her research was for resurrecting the dead. She wanted to use magic to bring her dead fiancé back to life."

"And you didn't tell her then and there? That what she was doing was impossible?" Heat asked with a stern glare.

"I just couldn't do it. I knew it was impossible, but I just couldn't bring myself to tell her the truth. She'd finally found the strength within her to stand up, so I was afraid she would relapse if I said anything."

Heat offered nothing in reply other than a rather bemused "humph."

"I couldn't tell her the truth after seeing the joy on her face when she brought a dead body back to life. I did try to tell her indirectly that without a soul, you couldn't say they were 'alive,' but once I did, her research became even more extreme. There was seemingly no end to it."

"Did that lead to creating a method for summoning people from other worlds?" asked Jade.

"Yes. When I told her that his soul might've gone to that world, she said that all she needed to do in that case was to bring it over. Granted, it's still not complete."

Jade then asked, "Why did she tell the method to Nadasha?"

"Nadasha? What are you talking about?" the Spirit of Darkness replied.

"You taught it to the land of Nadasha, didn't you? The summoning magic along with the Spirit Slayer magic and the magic circle."

"By Nadasha, you mean the nation neighboring the Nation of the Dragon King? If so, then no. She doesn't have a single tie to Nadasha."

The Spirit of the Darkness didn't seem to be lying. Jade tilted his head in confusion. So it *wasn't* the queen?

"Then what about the organization known as the Church of God's Light? She taught those people the resurrection method, didn't she? She handed them several of her items as well."

"No, she did nothing of the sort. She's never left the nation to begin with. She wouldn't have ties to any outsiders."

"What do you mean?"

Rin then flapped her wings over to the Spirit of Darkness and asked, *"Darkness, you've cut off communication with the other spirits for a while now, haven't you?"*

"Yeah, the smaller spirits clamor too much. I've had my hands full with her anyway."

"Read me and Fire's memories from a few days ago," Rin suggested. Spirits could share their memories with one another.

After a short silence, the Spirit of Darkness put his hand to his temple. "What is this…?" he asked.

"You don't know anything?"

"No, I didn't know this was happening. It wasn't her who taught them, and it naturally wasn't me. After all, I haven't left this land since she was born. And those people have never come here before."

"*Then who was it? If it wasn't you, then it must have been someone else who knew about it.*"

"The details of the research have never been disclosed to anyone—not even her aides. Not even I know the exact details behind it. Mostly because I was never interested in knowing, that is. The only other person who'd know is… No, but he wouldn't…"

"Do you have a hunch?" Jade asked, his face grim. He had been hoping that all this would end with the queen.

"Dragonkin blood is quintessential for the resurrection research…" the Spirit of Darkness said.

"Yes, I heard from Joshua. How did the queen get the blood to start with? It isn't something you can just obtain easily. Especially if the queen has never ventured outside of Yadacain."

"She received it from her collaborator."

Jade wasn't too surprised to hear that since Joshua had filled him in beforehand. Nevertheless, that begged the question of *how* the collaborator had obtained the blood. Since dragonkin were aware of the danger their blood contained, they wouldn't give it to others unless it was a serious emergency. And it would be very difficult to get it, especially from someone as strong as a dragonkin.

"He had also lost someone dear to him, and he hoped that her research would bring them back to life. The blood came from him. He helped her for a while, so I'm sure he'd be able to teach others."

"Who is this person? How did he get dragon blood?" asked Jade.

"I believe that you would know them better than I would," the Spirit of Darkness said, shooting a look at Jade.

"Me?" Jade repeated, puzzled. It was someone he knew? What did he mean by that?

"The one who had been collaborating with her and providing her with blood was a dragonkin."

"A *dragonkin*?!" Jade exclaimed, leaning forward in his seat.

Jade was surprised, but at the same time, this made sense. There was no need to get it from somewhere else if they were providing it themselves. But who in the world would do such a thing? If it was a dragonkin, then it was possible that Jade was familiar with them, as the Spirit of Darkness had said. No one came to mind, however.

As Jade contemplated who it could be, the Spirit of Darkness added some even more shocking information.

"I heard that he was the previous Dragon King. Seeing as how you're the current Dragon King, you must know him, correct?"

Jade's heart uncomfortably skipped a beat, like someone had grabbed it and squeezed.

"Quark, Rortz... No, Quartz, I think it was? Some name like that."

"Wh-What did he look like? Can you describe his appearance?" Jade asked, tightly clenching his fists. He was afraid to hear Darkness's response.

"A kind-looking man with silver-white hair and purple eyes."

Jade refused to believe it, but the Spirit of Darkness's description fit the bill for Quartz. A horrible dryness filled Jade's mouth.

"Master Quartz? That just…can't be…"

"He must have placed his hope into resurrecting the dead once he lost his mate."

It was true that Quartz had lost his mate, which would make him someone who would wish more than anyone to resurrect the dead, but how the queen and Quartz had met made no sense. They were both rulers, but the Nation of the Dragon King and Yadacain had no history of diplomatic relations.

"How did he connect with the queen in the first place?" asked Jade.

"Didn't you know? That man's mate was a witch of Yadacain."

The surprises kept coming, leaving Jade speechless.

"Seraphie, right? I'm pretty sure that was her name. My beloved one's mother and Seraphie were old friends. Apparently, he came to Yadacain for some sort of purpose, and when he found out that she had *also* lost someone important to her and was researching resurrection, he decided to become her collaborator."

The Spirit of Darkness also mentioned that Quartz had accepted all sorts of items from the queen as well.

In stark contrast to the Spirit of Darkness, who was nonplussed, Jade's expression was rife with tension.

"That man's eyes were horribly dark; they didn't fit his appearance at all. Even Light seemed worried about him…" Darkness said.

"Light? Why are you bringing up Light? You do mean the same Light I'm thinking of, right?" Rin asked, thinking of none other than their supreme-level spirit brethren, the Spirit of Light.

"It was because the Spirit of Light was conducting himself with Quartz. Apparently, Light formed a contract with Seraphie while she was still alive."

"*But Light wasn't around that man. Fire, did you see him?*"

"No, I didn't," Heat replied.

"*Do you think they've gone their separate ways now?*" Rin wondered, concerned about the Spirit of Light.

Jade, however, was more concerned about Quartz. "Why would Master Quartz do that…?" he asked, still unable to believe it. He told himself that it wasn't necessarily set in stone that it was Quartz, but the more he heard from the Spirit of Darkness, the more it seemed it couldn't have been anyone but Quartz.

"Since my beloved one wouldn't know, he is the only other individual I can think of who would be able to teach people about Spirit Slayer, and the methods for resurrecting the dead and for summoning. Although I'm clueless as to his reasoning."

If that was so, then just how far involved was Quartz? Was he behind Nadasha's raid on the Nation of the Dragon King? Was he behind the Church of God's Light's plot to assassinate Ruri? Was he behind the kidnapping of the dragonkin and the attack on the castle? If he had been involved in any of these things, Jade couldn't just let Quartz roam free.

The worst-case scenario was that Jade had ordered Quartz to…

Before Jade could finish the thought, he clenched his fists tightly in frustration.

21 The Kidnapping

If all that the Spirit of Darkness said was true, Jade needed to return to question Quartz immediately. Unfortunately, he had some unfinished business to attend to in Yadacain. While he was relieved to know that the abducted dragonkin were safe with Joshua and the other reconnaissance operatives, Rin and the other supreme-level spirits still wanted to get rid of the Spirit Slayer magic.

Since Jade couldn't talk to the queen, he set up a meeting with the nation's delegates and demanded they cease all use of Spirit Slayer magic moving forward. He added that they were to destroy all weapons and tools enchanted with Spirit Slayer, such as their ships and cannons, as well as any and all documents related to its creation or use.

The delegates were reluctant. They were witches, and they'd lived with Spirit Slayer magic their whole lives. There were going to be issues if they could no longer use it. Nonetheless, Jade couldn't back down either, what with Rin and the others being so insistent. If they couldn't accept these terms, the Nation of the Dragon King would have to take appropriate measures.

Jade told them that his soldiers could subdue all of Yadacain, but if they accepted Jade's demands, then Yadacain would be allowed to continue being Yadacain. He was threatening them.

The delegates realized that Jade's threats weren't idle—he was serious. Their faces turned pale, but they asked him to give them time to speak with the other witches, possibly because they couldn't make the call on their own despite being delegates.

According to Joshua's report, the people of Yadacain didn't have much direct relation with Spirit Slayer in their daily lives. Essentially, the only people who used it were the witches. However, there were other things that benefited from Spirit Slayer, like their ships and weapons.

There were no spirits in this country. Normally, the land would dry up and become uninhabitable, but Yadacain was self-sufficient and able to maintain regular plant growth. That was because they used Spirit Slayer to absorb mana from the world and return it to their land. The delegates argued that Yadacain would become uninhabitable without Spirit Slayer since there were no spirits.

Honestly, though, everyone from the Nation of the Dragon King thought they were getting their just deserts. They'd been creating all sorts of things, researching with no signs of stopping, while the world around them explicitly told them of the dangers. After all, the witches were the ones who made the land uninhabitable for spirits. But even though everyone thought that, they couldn't just ignore the nation.

The Spirit of Darkness proposed a solution to this problem, stating that he would bring in other spirits to compensate so long as the Spirit Slayer was destroyed. He said that spirits would naturally gather wherever a supreme-level spirit resided and that he planned on staying in the nation so long as the current queen was alive. Even when the queen died, the spirits would have settled in by then, meaning there should be no issues. It wouldn't affect the livelihoods of the people if Spirit Slayer were removed.

The question now was whether the witches would abandon the magic they'd been using for so long. If they said they couldn't, Jade would have to consider taking the nation with weapons, just as he'd declared to the delegates. Jade didn't want to do that, but the same issues would arise if things were left unchecked.

Rin and the other supreme-level spirits wouldn't be too pleased either since they originally said they wanted to destroy the magic themselves. Although they were deferring to Jade for the time being, if Yadacain continued using Spirit Slayer, then Rin and the others would step in themselves. If that happened, there was no telling how much they would lay waste to Yadacain. There would be less damage if Jade were to just take control of the nation by force.

Despite Jade's desire to hurry back to the kingdom and confirm things with Quartz, the proceedings weren't going as smoothly as he'd hoped. As he waited impatiently for the witches' decision, he ordered his troops to prepare so they could make a swift return. Things could take a lot longer, though, depending on their choice. He only prayed that they would make a wise decision.

After a considerable amount of time had passed, the delegates once again entered the room. They had decided to accept all of Jade's terms—albeit rather reluctantly. It was the obvious choice in Jade's mind, since he had only told them to stop using Spirit Slayer and not their brand of sorcery altogether. But for the witches, it must have been an arduous decision. They decided to agree to his demands rather than let the Nation of the Dragon King subjugate their nation.

After the delegates agreed, Jade immediately set out and destroyed the Spirit Slayer magic that had a hold over the entire island. With it gone, they could now use their magic. Next, he had the nation surrender all Spirit Slayer-related documentation and tools, such as their weapons and ships. Jade also mobilized all of his men to search the castle from top to bottom, just in case they had some secret storage.

The Spirit of Darkness helped with that. Since he'd lived in the castle for so long, he was familiar with where the documents were stored and where all the hidden spots were. All of the queen's documents had already gone up in flames with the lab, so they weren't a problem.

Jade's men gathered all the tools and documents, and Heat burned them with his flames. Doubts remained about whether this was really all of it, but from now on, the Spirit of Darkness would be taking responsibility and keeping a watchful eye to ensure Spirit Slayer was never used again. They could trust the nation if the Spirit of Darkness was watching. Spirits didn't tell lies.

It wasn't certain whether the queen approved of this situation, but the Spirit of Darkness said that he would keep a close eye on her. She had gone through the sorrowful process of losing her fiancé, but that still didn't excuse her for involving other people in her methods. She was unapologetic, and he'd like to chastise her more, but given her state, it was better to just let sleeping dogs lie.

The Spirit Slayer had been removed entirely. Jade was impatient to get back home as soon as possible. He gave his men express orders to proceed with their departure. But just as he was about to board his ship, he spotted a man and a woman arguing with one of his soldiers on the side of the boat. They were both dressed in Yadacain clothing, so they were presumably from here.

Jade contained his impatience and walked toward the dispute.

"What are you doing?" he asked.

The soldier looked relieved, but then he arched his eyebrows and explained, "Your Majesty. These people are asking to be taken to the Nation of the Dragon King on our ship."

The woman, who seemed to be in her forties but had neither young nor old features, looked at Jade's face. She blushed and excitedly said, "Oh my, what a *hunk*! If all the dragonkin men are handsome like this, then they're my dream race! *You* are especially hunkier than the rest."

Jade watched her, bewildered, as she squealed.

225

The slightly nervous-looking man with her tried to contain her outbursts. "Calm down, Riccia. Besides, he called that man 'His Majesty.' He might be the *king* of the dragonkin."

"What?! No way. Really?" the woman asked, leaning over in surprise.

Jade found himself shrinking back. "Well, yes, I am…"

"Eeek!" the woman shrieked, so loudly that the soldiers dropped their preparation work and turned to see what was happening.

"Omigod, this person is the handsome Dragon King that Ruri mentioned in her letter, isn't he? He really *is* a handsome one. He's giving me palpitations. Oh, this is no good. I'm a married woman."

"Ruri?" Jade repeated, surprised to hear her name.

That was when Rin came flapping over. "*Oh my, so you were here after all.*"

"A clione? It's so big, and it's flying!" said the woman, staring at Rin curiously. The man was also shocked at the creature's very un-clione-like size.

"*It's me, Rin,*" she said in greeting.

The woman's eyes widened once she heard her name. "Oh my, you're Rin? As in, the spirit Rin-chan? It's been so long. I didn't recognize you because you didn't have that body when you came to see me."

"*Jeez, what have you been doing all this time? Ruri was worried about you.*"

"If you're asking us that question, you're barking up the wrong tree," the woman replied. "But I'm glad we met up again!"

Still surprised from hearing Ruri's name, Jade looked at the woman's face once again, his adrenaline running high. Platinum blonde hair and blue eyes—features that reminded him of someone he adored. In fact, upon closer inspection, he could see a vague resemblance.

"Are you both Ruri's parents?" Jade asked. He'd been so hyper-focused on returning home that he'd forgotten that he'd also come to Yadacain to find Ruri's parents.

"Indeed we are! I'm Ruri's mother, Riccia, good sir~!" said the woman.

"I'm her father, Kohaku," added the man, greeting Jade politely with a bow.

Unlike Ruri's mother with her cheerful personality and similar hair and eye color to Ruri, her father was rather subdued yet slightly high-strung, and he had black hair and dark eyes. Since both bore a vague resemblance to Ruri, Jade could see that they were indeed her parents.

"Oh, so you *did* come to Yadacain after all, then?" asked Jade.

"That's right. Before we even knew what was going on, we ended up at Yadacain's castle. There were no spirits around, and we were positively lost," Riccia explained.

"*The queen must have conducted a summoning and dragged you here. Did they do anything harmful to you?*"

"No, they didn't. The people at the castle treated us very courteously. But when I wanted to go to the Nation of the Dragon King right away, they told me that I couldn't leave the island since their borders were closed and they had no relations with other nations. They said the only way to get out was to buy a ship and leave ourselves. So that's why we came here and worked for half a year, but we couldn't save any money. And figuring out *when* we'd make it the Nation of the Dragon King was becoming an issue."

"*If that's all, you can hop on the boat with us.*"

"Really? That's great. Now we can finally see Ruri!" Riccia exclaimed.

"*Ruri's grandfather is already back at the kingdom.*"

"Oh, dad already made it there? I was worried when we got separated. Then again, dad can survive no matter where."

"*Yes, he's apparently been on a rather leisurely journey this whole time.*"

Riccia followed Rin onto the ship, leaving Kohaku behind. Jade met his eyes and Kohaku said, "I apologize for my wife being so all over the place."

"No, it's fine. She seems to have a very different personality from Ruri."

"Well, since that's how her mother acts, Ruri grew up well-adjusted to compensate. How is she, by the way? Is she doing well?"

"Yes, she's doing just fine," Jade replied. "She was very worried about the both of you. But I'm glad you're both all right. Now then, please step aboard."

"Thank you very much."

Jade hadn't gotten this impression from Riccia, but it seemed that life here had been rough judging from Kohaku. He looked somewhat fatigued, but he also looked relieved to have met someone like Jade, who was willing to help.

This development was sure to make Ruri happy. Jade was pleased to have such a fine present to give to her, but once he remembered that he needed to speak to Quartz, his mood grew dour. Nevertheless, he had to speak to him—as Dragon King and as someone who knew Quartz well.

After a final check to see if everyone had boarded, Jade and the others left Yadacain.

As they sailed along with Rin's powers pushing them through the seas, Rin suddenly yelled, "*What do you mean?!*" Her outburst echoed on the deck of the ship.

"What's the matter, Lord Rin?" Jade asked Rin, feeling an unusual sense of concern. Heat was furrowing his brows as well. Just then, the ship started to go even faster than before. Everyone stumbled in place. "Lord Rin?"

"*This is bad. We need to get home quickly. Blasted Kotaro, what were you even doing? I swear,*" Rin cursed.

"Lord Rin, did something happen?"

"*Ruri has been kidnapped. By that Quartz guy!*"

Jade had no idea what he was hearing for a second. "What do you mean?"

"*It's as I just told you. He made off with Ruri. Kotaro is looking for her, but he can't find her.*"

"Ruri was kidnapped...?" Jade repeated, clueless.

What was Rin even talking about? Where would he have taken her and for what purpose? What in the world was the meaning of all this? What was going on?

Before Jade could ask any of these questions, Rin said, "*I'm going to concentrate for a while, so don't talk to me.*" She focused on increasing the speed of the ship, so Jade couldn't get any more information out of her.

Heat was also scowling, looking very much like he wasn't in the mood for conversation.

Jade and his men returned to the Nation of the Dragon King at breakneck speed. He left the unloading up to the others and rushed to the castle. It was faster for him to turn into a dragon and fly from the port straight to Sector One than to run all the way there. He let Rin and Heat hop on his back and took off.

When they arrived, the inside of the castle seemed no different than usual—nary a sign of disturbance. Jade was telling himself that it must have been some sort of mistake, but he never once slowed his stride. He followed Rin, who was leading the way, and they arrived at Ruri's room. The window had a big hole in it. The room was a mess, and right in the middle of it was Kotaro, his eyes closed and concentrating. Chelsie, who was sitting in the chair beside him, stood up once Jade and the others came in. Ruri was nowhere to be seen.

Jade asked, "What happened to Ruri?"

Chelsie turned her eyes away, awkwardly.

"Where's Ruri?!" Jade shouted, unable to contain his panic.

Kotaro finally opened his eyes, only to be met by Rin rushing him.

"*How could this happen while you were here?!*" she yelled.

Kotaro lowered his tail. His whole body slumped, and he replied, "*I'm sorry…*"

Jade, however, just wanted to know about Ruri. "What happened here?"

"*The previous king took Ruri away.*"

"Why? How did it come to that?"

"*Ruri was worried about you and couldn't calm herself down, so Quartz offered to brew her some tea,*" Kotaro said, going on to explain what had transpired.

It had all happened while Jade was on his way back from Yadacain. Ruri had been restlessly pacing around the room, fearing for Jade's safety. Chelsea had told her to calm down, but she couldn't, which prompted Quartz to offer to make tea. Ruri had been more interested in the tea Quartz was making than whether she should be letting the previous king do such a thing, so she'd gladly accepted the show of goodwill. Once Quartz came back, he'd placed the tea in front of Ruri and Chelsie. He had even prepared some for Kotaro, and he placed his cup on the floor to make it easier for him to drink.

The vibrant color of the tea amazed Ruri. "It smells great," she said.

"I also brought some snacks. Eat as many as you'd like."

"Thank you very much, Quartz-sama."

"Chelsie, feel free to help yourself as well."

"Aye, thank you very much," Chelsie replied.

After Ruri took in the fragrant aroma, she took a sip—but she noticed something was amiss and paused. "Hm?"

"What's the matter, Ruri?" Quartz asked.

"Oh, no. It's just that this seems to be more than just black tea. There's some sort of...aftertaste?"

"Ah, yes. Possibly the herbs. I placed some herbs only in your cup to help calm your nerves, you see," explained Quartz.

"Oh, is that so? I very much appreciate that," Ruri said, impressed by Quartz's meticulous care as she took another sip.

"You're very good at making tea, aren't you, Quartz-sama?"

"Heh, heh, heh, flattery will get you nowhere."

"No, I'm serious."

"Seraphie liked it. So I had a lot of practice."

"Wow, your mate sure was a lucky woman. Someone as kind and gentle as you must have fawned over her."

"Yes, well, I'd be happy if she thought so."

The genial conversation continued. Ruri took another sip of her tea, oblivious to Quartz staring at her.

After a while, Ruri noticed that her body felt strange. "Huh?" she uttered. Her fingertips felt prickly and numb. She thought it was her imagination at first, but the numbness gradually started to spread from her fingers to her arm to her entire body. Eventually, she couldn't hold the cup anymore and it fell from her hand with a loud crash.

"Hey, what are you doing, child?" Chelsie asked, under the assumption that Ruri's hand had simply slipped. However, soon after, Ruri went limp atop the table. Warning flags waved in Chelsie's head. "Ruri?"

She stood up and reached over to her, but someone swatted her hand away—Quartz. Chelsie looked at him, demanding answers, but Quartz just smiled. It was the same smile as always, but there was something vaguely sinister about it this time around.

Ruri was clearly conscious, but her body was completely immobile. Quartz pulled out a dagger. Chelsie swallowed her breath, and Kotaro bared his fangs. Fortunately, Kotaro still had a barrier up, so it was impossible for Quartz to hurt Ruri.

In the next instant, Quartz foiled that saving grace by saying, "Would you mind taking down the barrier around Ruri?"

"*There's absolutely no way I would do that.*"

"I'm not going to harm Ruri."

"*Like hell I believe you. Away from Ruri, you scoundrel.*"

Without so much as flinching at Kotaro's snarls, Quartz let out a sigh. "Are you sure? If you don't, Ruri will die."

Kotaro and Chelsea both gasped in surprise.

"I fed Ruri poison. If I don't give her the antidote, then she'll soon die. But I'll give it to her if you agree to lower your barrier."

"*You* what?" Kotaro asked, incredulous.

"Come now, Ruri is a goner if you don't hurry," Quartz said. His unchanging angelic smile looked eerie given the situation.

Kotaro looked at Ruri. She wasn't moving. He didn't know how much he could trust Quartz, but if he was telling the truth, Ruri would actually die. Kotaro made the arduous decision to drop the barrier.

"*There. I've lowered Ruri's barrier. Hurry and cure her.*"

"Yes, I certainly will. *After* I've made my getaway, that is," Quartz said, turning into his dragon form. He picked Ruri up with one of his claws and took to the skies.

Kotaro had tried to chase after him, but Quartz's words stopped him in his tracks.

"Don't follow after me. If you want to ensure Ruri's life, that is."

And with that, Quartz had carried Ruri off.

"*You moron!*" Rin screamed, tackling Kotaro between his eyes with all her might. It was a critical hit.

"*I'm sorry,*" said Kotaro.

"*Why would you ever follow his orders?!*" asked Rin.

"*Because if I didn't, Ruri would have died.*"

"*You didn't know if the blasted poison was even real!*" shouted Rin.

Chelsie came to Kotaro's aid, saying, "But what if it was real? If it was really poison, then Ruri would have died if Kotaro had interfered. I tried to stop him as well, but Master Quartz lives up to his reputation. He left me with no opportunity. So Kotaro is not the only one at fault."

"*Grr...*" Rin grumbled, stopping herself from saying anything else.

"*I also thought I could get her back right away,*" Kotaro said. "*I figured he was only a dragonkin, so I would be able to get her back once I spotted an opening. But as I was following him via the wind, he abruptly vanished.*"

"*Vanished? What, Spirit Slayer again?*" Rin asked.

"*No, that stuff emanates an unsettling aura when you use it. You can tell where it's active because any place that uses it winds up being invisible to us. No, what he did was different. His entire presence just vanished.*"

"*You can't find him with your wind powers? Well, aside from Spirit Slayer, I don't know of any other... Aaah!*" Rin shouted partway through her sentence, as if something had dawned on her.

"*It's Light. Now that I recall, Darkness said that Light had been with that man. With Light's powers, he'd be undetectable even to you, Kotaro.*"

"*So this is Light's doing...*" Kotaro said, comprehending the situation.

Jade, who had been listening to the conversation, cut in. "You won't be able to find Ruri?"

"*Light's barriers are impervious to our powers. Not even Kotaro's wind powers can search for her,*" replied Rin.

"That can't be... Then what do we do to save Ruri?!"

Kotaro and Rin didn't offer any response.

"Ruri..." Jade muttered to himself, standing stock-still inside the room as wind poured in from the broken window.

22 Truth

Quartz had flown off in dragon form, carrying Ruri in one of his claws. He left the castle and capital behind, heading for parts unknown.

Ruri's body was immobile, but she was fully conscious, so she had made an incredibly calm and composed assessment of the situation. Her eyes were the only things she could move. She wanted to see where they were heading, so she decided to stay still—or rather, she had no other choice but to stay still since she couldn't move anyway.

Suddenly, the air around Quartz started to sparkle. Ruri blinked in surprise, but Quartz didn't seem fazed. After flying for a little while more, he began to descend. He slowly landed on the ground below.

Quartz returned to his human form and picked up the still-paralyzed Ruri in his arms. Ahead of them was a charming house, which he walked into without hesitation.

Was this Quartz's house? Ruri wanted to ask, but she was physically incapable of speaking.

Quartz walked her up the stairs to the second floor, entered a room in the back, and laid her down on the bed there. He then put his hand under her chin to nudge her head up a little. He pulled a small vial of liquid from his pocket and slowly tilted it to her lips, making her drink the contents. Once he let her chin fall back in place, Quartz took a seat in a chair near the bed and peered at her.

Quartz's stare was practically burning a hole through her, making her feel extremely uncomfortable. That was when Ruri noticed someone else standing near the door, throwing her for a loop.

It was a small girl. She walked closer, but without making a single footstep. Her hair was golden, her eyes sky blue. Her wavy hair was as shiny as thread, and her features were as adorable and immaculate as a doll.

"What is this girl's story?" the girl asked.

Without so much as a glance at the girl, Quartz spoke as if talking to himself. "She was singing the song, so I brought her here."

"You think that she is the one?" the girl asked.

"That's the only other explanation. That song was a secret between her and me," Quartz replied.

"But she herself doesn't realize it, right?"

"That's why I'm asking you, please. Make sure she doesn't go outside of the barrier."

"Keep her locked in? Well, if that's what you want to do, so be it," the young girl said, sighing in resignation and walking over to Ruri. She stood by Ruri's side and held out her hand. A vine of light grew from the girl's hand, wrapped around Ruri's wrist, and disappeared. "There. Now she can't go outside."

"I appreciate it."

"Call me if anything comes up," the girl said before silently exiting the room, leaving the two all by themselves once more.

"The medicine should be working. You should be able to speak now, yes?"

Ruri tried to speak. "Ah, aah, aaah." She was indeed able to produce sounds. Her body still couldn't move and her voice was a tad raspy, but she could speak. "Why...did...you do this?"

"You're awfully calm. You do realize I've kidnapped you, right? I thought you'd show a little more fear or panic."

Ruri was indeed calm—so calm that it surprised even her. She knew that she'd been kidnapped since she was conscious the entire time. Even so, she didn't feel any need to be on guard with Quartz despite her predicament.

"I realize you did. But I'm still oddly calm," she explained.

"You don't think that I'll do something to you?"

"No, I don't think you'll harm me, Quartz-sama. Um, maybe," Ruri said, a tad unsure. But she deduced that Quartz had had plenty of chances to hurt her already if he'd wanted. She also didn't sense any kind of hostility or ill intent coming from him. In fact, Quartz was acting so much like he usually did that it made her doubt if he'd even kidnapped her in the first place.

"You either have no sense of apprehension or you're entirely too trusting," Quartz said, suddenly scowling. "Tell me, Ruri, you came to this world because of Nadasha's summoning magic, didn't you?"

"Yes, that's right. But what of it?" Ruri asked in reply, curious as to why he brought up Nadasha.

"What if I were to tell you that *I* was the one who taught the Nadashians the summoning magic?"

"Huh…?" Ruri looked at Quartz, her eyes going wide.

"And it was me who taught that strange cult how to resurrect the dead."

Ruri was speechless.

"I also gave them all those Spirit Slayer tools as well. Though I never thought they would use them to assault a Beloved. I wonder if Jade has learned this in Yadacain by now. What do you think he'll do?" Quartz said as if speaking about someone else's problems.

"Why would you do that?!" Ruri asked.

"To meet Seraphie. Yes, that was what it was at first," Quartz said as he started to explain. "Seraphie was a witch from Yadacain. I visited Yadacain with the reasoning that she might be reborn in the same place. There I found that the queen had lost someone dear to her, just like me, and was conducting a certain type of research. Research into bringing people back from the dead with magic."

Ruri listened to Quartz's tale, transfixed.

"Then it hit me like a slap in the face. I had been so preoccupied with finding Seraphie's reincarnation that I'd never considered that I could bring her back to life as she was. Nothing would make me happier than seeing Seraphie coming back in the flesh. I decided to help the queen with her research. I even gave her dragon blood. In return, she gave me a variety of tools that used Spirit Slayer."

The bracelet that turned people into rats, the one that the Church of God's Light had used, was crafted by Yadacain witches, so it was possibly one of those tools as well. If Quartz was the one who'd taught the Church of God's Light magic, then he most likely was also the one who'd given them the bracelets. Even if it wasn't intentional on Quartz's part, the danger that Ruri had faced as a result of his actions left a bitter taste in her mouth.

"But, you see, the research never took off; it just added more bodies to the pile. Feeling that the queen's knowledge wasn't enough, I taught a cult how to resurrect the dead. I figured it would be more efficient to have more people researching it aside from just the queen. I even threw in some dragon blood," Quartz said, explaining how the resurrection method had ended up in the hands of the Church of God's Light.

The church must have kidnapped the dragonkin during Ruri's assassination attempt because they'd run out of Quartz's sample platter of blood. But though they had also conducted research, they hadn't been able to produce anything more substantial than what they were initially taught.

"After much digging, I found out that people couldn't be revived without a soul. It was a complete waste of time and effort. After all the hope I placed on this research, I was devastated. But I still had my eye on another of the queen's research projects. Magic to summon people from another world."

At first glance, this didn't seem to have anything to do with Seraphie, but it did to Quartz.

"Souls are always in cycle. However, sometimes reincarnation sends souls to the other world instead. What if that had happened to Seraphie? You can't go from this world to that one. If Seraphie was on the other side, I would lose my chance to see her forever."

"And...that's where summoning comes into play?" Ruri asked. "But that magic can't bring over a specific person."

"Yes, at least the version I taught the Nadashians can't. It was still in its incomplete phase. That magic can actually bring over people from the other side who possess mana. Apparently, there aren't many people in the other world who have mana, so if I bring them *all* over, Seraphie might be among them."

"That's mad," Ruri said.

He didn't know how many people in the other world possessed mana, but he was going to summon them all—regardless of whether those people who weren't Seraphie wanted to come over. Seeing as how Ruri had been dragged over herself, this news only enraged her.

"Mad? Yes. But I want to see Seraphie no matter how many people I must sacrifice. That's why I taught them the unfinished technique with the stipulation that they use it for research. Yet those Nadashian priests ended up using it to suit their own desires with barely any research themselves. Then again, the fact that they brought you over was a stroke of luck. For both Jade and myself."

"Why would *you* be happy about that?" Ruri could understand Jade being happy. Thanks to her summoning, the two of them were able to meet. But why Quartz?

"So, tell me, Ruri, let's say that I found Seraphie after all my searching, but not only does Seraphie not remember anything about me, she actually is in love with another man. What do you think I would do in that situation?"

"That's not a question I have an answer to," Ruri replied.

Quartz suddenly took a tuft of Ruri's hair and softly kissed it. "Tell me, what should I do?"

As he looked at her with those entrancing, gem-colored eyes, Ruri started to get the gist of what he was asking.

"You're not saying that I'm the reincarnation of Seraphie-san, are you?"

"I would hope that you are. It'd be a nightmare if it were you after Jade picked you as his mate, but you're the only likely choice."

"It isn't me. It *can't* be me."

"How can you deny it if you don't remember anything from your previous life?" Quartz pointed out.

Ruri paused momentarily. That was impossible, though. There was certainly nothing wrong with Quartz, but Ruri didn't feel anything toward him.

"I assure you, it's not me," Ruri said.

Her frankness painted Quartz's eyes with sadness. Seeing that made Ruri recoil; it almost felt like *she* did something wrong.

"You might regain your memories if you stay with me. Seraphie said it herself. She said that she would always remember."

"Okay, but that's only if I *am* Seraphie-san."

"You're the only person I can think of. Especially since you know something that you shouldn't know otherwise."

CHAPTER 22: TRUTH

"What do you mean 'something I shouldn't know otherwise'?"

Quartz stood up from his seat rather harshly, as if saying that he couldn't speak of it anymore. "You'll remain here until you remember," he said as he exited the room. His face was tinged with sadness, looking like he would cry at any moment, but Ruri couldn't see it.

The room was cast in silence.

Ruri could finally start moving her hands. "Seriously...?" she muttered and then sighed deeply.

Ruri being a reincarnation of Quartz's late mate? She wanted to know what in the world he was basing that assumption off of. She hadn't done anything to him. He'd seemed his usual self until just before he'd kidnapped her. What on earth was going on here?

There was no way that Ruri was the reincarnation of Seraphie. She didn't have any memories of her previous life, but she could say that for sure. And even if she were Seraphie, she wouldn't feel anything for Quartz. That was because the person Ruri loved was...

Be that as it may, it was hard to staunchly deny that assertion once she saw that sadness on Quartz's face. It almost made her feel as if *she* was wronging *him*. She needed to talk things out with him. If she did, he would come to understand that Ruri was nothing like Seraphie.

First, however, she needed to contact Kotaro and the others. She could finally move her body again, so she sat up. They were all surely worried after the way she'd left the castle.

Just then, Ruri decided to break things down in her head. She'd been abducted and brought to this world because of the king and priest of Nadasha, which was why she sought appropriate revenge against them. But since Quartz was the one who'd told them about the summoning magic in the first place, would that not make *him* a target for her revenge?

241

"That's actually starting to kinda piss me off," Ruri said to herself, realizing that the root of the evil that had brought her to this world lay in Quartz.

Ruri couldn't let that go unsettled, but now wasn't exactly the time for that. She opened and closed her hands to make sure her body was no longer numb. Then she slowly got up and looked out the window of the room. The house was surrounded by a forest, reminiscent of Chelsie's place. She couldn't tell where exactly she was just by looking outside, though.

Confirming that the window easily opened, Ruri took out her bracelet from her pocket and transformed into a cat.

"Nyeow!" she cried as she jumped out of the window onto a tree directly across from it. She then slid down the tree and began to run. Just as it seemed her escape was assured, she bumped into something blocking her path.

"Meow!" Ruri cried, almost as if saying "ow." She rubbed her sore nose. She looked in front of her to see what she bumped into, but there wasn't anything there. She absolutely bumped into something, though.

Feeling something was off, Ruri reached out to find that despite being invisible to the naked eye, there was something akin to a wall there—a wall similar to the kind that Kotaro would form out of the wind.

"Is this...a barrier?"

She tried banging on it, but it showed no signs of cracking. She tried to use magic to break it, but her magic wouldn't activate. She thought of whacking the wall with a weapon from her pocket space, but it wouldn't open either.

"Huh? But why?!"

Her actions were completely limited. There also didn't seem to be any openings anywhere on the barrier. If she had the physical strength of a dragonkin, she might've been able to crack it, but she had nothing of the sort. She was utterly powerless.

"I guess I'll just have to wait until Kotaro and the others come and rescue me, then?"

"That isn't going to happen," sounded a voice behind Ruri.

Ruri jumped in surprise. She thought it was Quartz for a second, but the voice sounded far too young. Turning around, she saw the cute doll-like girl who had been standing in the room a second ago.

"You're inside a barrier I created to block your escape. You may have contracted Wind and Water, but neither of their powers can break this barrier. In fact, they can't even pinpoint this location in the first place. So, give up and stay here."

"Who are you?" Ruri asked, positive that she wasn't as ordinary of a girl as she appeared.

"I'm a brethren of Wind and Water, the two spirits you share a contract with—the Spirit of Light."

"The Spirit of Light?!"

It was shocking, but if she could put up a barrier of this caliber, then it made sense she was a supreme-level spirit.

"Let me out of here, please."

"I can't do that," the Spirit of Light said, flatly refusing.

Ruri scowled. *"What is the Spirit of Light doing here to begin with?"*

"I had a contract with Seraphie, and she entrusted Quartz to me before she died. Which is why I'm helping him."

"Then you should tell him! Tell him that I'm not Seraphie-san!"

"It's pointless. There's nothing I can do as long as he thinks you are. You can try to convince him. Though I doubt he'll accept it as fact. I'm simply granting Seraphie's wish."

"*Her wish?*"

"To watch over him and make sure he doesn't break. Though it may already be too late." The Spirit of Light looked toward the house and let out a tiny sigh.

"*Too late...?*"

"Dragonkin are wholly dedicated to their mates. And Quartz was particularly dependent on Seraphie. It's been decades since he lost her... His mind is already at the breaking point. Seraphie left quite an unfair wish behind. It would have been better for him if he had just forfeited his life along with her," the Spirit of Light explained, looking like a concerned mother—an expression unfitting her youthful appearance.

The Spirit of Light looked back at Ruri and lifted her by the scruff of her neck.

"Meow!"

"Come on, back we go. If you want to go home, then you'll have to convince him."

"*Whaa?!*" Ruri telepathically exclaimed as she was hauled off back inside the house.

23 Quartz's Wish

A few days had passed since Quartz kidnapped Ruri—a few unfortunate days. There was no sign that anyone was coming to her aid. Perhaps Kotaro couldn't locate her, as the Spirit of Light had said. The Spirit of Light wasn't going to do Ruri any favors by letting her go either. Instead, she had told Ruri to negotiate with Quartz. Ruri did resign herself to that and had spoken to Quartz, but their talks had gone nowhere.

"Hey, Quartz-sama, let's go back to the castle!" Ruri said, tugging on Quartz's arm. But Quartz remained seated in his chair, book in hand, and merely smiled at her pleading. "Jade-sama is worried about you too. I'll join you in apologizing for passing on magic to Nadasha and the Church of God's light, so let's go back, okay?"

"Have you regained your memories?" Quartz asked.

"Ughhh, *for the last time*, I am *not* Seraphie-san, so there are no memories to regain! Now, let's go back! There's no point in staying here forever!"

"Hmm, I'll think about it *after* you regain your memories."

"Argh, your head is harder than I ever imagined!"

That was pretty much how their talks played out; he wouldn't listen to reason. Even so, Quartz was as kind to Ruri as he always was, and he showed no signs of wanting to harm her. Because of this, Ruri didn't feel threatened despite being held against her will, and the mood remained rather nonchalant. If it weren't for the situation being as ugly as it was, Ruri might have felt like she was on an excursion of sorts. But considering Kotaro and the others were worried sick about her back at the castle, she couldn't afford to stay complacent. Jade was most likely back from Yadacain by now and was surely concerned for her. He would definitely be worried about Quartz as well.

"Aaaah! What the heck do I dooo?!" Ruri exclaimed, clutching her head. She was getting impatient and feeling like she needed to get back to the kingdom fast. But now that her magic was disabled, she couldn't destroy the Spirit of Light's barrier. No, even if she could use her magic, she probably didn't stand a chance against supreme-level power.

Above all else, Ruri didn't want to go back just by herself. If she was going, it would be with Quartz. She didn't want to leave him alone. There were far too many people worried about him—Jade and Agate, for starters. The only thing on his mind was Seraphie, Seraphie, and Seraphie, but she really wanted him to realize that there were *other* people who cared for him.

Quartz spoke like nothing else but Seraphie existed, and that didn't sit well with Ruri in the slightest. Jade's face would light up around Quartz like Ewan's did around Finn. Agate, Finn, and Claus also looked at him with admiration. And all of the soldiers delighted in training with him. Every single one of them were likely worried about Quartz.

It was true that Quartz's actions were harmful. He had inadvertently incited wars and assassination attempts. Still, he'd only given Nadasha and the Church of God's Light information; he wasn't involved in any of those matters himself. He was entirely dedicated to getting Seraphie back, and he'd placed his hopes on magic research that seemed likely to work. It was honestly a mystery as to why he'd chosen Nadasha and the Church of God's Light, but perhaps no one else would willingly involve themselves with Spirit Slayer magic.

And Quartz didn't share this information without due consideration either. He'd said that when he asked the Church of God's Light why they wanted the magic, they had tearfully replied that it was to help those who'd lost their loved ones. Then again, had he done some proper research, he would have figured out that it was a blatant lie. But considering he'd also lost someone dear to him, he'd ended up sincerely empathizing with their cause.

By Quartz's account, he'd taught Nadasha the summoning magic, but he'd never imagined it would lead to war. However, Nadasha's head priest was more well versed in arcane magic than he let on, so Quartz had figured that the head priest might be able to produce some form of results.

Quartz had never expected any of these outcomes at all. Nevertheless, even if teaching Spirit Slayer magic wasn't a crime, he would probably need to be punished accordingly. If the fear of being reprimanded was the reason why Quartz was so reluctant to return to the kingdom, Ruri could apologize right alongside him.

After Ruri had spent a few days together with Quartz, she started to suspect something. Quartz had said that she was the reincarnation of Seraphie and that he wanted her to recall those memories, but Ruri got the feeling that he didn't want it all that much. She didn't feel any sense of urgency behind his pleas for her to hurry and remember. For someone who desired to see his beloved again so much that he willingly gave up his throne and his kingdom, Quartz didn't seem all that anxious for results—despite pleading with her to quickly recall her memories. It was as if he didn't really care if she did remember.

Ruri doubted whether Quartz really thought that she was Seraphie in the first place. But in that case, why had he kidnapped her?

Ruri sighed. "What do I do?" she muttered to herself as she walked around outside. She was looking for any tears in the barrier, but there were no such conveniences. She was completely trapped inside this space, cut off from the outside world. She kicked at the barrier in frustration, but her foot didn't make so much as a dent. It only made her foot sore.

"Grr! If I could at least use my pocket space, I could go to Lydia's and ask her to communicate with Kotaro and the others. I suppose I'll have to convince Quartz after all…"

Ruri was reluctant to try this. Anything she said only garnered a smile from him, and despite seeming kind, his mind was as hard as steel. He wasn't likely to change his mind. Still, she couldn't afford to let things go on like this.

With heavy steps, Ruri walked back to the house and went to Quartz's room. She knocked on the door, but there was no response. Wondering if he was in, she slowly cracked the door and entered to find Quartz lying on the sofa, asleep.

Ruri saw his face and halted in her tracks. His eyes were closed, but a trail of water dripped from them. Quartz was crying in his sleep. Perhaps he was having some sort of sad dream.

Ruri felt that she'd seen something she wasn't supposed to see and carefully tried to leave the room, but Quartz's eyes started to slowly open.

"Ruri?" he asked.

"Um, I'm sorry. You didn't answer, so I just came in."

"No, it's fine. What did you want?"

Quartz still hadn't realized that he'd been crying, but once he sat up and felt the wet trail leading down his cheek, it was clear. He wiped his eyes and turned his face away in embarrassment.

"Seems you've caught me at my worst."

"Oh, no. Were you having a sad dream?"

He hesitated for a second but replied, "I was having a dream about Seraphie."

Any time Quartz talked about Seraphie, his voice always sounded sad and happy at the same time.

"You really love Seraphie, don't you, Quartz-sama?"

"Yes. Seraphie is my everything. I can't live without her. And yet...I have to wonder why Seraphie insisted I not follow her in death."

"Quartz-sama..."

"You see, I regret it. I put up a front and complied with her wish, but I should have turned it down. I never thought that every day without her would be such torture. I should have never been born a dragonkin. Our life spans are long, and we are so very dependent on our mates."

Quartz was looking down, so Ruri couldn't see his expression, but she was sure he was on the verge of tears. She stroked his head. She felt compelled to do so; Quartz almost looked like a lost child to her. Quartz allowed her to do as she wished, never trying to shake off her hand.

"I can no longer bear to be in a world without Seraphie..."

Ruri's heart tightened. Dragonkin truly were devoted to love.

If she were to die first, would Jade end up like Quartz? Would he try to follow in turn? If he did, would she tell him not to die, just as Seraphie had? On the other hand, that wish was

249

the reason behind Quartz's great sadness and anguish. If this was how it would turn out, then perhaps it was for your partner's own good to take them along with you.

Ruri wouldn't want any partner of hers to do that, though. Jade had so many other people who also cared for him. They would inevitably be saddened if Jade were to die. Ruri also had no desire for him to follow after her in the afterlife, so she was certain that she would follow Seraphie's example and tell him not to die.

After giving it some thought, Ruri could understand why Seraphie had wished for Quartz to live. It was too painful to know someone you loved had followed you into death.

Ruri had an irresistible urge to see Jade right now. Jade needed her as much as Quartz needed Seraphie. Plus, Jade had given her his dragonheart. That made her want to cry with joy. She missed him so much. She had been fretting and giving all sorts of excuses up until now, but she just wanted to be by Jade's side—the man who needed her. That was the most important thing.

Ruri was confident she could honestly tell Jade how she felt about him now. She needed to see him.

"Ruri, I—"

Just as Quartz started to speak, they both heard a noise like glass shattering.

"What was that?" Ruri asked, looking around the room.

Quartz lifted his head and stood up, seemingly unsurprised.

"Guess they're finally here."

"Huh?" Ruri gasped, bewildered.

Quartz took her wrist and started walking. They walked out of the room, down the stairs, and outside the house. The Spirit of Light was there waiting for them.

Once Ruri saw who else was outside, her eyes widened. Standing there was Jade, Kotaro, Rin, and an unfamiliar man. She had no idea how all of them had gotten through the Spirit of Light's barrier.

Ruri was puzzled, but she was glad to see that Jade had returned from Yadacain in one piece. Yet a scowl adorned Jade's face, making it clear that he was *very* upset. That anger didn't seem to be directed at her, but it made her want to do an about-face nonetheless.

The Spirit of Light looked at the other man with a content expression. "So you've brought Darkness with you."

"Darkness? *He's* the Spirit of Darkness?" Ruri asked.

"Yeah, my brethren, the Spirit of Darkness. For light, there is darkness. For darkness, there is light. The only one who can find and break my barrier is the Spirit of Darkness. They must've brought him along from Yadacain."

Ruri realized that the sound from a moment ago must have been the barrier shattering.

"Master Quartz," Jade said. He was staring arrows into Quartz.

"That's quite the scary look, Jade," Quartz responded.

"Please, return Ruri. I also have many questions for you."

"Hate to be the bearer of bad news, but I can't return her. She will continue to live here."

"But why?! Why did you take Ruri?!"

"Because I thought that she might be Seraphie."

Jade was extremely shocked by that, but he quickly regained his composure and stated, "Ruri is Ruri. My mate and my one and only. Even if what you say were true, Seraphie isn't her anymore. She's *Ruri*. I cannot hand her over to you."

"Do you know how badly I desire Seraphie?" Quartz asked.

"Yes. I know all too well. Still, Ruri is Ruri and *not* your mate. You've spent enough time together now that you should know this. I can't just let you have her."

"Care to reclaim her, then?"

Quartz pulled a sword from his pocket space. It seemed pocket spaces were usable now that the Spirit of Light's barrier had been destroyed.

"If you want her back," Quartz continued, "you'd best come at me with sights to kill. Otherwise, I'll seek Seraphie for as long as I draw breath."

The look in Quartz's eyes—he wasn't joking. He was dead serious.

Jade gritted his teeth and bitterly stared at Quartz, but he took a deep breath to regain his calm and pulled out his sword.

"Wait a minute, both of you!" Ruri screamed, but before she could stop them, their swords clashed.

Their fight reminded her of a match back at the tournament, violently crossing weapons over and over. She needed to stop this, but she was too stunned to do anything about it. That was when Kotaro and Rin ran up to her.

"*Ruri, are you okay?!*" Kotaro asked.

"Kotaro, Rin! Yeah, I'm fine, but we have to stop those two."

"*What are you talking about?! You were kidnapped!*" Rin exclaimed.

"But he never did anything to me. This is all a misunderstanding. If you talk to Quartz-sama, I'm sure he'll understand."

Kotaro and Rin only saw Quartz as an enemy since he'd kidnapped Ruri, but Ruri saw it differently. Quartz hadn't done anything to her; he'd just taken her a little farther away. Then again, it might be hard to argue that he *wasn't* confining her, but Ruri

252

hadn't experienced anything bad here. Quartz had been as much of a gentleman as he always was; he hadn't done anything that she didn't like. He just wanted to see Seraphie, albeit a little bit too passionately. But that was honestly all there was to it.

Everyone could get on the same page if they just talked it out—or so Ruri thought. However, the battle between Jade and Quartz was growing fiercer, and neither were likely to listen to her pleas even if she voiced them. Jade seemed so enraged that he wouldn't listen to what *anyone* had to say.

Ruri glanced at the Spirit of Light standing next to her. She was staring at the ensuing battle, clutching her skirt and looking extremely sad.

"Why do you look so sad?" Ruri asked, unable to help herself.

The Spirit of Light, her eyes still fixed on the battle, said, "Dragonkin are devoted to love, especially with their mates. It's not uncommon for them to follow after their mate in death. Quartz only chose to live because Seraphie had wished for him to. But that was the beginning of his personal hell. He persisted in a world without Seraphie. He's reached his limit. He wishes for death."

Ruri gasped.

"He can't die by his own hand due to his promise with Seraphie. That's why he chose someone of equal strength, someone capable of killing him. He returned to the Nation of the Dragon King for that very purpose—to get someone he loved like a little brother to kill him."

"Kill... Do you mean he wants Jade-sama to kill him? Don't tell me *that* is why he kidnapped me. So that Jade-sama would get angry? So that he would challenge him to battle?"

The Spirit of Light nodded. "That's right. I've doubted whether you were Seraphie, but that doesn't matter anymore. I gave up. I just wanted to end it."

"What do you mean?!" Ruri asked, unable to hide her frustration.

It was clear from listening to Quartz that Seraphie was the most important thing in the world to him. It was also clear that he'd fallen into despair and had anguished over multiple dead ends. None of his attempts to find or regain Seraphie had worked. That anguish—that sadness—was probably far beyond Ruri's imagination. Even now, no one would have blamed Quartz if he'd succumbed to it.

That had nothing to do with this, though. Jade looked up to and cared for Quartz. How could Quartz ever force Jade to kill him?

Ruri was exploding with anger. Meanwhile, Jade and Quartz were still fighting. Little by little, Jade was starting to overwhelm Quartz.

A faint smile formed on Quartz's lips. He purposely left a gap in his defense, at which Jade unwittingly took a swing. Quartz then left himself to the mercy of Jade's incoming blade.

Jade sensed something was amiss. And then Ruri slipped between them, her arms spread out. All three held their breaths in shock. Jade tried to stop his sword, but the momentum proved too much for him to pull back the reins.

Just when Jade was convinced that he would hit Ruri, Quartz lunged forward and covered her from behind, letting the blade fall upon him instead. The whole event seemed to take place in slow motion. Unable to fully stop his sword, Jade felt it cutting into flesh.

"Ruri! Master Quartz!" shouted Jade. He dropped his weapon and ran over to them.

Red blood steadily dripped onto the ground.

Ruri stood up. Jade breathed a sigh of relief, glad to see that she wasn't injured anywhere, but then he looked at Quartz. Blood was coursing from his arm. He was wounded for sure, but since Jade had changed the direction of his strike at the last moment, it wasn't fatal. It was just a scratch to a dragonkin, which put Jade's mind at ease.

CHAPTER 23: QUARTZ'S WISH

Jade then glared at Ruri for pulling such a stunt. "Ruri, do you know how dangerous that was?! How could you do such a thing?! One wrong move and a serious injury would have been the least of your problems!"

Though Jade was yelling at her, Ruri didn't even look his way. She instead grabbed Quartz by the lapels and rammed her head straight into his face with a blunt and nasty-sounding thud.

"Grk!" Quartz yelped.

"Urgh~" bellowed Ruri.

Ruri's headbutt had caught Quartz off guard, and he accidentally bit his tongue a little. Quartz rubbed his jaw, and Ruri rubbed her head. Jade looked down at both of them in exasperation.

"What are you doing, Ruri?" asked Quartz.

Ruri didn't answer him. Instead, once she'd recovered, she slapped Quartz across the cheek. It was loud and sharp, and Quartz blinked in surprise.

"You *idiot*!" Ruri yelled, bringing down the thunder. She grabbed his collar, visibly angry. "What were you trying to get Jade-sama to do?! You should know better than *anyone else in the world* just how much Jade admires and adores you, right?! Yet here you are, trying to make him *kill you*?! Enough of this *nonsense*! Did it never occur to you how Jade would blame himself and suffer as a result of that?!"

Quartz winced. Ruri was indignant. If he was going to make a face like that, then why did he do this in the first place?

"I had no other choice…" Quartz replied. "I can't die by my own hand because of my promise to Seraphie. So, I'm telling you that—"

"And I'm telling *you*, don't make Jade-sama do that!"

Quartz hung his head in guilt, but that wasn't enough to quell Ruri's rage. If he felt so bad about it, he shouldn't have done it to start with! Quartz knew what he was doing was wrong. This form of betrayal was beyond cruel.

"Why can't you get a grip?! Always going on about Seraphie this and Seraphie that like you've hit rock bottom! You're utterly *insufferable*!"

"I-Insufferable…" Quartz repeated in shock, his face tensing.

"Aah, Ruri, that might be going a little too far…" Jade rebuked.

Ruri didn't pause and instead continued her tirade as she said, "Seraphie-san *isn't* everything!"

"What do you know? How would a human like you know how much a dragonkin values their mate?"

"I know that you value Seraphie-san. I may not understand how it makes you want to follow her into the grave, but I do know that's just how much you love her, right? But, please, consider the people who would mourn your death. And I don't mean just Seraphie-san. You have so many other people besides her who care, don't you?!"

"I'm not sure if I can live in a world without Seraphie, though."

Ruri, her brow tense, slapped Quartz across the cheek again. "Quit behaving like a petulant child. Open your eyes and take a good look around you! It's true there's no replacement for Seraphie, but you have plenty of people in your life, don't you? Jade, Agate, Claus, and Finn—they're all worried about you. There are so many people who would shed tears if you died. So please, *think*. Why did Seraphie-san tell you to keep living? She said that because she knew you better than anyone else in the world, right?"

"I don't have a clue," replied Quartz.

"Neither do I, but if I were going to die soon, I think I would tell Jade-sama to keep living too. I'd want him to live. I'm not the only person Jade-sama has. So many people care for him. I just couldn't ask him to die with me if it meant making those people sad."

"B-But I…" Quartz stammered, still irresolute.

"For crying out loud, are you going to be wishy-washy forever?! I'm going back to the castle! Everyone will be waiting for you there. Did you feel nothing while you were in the kingdom? Were you just suffering the entire time? You had fun there too, right? You forgot about Seraphie-san and laughed, if only for a few seconds. You don't just have Seraphie-san; you have everyone in the castle."

"That's…" Quartz started, seemingly coming to that realization. He offered no rebuttal.

"And you have Seraphie-san's promise to keep! You would lose your honor as a man if you just gave up on it. You need to see it through to the end!"

While it might have been a cruel thing to ask of someone who was so exhausted from searching for the love of his life, Quartz still had Seraphie as emotional support.

"What kind of dragonkin male would you be if you couldn't grant your mate's dying wish? If living without Seraphie-san is too much to bear, then you can come back to the castle. If you get lonely, I'll sit down with you for a cup of tea. I'll listen to you reminisce about Seraphie-san, even if it does get insufferable. We all love you. So please, live your life. Everyone will be waiting for you."

Ruri finally finished her rant, panting hard. She had worked herself up so much that her face was flushed, but she had said all that she'd needed to say.

Quartz bit his lip. Just then, Jade extended his hand to him.

"Let's make our return, Master Quartz. If there's anything I can do, you have my help."

Quartz looked on the verge of tears, but he took Jade's hand and said, "Yes, sounds good. Let's go back."

Seraphie

The case was technically closed, but instead of going straight back to the castle, they all decided to go inside the house and talk. Jade had many questions he wanted to ask—mainly about Spirit Slayer.

While Ruri prepared tea for everyone, so that they could relax while talking, Jade listened to what Quartz had to say.

"Is that so? You simply passed on the magic to Nadasha and the Church of God's Light?" asked Jade.

"Yes. I had absolutely nothing to do with the war they incited or that assassination plot. I did teach them the magic, but I had very little to do with them thereafter. I would only check on their research from time to time, but they weren't producing anything greater than what I gave them initially, so I left them be for a few years. When I came back to the Nation of the Dragon King, I was surprised to hear that they were the instigators of such a huge incident."

"I am relieved to hear that you were not involved in anything. However, Spirit Slayer is forbidden magic, and teaching it to others arbitrarily is impermissible conduct."

"I'm well aware. I'll accept my punishment," Quartz said, comfortable with that fact.

The Spirit of Light, on the other hand, furrowed her brow. "Wait, I'm also responsible for not stopping the Spirit Slayer magic even though I knew it was harmful to spirits everywhere. Isn't that right, Darkness?"

"Yes, indeed it is," the Spirit of Darkness replied. He too was also responsible for allowing Yadacain's queen to continue her research.

"If you're going to pin the blame on Quartz, then Darkness and I need to be punished as well."

"U-Um, no, but…" Jade stammered.

The Spirit of Light was demanding to be punished if Quartz was, but not even a Dragon King could ever punish a spirit. If he tried, every nation in the world would be at his throat. The Nation of the Beast King would be especially opposed given that all their people were very spirit-religious. The Spirit of Light would not sit idly by if Jade only punished Quartz. At the same time, Jade couldn't let Quartz go scot-free just because he couldn't punish the Spirit of Light.

Seeing as how the incident with Nadasha had harmed Ruri the most, the punishment was up to her discretion. But the real issue here was that Quartz had taught the Church of God's Light the Spirit Slayer magic. That entire incident had started because of that, and the results had involved the Nation of the Beast King as well. To make matters worse, Celestine had been assaulted by the tools Quartz had given them. The Nation of the Beast King wouldn't stand for it if Jade were to completely pardon Quartz.

Actually, since the Spirit of Light was adamantly defending Quartz, and since the nation was so spirit-religious, perhaps they would forgive Quartz if the Spirit of Light were to give them a proper apology.

"But I kidnapped Ruri. That is absolutely a crime," Quartz stated.

Kidnapping a Beloved and forcing them to drink poison— Quartz was undoubtedly guilty of both. Not even Jade could cover for him in that. It also didn't help that the laws had been amended after Ruri's run-in with the Church of God's Light. Now, anyone who harmed a Beloved was subject to serious punishment. Quartz, though a former Dragon King, wasn't above the law.

Ruri looked at Jade and Quartz vacantly and said, "Oh, you two. What are you talking about? I wasn't *kidnapped*!"

"Huh?" Jade asked.

"What are you talking about, Ruri?" Quartz followed.

The both of them stared at her, puzzled.

"Why, I just asked Quartz-sama to bring me here to meet the Spirit of Light."

Jade smiled in relief as he realized what Ruri was trying to say. "Right, I almost forgot. Did you enjoy yourself?"

"Yes. But I think it's about time we start heading home."

"I agree. That's a good idea," Jade replied.

Quartz listened to their conversation in stunned silence. Ruri was indirectly saying that she would pretend Quartz's recent actions had never occurred. There had been no "kidnapping" to begin with, and you couldn't punish what never happened.

"Ruri, are you sure about that?" Quartz asked.

"Oh, I'm sure," Ruri declared as she handed Quartz the tea she'd prepared.

"Thank you," Quartz uttered softly, taking a sip from the cup. "That reminds me. Whatever happened with Yadacain?"

Since the kidnapping occurred before they'd received any reports from Yadacain, neither Quartz nor Ruri knew what had transpired. Quartz was curious to know since the queen was an acquaintance of his.

"We destroyed anything related to Spirit Slayer," Jade explained. "I made them promise that they would never use it again or leave any trace of it for future generations. The rest will be under the Spirit of Darkness's supervision."

"And the abducted dragonkin?" Quartz prompted.

"They're all safe. No serious injuries."

"Good to hear," Quartz replied, a soft smile on his face. He had been worried about his kinsmen.

Ruri was also relieved to hear that they were safe.

"What are you going to do about the queen?" Quartz asked. After all, she had abducted dragonkin. The Nation of the Dragon King couldn't just take that lying down.

"To be honest, I wasn't able to talk much with the queen," Jade replied. "I talked with the delegates and the Spirit of Darkness instead. Considering the Spirit of Darkness was the one who did the abducting, there isn't much we can do in the way of a formal punishment."

"Very true," Quartz murmured.

Just like with the Spirit of Light, a mortal couldn't possibly punish a spirit.

"Be that as it may, I couldn't just leave things at that, so I came to the decision to have Yadacain pay reparations."

"That seems fair. But the queen is going to comply with the eradication of Spirit Slayer?"

Jade shot a quick, awkward glance at the Spirit of Darkness and then turned his eyes back to Quartz. "As for that, Joshua set fire to the queen's laboratory and burned it to the ground. With all of her research reduced to ash, the queen went into shock. I wasn't able to speak to her, so you could say it's more retrospective approval, if anything. Anyway, the Spirit of Darkness said he would watch over the queen from now on, so I'll be leaving things to him."

"Well, you sure were thorough. Reducing her research to nothing and restricting her from conducting it ever again is the greatest form of punishment she could possibly receive. Though I doubt the Spirit of Darkness will take it lying down," Quartz said, inquisitively glancing at the Spirit of Darkness.

Obsessive devotion to a loved one was an emotion that Quartz knew all too well. It wasn't something you could just give up on.

"That won't be a problem. I will convince her, sure enough. The next opportunity I have, I assure you," the Spirit of Darkness said, his jet-black eyes filled with determination.

He'd sat on the sidelines this entire time out of sympathy, but he actually should've reprimanded her long ago—just as Ruri did with Quartz.

"I'm sure she will be fine," the Spirit of Darkness said. "Despite how she may appear, her vassals adore her. She won't be alone. She has me. I will keep telling her that she isn't alone until she understands."

"I see. I hope she comes to realize that, then," Quartz said.

And with that, they had tied up all loose ends, bringing things to a conclusion. Or at least, that was what everyone thought, but Ruri wasn't about to let this end on that note. She abruptly stood up. All eyes landed on her.

Ruri smiled at Quartz and said, "Quartz-sama, would you stand and come over here for a second?"

"Huh? Oh, sure," Quartz replied. He was perplexed, but he walked away from the table as instructed.

"I am angry. I've always thought it was Nadasha's king and priests' fault that I wound up summoned to this world. And while I do feel better after enacting my revenge on them, I've learned a rather shocking piece of truth."

Everyone seemed to know what Ruri was getting at.

"To think that *you* were the root of this evil, Quartz-sama, is shocking, saddening, and *infuriating*. That basically means *you* are the target of my revenge. So, on that note, I humbly ask that you allow me to land one free hit on you."

Ruri was smiling sweetly, but Quartz's jaw tensed. "Huh? But you hit me pretty hard just a moment ago. One headbutt and two slaps across the face, to be exact…"

"That was that. This is this. The reasons are different."

"Hmm. Well, fine. I did cause all of that. I'll accept a punch—even two or three, if that's what it takes."

Quartz set his resolve and accepted his fate.

"Okay, then I implore you to close your eyes and grit your teeth."

Quartz closed his eyes as Ruri instructed. His assumption was that her punches wouldn't pack much force since she was merely a human girl—a misguided assumption on his part.

Ruri tightened her fist. Next, after checking to see if her magic was available, she secretly wrapped her legs in wind power. She made it seem as though she was going to throw a punch at Quartz's face, but she instead delivered a roundhouse kick to his gut. The force of it was unlike that of a woman, and he went flying into the wall.

"Oof!" Quartz grunted, blindsided.

Jade grimaced in terror at the sight that played out before him, but Kotaro, who still had a bone to pick with Quartz for kidnapping Ruri, smiled in delight. In fact, if he were in human form, he would have been grinning ear to ear.

"Urgh," Quartz coughed, clutching his stomach.

Ruri watched his reaction, grinning in satisfaction.

Quartz reproachfully looked up at Ruri. "You told me to grit my teeth! I wasn't prepared for a *kick to the gut*."

"I don't want any complaints. Punching a dragonkin would just end up hurting my hand. And since I lacked the force, I made up for it with magic. I suggest taking that minor bump in stride. After all, you made it so I can never return to my homeworld ever again."

Ruri had laid it all out, and Quartz couldn't argue with it. He made a sour face but then bowed his head and said, "Yes, you're right. I'm truly sorry for that."

Ruri was more than satisfied with this outcome, seeing as how it was too late to change what had happened. She forced herself to come to terms with the fact that this was the final chapter of her revenge.

"Speaking of homeworlds reminds me," Jade interrupted. "I found your parents in Yadacain, Ruri."

"Huh? You did?!"

"Yes, they seem to be doing well."

"Thank goodness. That's great," Ruri said in relief. She had been worried about their well-being since they had gone missing, but they had apparently stuck it out and survived, just like Ruri's grandfather had said.

Now that all of Ruri's worries were gone, she was going to suggest going back to the kingdom. But just then, Rin spoke up.

"*Say, by the way, whatever happened to Ruri possibly being your mate?*"

"Oh," Ruri gasped. She'd almost completely forgotten about that.

Jade looked at Ruri with concern. What would happen if that *were* true?

"*So what's the actual deal here, Light? Is Ruri her?*" Rin asked.

"No, that girl is not Seraphie."

"Huh? I'm not?"

Despite swearing up and down this whole time that she wasn't Seraphie, Ruri was still taken aback at how quickly the Spirit of Light refuted the idea. Once Ruri thought about it, though, she realized that the Spirit of Light had never once called her "Seraphie" during her stay.

"Spirits know just by looking. Your soul isn't the same."

"In that case, why didn't you tell Quartz-sama that sooner?" Ruri griped.

"Because Quartz was convinced. I didn't think he would listen even if I told him. Also, he brought you here in the first place to anger the Dragon King, so he wouldn't have let you go no matter what I said."

That was true, but it didn't necessarily mean that Quartz knew she wasn't really Seraphie. Ruri wondered why she'd spent all that time fretting over whether she actually was Seraphie's reincarnation. She looked scornfully at the Spirit of Light, wishing she had just told him that wasn't the case.

"Why did you think I was Seraphie's reincarnation in the first place, Quartz-sama?" Ruri asked. That question had been on the forefront of her mind, but Quartz had only answered in vague responses until now.

"You sang the song," Quartz stated.

"Song? Me?" Ruri cocked her head. She didn't remember singing for him.

"During the tournament, you were humming a song," Quartz explained. "That was a secret song that only Seraphie and I knew. Since no one else knows it, and you were singing it, I figured you were Seraphie."

Jade looked at Ruri and asked, "Ruri, can you explain?"

Ruri remembered that she'd started humming when Jade made it through the tournament, but the song she'd hummed back then was...

"I picked up that song. It wasn't one I already knew," Ruri replied.

"That's impossible. Seraphie wrote that song, and she's the only person other than me who knows it. She didn't even sing it in front of the Spirit of Light, and she had a contract with her. You can see why I would assume you were Seraphie given that you knew something only she would know."

Quartz's argument was convincing, but what was wrong was wrong.

"We had never met each other before I returned to the Nation of the Dragon King, so where in the world did you learn that song?" Quartz asked.

"It's the song that the ghost in the pocket space sang," Ruri replied.

"Ghost in the pocket space?"

"Yes. There's a room that no longer has an owner in Lydia's domain. Lydia usually checks inside those rooms and erases them, but there's one where a ghost has taken up residence. It's spooked her so bad that she's left it alone. But sometimes you can hear an extremely beautiful song coming from there, so I've been going to hear it on occasion."

"And that was the song the ghost was singing, you say?"

"That's correct."

"You have to take me there!" Quartz insisted. "Take me to the room, please!"

Quartz jumped to his feet and grabbed Ruri's arm in such a frantic manner that he forgot to control his strength.

"T-That hurts, Quartz-sama!" Ruri screamed.

Quartz came back to his senses and let go of Ruri's arm. "Sorry about that. But could you please take me to this place? I beg of you."

"Hmm, while I'd love to take you there, only Lydia and her contract-bearers can go there, so I don't think you'll be able to."

"That can't be…" Quartz said, looking painfully dejected. His shoulders slumped.

"Don't worry, I'll go check it out. The idea of meeting with a ghost scares me, but I'll do my best."

"I'd appreciate that."

Ruri opened her pocket space and jumped inside. Lydia was waiting for her, distress written all over her face.

"*Ruri, are you really going in?*" Lydia asked. She'd apparently heard the news from Kotaro and the other supreme-level spirits. That helped cut a rather long story short.

"Of course. Come on, let's go, Lydia."

"*Aww, what? But what if the ghost attacks us?*"

"They're not a zombie, so we'll be fine. If it comes attacking us, then we just book it outside and erase the whole room."

"*They won't end up haunting us?*"

"I don't think so. Not someone who sings a song that beautiful, at least."

Ruri was honestly afraid that she might get haunted, but she had no other choice. She had to do this, for Quartz's sake.

Lydia brought her to the room where the ghost resided, but neither of them could hear singing. Ruri was about to reach out to the doorknob, but her hand stopped.

"*Hey, Ruri, we can still turn back now.*"

Even though spirits and ghosts were similar, Lydia was considerably freaked out. She was really afraid of getting haunted. Ruri was similarly afraid and didn't really want to go in herself, but she couldn't just leave without venturing inside.

"Ughh… Women have guts! Women have guts!" Ruri repeated like an incantation and then swung the door open.

Unlike Ruri's pocket space, the inside of this room was quite small—though it wasn't a fair comparison since Ruri's space was by no means standard. From Lydia's perspective, a spirit who knew other pocket spaces, this size was average.

"Hello, is anyone home~?" Ruri called out as she and Lydia timidly looked around the room. They found neither hide nor hair of any ghost. "Did we get the wrong room?"

"No, this is the room all right."

Be that as it may, there was no sign of a ghost at all. But just as Ruri considered leaving and trying again, it happened.

"Who are you two?" asked a voice belonging neither to Ruri nor Lydia.

They both slowly turned around to see a woman dressed in white clothes—her body transparent.

"Eek! There it is!"

"Eeeeeeeek!"

Ruri belted out a loud scream and ran toward the exit, but as she reached the door, she finally came to her senses and stopped. Her sense of duty had prevailed over her fear. She nervously turned around to see...a transparent ghost. Lydia was also transparent when she wasn't in her material form, but Ruri could sense a strong life force or aura from Lydia. The woman before her had none.

The ghost cocked her head, her look vacant.

Even though Ruri didn't feel any hostility from the woman, she couldn't help but fear that she might suddenly attack. It was taking all of Ruri's courage to even face her.

Taking a big gulp, Ruri summoned up the courage to ask, "You're a ghost, aren't you? You've been singing here this whole time, right?"

"Yes, that's right," the ghost woman replied. "That's probably right, since my body died. Have you been listening to my song? I have to say, knowing that people have been listening is quite embarrassing."

"What are you doing here?"

"Oh! You'd actually like to hear about that?!"

The ghost enthusiastically slid up to Ruri's face. Ruri gasped and drew back, but she regained her composure and nodded.

"Okay, so I ended up falling ill. I wasn't so much afraid of dying, but I have a husband, you see. He is utterly hopeless without me around, and he said that he would follow after me if I were to die. I thought, 'What kind of nonsense is he talking about?' But then I realized, that must be how much he really loves me. It sparked a bit of joy in my heart, I'll tell you."

She was rapid-fire talking. Ruri was so stunned that the fear left her mind.

"Say, are you listening to me?" asked the ghost.

"Yes, I am."

"Good. So, yeah, I was worried that he really *might* follow me, so I did some convincing and got him to agree to a promise. I told him to look for me after I was reincarnated. Encountering the same beloved after being reincarnated is a scenario girls tend to like, you know. Tee, hee, hee. But even though I made him promise that, I knew he would find the process unbearable, so I needed to do something."

Ruri couldn't help but think that this story sounded awfully familiar.

"And so what I came up with was—"

"Ah, wait a second! Before I hear the rest, could I ask for your name?"

Ruri had cut her seemingly long life story short. That prompted the ghost to come to her senses and speak a little more calmly.

"Oh my. Yes, I'm sorry. You're right. First-time greetings are very important. It's just been decades since I've talked to anyone. I got a little carried away. I'm Seraphie. And you two are?"

Ruri was taken aback. She hadn't wanted to believe her hunch at first, but the ghost's story, including what she'd said about the song, was extremely similar to what she'd heard from Quartz.

"Seraphie?! Your name is Seraphie?!"

"Yes, it is."

"Then you're Seraphie-san, Quartz-sama's mate?"

The ghost was surprised. "Do you know Quartz?! Please take me to him!"

"I'm back!" announced Ruri as she returned from her pocket space.

Quartz, who had been waiting on bated breath, rushed over to her in a mix of expectation and anxiety.

"Well? How did it go?!"

Ruri simply unfurled her hand in front of him. Although confused, Quartz instinctively stuck out his own hand. Ruri plopped something into his palm. It was a ring—a familiar ring.

Quartz's eyes widened. "But this is Seraphie's ring. How did something stolen by grave robbers end up with you, Ruri…?"

Quartz stared at the ring in disbelief a few seconds more and then raised his head, only to find something even more unbelievable staring him in the face.

"Sera…phie…"

She was lacking a physical body, and her entire form was see-through, but standing there was indeed Quartz's beloved mate, Seraphie.

"Am I...dreaming...?" Quartz asked in a daze, unsure if this was real.

"Hee, hee, hee, it's no dream. We meet at long last, dear."

That same tender smile as when she was alive—the smile that Quartz had searched years for—was really there.

"Ngh... Seraphie...!" Quartz exclaimed, clinging to his beloved mate. Or, at least he would have clung to her if she'd had a physical form. But instead of taking her into his arms, he passed right through her and stumbled forward.

Seraphie giggled, finding Quartz's actions comical. "Silly, you obviously can't do that when I don't have a physical body."

Quartz couldn't touch her, but he was still happy to see her laughing and smiling. His lips stretched into a wide smile, and tears rolled down his face.

"Ruri, what in the *world* is going on here?" Jade asked. He assumed that the ghost before them was Quartz's mate, despite never having met her before, but he didn't know how she had become a ghost.

"Well, it's certainly a long story..." Ruri started.

"Allow me to explain," Seraphie interjected, volunteering to elaborate. "Hey, Quartz, do you remember? After my death, you buried my favorite ring with my body."

"Right, *this* ring," Quartz replied, referring to the ring Ruri had just given him.

"I was inside of that," Seraphie stated.

"What do you mean?"

"I made you share a promise with me before I died. Without it, you would have followed me right into the grave. I couldn't allow that to happen."

"Seraphie…"

"But I watched you wither away as you saw me grow weaker by the day, and I knew that you couldn't bear to live alone. Once I decided that I needed to do something, I came up with a way to be by your side even in death. That being the magic to move souls to items."

"That sort of magic exists?" Quartz asked, dumbfounded.

"Despite appearances, I am a very capable witch. Witch sorcery has a spell with that effect. The problem is, it has a *very* low success rate. I knew that if I gave you hope and it didn't work, you would fall into despair, so I kept it a secret. And just before I died, I initiated the magic. I managed to safely transfer my soul into the ring. But there was one problem."

"What was that?"

"Well, I was convinced that you were going to *keep* the ring. I figured you would keep it by your side since you knew it was my favorite piece of jewelry. So the issue was, even though I picked the ring to house my soul, *you* decided to *bury* the darn thing along with my body! It ruined the whole plan!"

Though Quartz could have never known Sophie's intentions, she was unreasonably blaming him.

"S-Sorry…" Quartz apologized as though he were in the wrong.

"I wasn't able to go outside because my soul hadn't fully affixed itself to it yet, which was an unfortunate consequence… But to make matters worse, grave robbers came and took off with the ring. Then it got tossed into one of their pocket spaces. I assumed that the grave robbers would eventually sell it somewhere and I would be able to get to the outside world, but that never happened and I spent decades inside of there. What happened to them?! I mean, honestly!"

To put it bluntly, luck just wasn't on their side. Grave robbers weren't an everyday occurrence. Not to mention that the ring was the only thing that had gone missing out of all the pieces of jewelry in the grave.

"I tried to get the ring back from the grave robbers," Quartz said, "but one of them died in a falling-out with his cohort. It was still inside his pocket space, which meant I couldn't have reclaimed it."

Quartz was absolutely not in the wrong, but he felt sorry nonetheless seeing Seraphie fuming mad.

"Well, what's done is done. I'm able to see you now, so we'll just say it worked out. Sorry for keeping you waiting, Quartz."

Seraphie gave him a beaming grin. Quartz squinted like he was looking straight at something overwhelmingly beautiful and dazzling and smiled. But then he awkwardly looked away.

"Seraphie, I have to apologize to you. I wasn't able to bear living without you, in spite of our promise. I tried to seek death as an option."

Seraphie cheerfully smiled. It was like she knew that but was willing to forgive him for everything. "Yes, I thought so. You're hopeless without me around, after all. But now I'm able to see you—alive. That's all that matters, right?"

"Right. And it's all thanks to Ruri. Without her help, I probably wouldn't be here right now," Quartz stated.

"Thanks to Ruri's headbutt, you mean," Jade jokingly quipped.

As soon as Ruri gave it some real thought, she felt embarrassed. She had been face-to-face with the former Dragon King, and she'd run the gamut—punched him, kicked him, headbutted him, and even gave him a stern lecture.

"Thank you, Ruri," Seraphie added. "I wouldn't have been able to see Quartz if not for you." If Ruri hadn't come along, Seraphie might have spent all of her days singing in that room.

"Then you would call this a happy ending...right?" Ruri asked, smiling and looking up at Jade.

"Yes, I think I would. Fine work, Ruri," Jade replied, smiling back at her and rustling her hair.

Emotions Bound

After witnessing the reunion decades in the making, Ruri and the others decided it was time to head back to the castle. The Spirit of Darkness needed to return to Yadacain, so Kotaro was going to take him back.

Jade bowed his head to the supreme-level spirit and said, "Thank you very much for all of your help." Without Darkness's powers, the Spirit of Light's barrier would have prevented them from finding Ruri.

"Don't mention it," the Spirit of Darkness said, sounding debonair. "Consider it my thanks for causing you so much trouble." Then he hopped on Kotaro's back and they left for Yadacain.

Meanwhile, Quartz was having a tiny dispute. The Spirit of Light was clinging to Seraphie's ghost right in front of him. He watched as his body shook in frustration. He couldn't lay a single finger on Seraphie because she was a ghost, but the Spirit of Light was touching her just fine. In fact, the spirit was lovingly embracing her—a sight that Quartz couldn't tolerate.

"How are you able to touch Seraphie?!" he asked, demanding an answer.

"Hmph, 'cause I'm a spirit," the Spirit of Light said with a smirk. She clung even tighter to Seraphie, as if to show off.

"What does she mean?" Ruri asked Rin.

"*Spirits are also beings composed solely of power. They don't have physical bodies. You know how even the little spirits without bodies can touch things that contain mana, right? It's the same as that. Souls contain mana. Even if someone seemingly has none, all manner of beings possess trace amounts of mana. The Spirit of Light is touching that mana right now.*"

"Hmm, so would it be possible for Quartz to touch her as well?"

"*I certainly can't help.*"

"*You* can't?" Ruri asked. Rin's emphasis on herself had drawn Ruri's attention. "So someone other than you *can*, Rin?"

Quartz, who had been listening to the conversation, was looking on with hope in his eyes. Things would get ugly if they embellished the truth.

"*Light, why don't you stop being mean and tell him?*"

"Oh, come on. I was trying to tease him. You're no fun," the Spirit of Light grumbled, jutting out her lips. She took Seraphie's hand and circulated power into it. Just then, Seraphie's body started to sparkle. "There, have at it."

The Spirit of Light went behind Quartz and shoved him hard. He lost his balance and fell forward—bumping right into Seraphie. Quartz ended up clinging on to her. His fingers were definitely grabbing hold of her.

"What's going on?" Ruri asked.

Quartz was touching Seraphie even though she was a ghost. Ruri wanted to check it out, but she didn't have the courage to interrupt the happy and joyful couple.

"*Light wrapped her power around her soul. I could explain further, but I don't think you'll be able to understand as a human, so I'm curtailing some of the details. But you can pretty much think of it as that.*"

"Hmm…"

"Well, I'd like to head back home now, but..." said Jade, awkwardly looking at Quartz and Seraphie. The two of them were cuddled up and ignoring everything else around them.

"If you have the courage to step up to them being all lovey-dovey, then by all means," Ruri prodded.

"I can't. I know better than to do something like that."

"Well, I don't want to either. I'd rather not face the backlash for trying to break them up."

As Jade and Ruri quibbled over calling out to them, Quartz's hand slipped through Seraphie once again. It seemed he could only touch her while the Spirit of Light's powers were still active. Quartz looked disappointed, but happy nonetheless—a natural response given that he'd found his mate after years of searching.

Quartz wanted more cuddle time, but Ruri pulled him away and they all returned back to the castle.

Chelsea had been quite worried, but Jade explained the situation to her. In the end, she reluctantly smiled and accepted it.

It was fortunate that Euclase had thought to issue a gag order, so the kidnapping didn't turn into a huge panic. Everyone bought the story that Quartz and Ruri had gone to see the Spirit of Light, especially since they had brought the Spirit of Light back to the castle.

The problem now was how the Nation of the Beast King would react to Quartz's deeds. But once the Spirit of Light bowed and apologized to Arman, the king of the spirit-religious nation felt nothing but shame. Celestine even got angry at him for making the Spirit of Light bow her head in deference.

Now that the Spirit of Light and the other supreme-level spirits had stepped forward, the Nation of the Beast King wasn't able to openly punish Quartz. If they did, the Spirit of Light would come forward and say she was to blame as well.

Nevertheless, Quartz felt a simple apology to the Nation of the Dragon King or the Nation of the Beast King wasn't enough. After discussing it, it was decided that Quartz would help Jade out with his work for free, at least for the time being. The Nation of the Beast King, however, couldn't come up with any ideas right away, so they asked for time to think about it. Even so, they probably couldn't cast any unwise requests upon him since the Spirit of Light was silently pressuring them from behind Quartz.

Arman started to feel his stomach turn, so he decided to go back to his kingdom and think it over there.

The fact that Quartz was the previous Dragon King meant that the Nation of the Dragon King owed the Nation of the Beast King a great debt. That fact depressed Quartz, but with his beloved mate by his side, things would work out just fine.

Once everything else had been settled, Ruri finally made up her mind and went to visit Jade. Her heart was beating out of her chest. She wanted to give up this very second, but she squashed her trepidation and kept walking up to the door of the royal office. She took a few deep breaths to calm herself, but she was so tense that she felt sick.

After she knocked on the door, a voice from inside gave her the okay. Ruri slowly opened the door and found Jade and Claus hard at work.

The corners of Jade's lips gently raised into a smile once he saw Ruri enter the room.

"Jade-sama, I need to talk to you, but is now a good time?"

"Yes, perfectly fine. I was just about to take a break anyway," Jade stated, but he seemed to be fibbing.

Claus grinned, looking resigned. Ruri felt sorry for him, but his compliance was helpful. It had taken her quite a while to make up her mind to come here. If she had been sent away, then she didn't know when she'd ever make up her mind again.

Jade placed his pen down. "So what did you want to talk about?"

Ruri peeked at Claus. "Well, I'd like to talk alone, if possible…"

Jade threw a look at Claus. Understanding what that meant, Claus stood up, bowed, and left the room.

With the both of them alone and the room quiet, Ruri felt herself getting even more nervous.

"Okay, what's on your mind?" Jade asked, oblivious to Ruri's tension.

Although he had no idea what Ruri was about to tell him, he was genuinely happy that Ruri was visiting. Nevertheless, he started to suspect something was wrong with her when she refused to say anything.

"What's the matter, Ruri?"

Ruri remained silent and put her hand on the dragonheart around her neck. Then she took it off and held it out to Jade.

Jade looked puzzled, not understanding the meaning behind Ruri's actions. She took Jade's hand and placed the dragonheart on his palm. As soon as the pendant touched his hand, his face immediately tensed.

"Ruri, what does this—"

Ruri had returned the dragonheart, an act that painted an unpleasant conclusion in Jade's mind. Ruri interrupted him before he could finish his sentence, though.

"When I first learned this was a dragonheart, I thought it was unbelievable. I always thought I was just a cat—a pet—to you, Jade-sama. I'm not from this world, so I don't know what logic dictates this world or dragonkin. Nothing strikes a bell when you tell me what a dragonheart is either. Because I'm not from this world."

"Master Quartz told me the same thing. He said that I needed to tell you plain and simple. But since you were being so proactive afterward, I thought you *did* get the message."

"I see your point, but you didn't deliver the message to me *clearly*, did you?" Ruri stated with conviction. She looked into Jade's eyes and thought about the thing that had been on her mind the entire time—her wish. "Please put it into words and say it. Don't say it in some special dragonkin way. Say it so that even someone ignorant of the ways of this world can understand. I want you to tell me in your own words, Jade-sama."

She'd said it. She had actually said it. She had put all the feelings stuck in her chest into words. But now a new fear arose. How would Jade react?

Jade had been silently staring at Ruri, but he stood up and pulled on Ruri's hand, bringing her closer. They were both *extremely* close now. Ruri's reflexes kicked in, and she tried to back away, but Jade wrapped his arms around her waist.

As Ruri stood flustered, Jade calmly said, "What you're saying is right, Ruri. Looks like I was imposing my own logic onto you and not considering yours at all." Jade offered her the dragonheart that she'd returned to him. "Ruri, you are precious to me. And not because you're a cat. I want you by my side as a woman. So, I ask you…please accept this. I want you to be my mate—my one and only for the rest of my days."

His shining jadeite eyes, filled with sincerity, had captured Ruri and wouldn't let go. They were urging her for an answer. His arms around her tightened, and she could feel his nervousness. He was probably anxious about how she would respond. He was anxious for no reason, however. Ruri already had her answer.

"I will," Ruri said, taking the dragonheart and wrapping her arms around Jade tightly.

"Is that it? I told you everything on my mind. I'd like you to do the same," Jade said in vague dissatisfaction as he squeezed her just as tightly.

"When I witnessed Quartz-sama's deep love for his mate, I wanted to be with you so badly. The thought that you loved me just as much filled me with sheer delight. It made me want to be there with you—to fill the place by your side." Ruri looked up at Jade with a wide smile. "I love you as well, Jade-sama."

A gentle smile formed on Jade's face as he squeezed her even more. "The day is finally here. I've been waiting all this time for the moment you'd come to me. But as much as I waited, you never came. In fact, you started avoiding me as of late."

"That is your fault, Jade-sama. After all, I've been worried that I had the wrong idea this whole time."

"Is that so? I should have been quicker about getting the message to you, then."

"But thanks to that, I had time to think it over, so I'm grateful in a way," Ruri said. She was sure that if Jade had confessed to her when he'd given her his dragonheart, she wouldn't have been able to respond right away.

"Ruri, now that you are my mate in both name and reality, I take it you've also agreed to marry me?"

"Yes. I'm prepared to walk the aisle. Besides, if I said no after becoming your mate, Agate-san and the others would raise a huge commotion."

"They're apparently already going through with preparations. I'm sure they'll be pleased to hear you've agreed. They've been putting more effort into this wedding than any other before."

282

"Then again, I am a little nervous about leaving things to them…" Ruri said, sounding hesitant.

"Yes, I can certainly see why," Jade agreed.

If the people insisting that Ruri change her wardrobe five times were to spearhead the ceremony, then it was anyone's guess as to how it would turn out.

"I wish they'd allow me a little more leeway to interject. It is *my* wedding, you know…" Ruri added. She was afraid that the elders were going to hold a ceremony by the elders, for the elders.

For now, Ruri put that matter aside as she and Jade snuggled together, their emotions finally bound.

There were eyes secretly staring at Ruri and Jade's exchange. Rin, Kotaro, Chi, and a number of smaller spirits were peeking inside through a tiny crack in the door. Standing off to the side was Claus, watching them in exasperation.

"May I remind all of you that eavesdropping is in bad taste?" Claus said, chiding them, but none of the spirits showed any signs of caring.

"*Ruri's business is our business. Now, you better plant a kiss on her, you lousy king,*" Rin said, launching into her frustrations and forgetting that she was being a Peeping Tom.

"*Good job, Ruri,*" Kotaro whispered in congratulations.

Chi added, "*Yeah, all's well that ends well!*"

"*Hooray!*" the other spirits cheered above their heads, high-fiving each other in celebration.

"Hmm, I can only hope that the elders do not go overboard…" commented Claus. He was overjoyed at their newfound relationship, but he also pictured Agate and the other elders flying into a frenzy at this.

The Party

A party was being held at the castle today to celebrate Jade's continued reign as the Dragon King. It had already been postponed once because of Yadacain's attacks.

Jade was naturally the star of the party, but another guest occupied most of the huge reception hall where the party was being held—Ruri's long-awaited kraken. The kraken was far too big to fit in the hall, so only its leg was present, which was plenty. Because it had been immediately stored in pocket space after it was killed, it was still twitching around—a good sign that it was fresh.

"I finally got the octopus I always wanted!"

"Yeah, you should be grateful," Ewan said. "I made sure to notify the men that you wanted the kraken."

"But it's not like *you* caught it, Ewan. Don't act all smug."

"I was fighting out there too, you know."

At the time, Ewan was battling Yadacain's ships *and* commanding the soldiers to capture the kraken, so he'd had his hands full. Ruri was grateful that he'd remembered amidst that huge commotion.

"Well, thank you. Okay, time to kick this takoyaki party off with some kraken!" Ruri shouted.

Just one of the kraken's legs was more than enough to fill the bellies of everyone in attendance. The rest of its legs and body would be used to make takoyaki at the hot spring facility. The massive kraken that the soldiers had reaped from the last battle would stave off Ruri's octopus woes for a good while.

It was surprisingly difficult to flip takoyaki. Even if a well-trained cook could handle it, it was still a challenging feat for a beginner. To help with the flipping, Ruri had brought in the slum children who handled the takoyaki equipment at the hot spring facilities. With their pristine clothes and tidy appearances, none of them looked like they came from the slums. They looked uncomfortable among the glitz and glamour of the castle, but it would be a good experience for them nonetheless.

The takoyaki was generally well received, and Ruri was very happy to see everyone enjoying their meal. She wanted to feed some to Jade as well, but the man of the hour was nowhere to be found. She searched the hall, only to find him standing alone on the terrace, holding a glass of wine and lost in thought.

"Jade-sama?"

"Oh, it's you, Ruri."

"What are you doing out here all alone? Shouldn't you be with everyone else?"

"It should be fine. This party may be for me, but it's pretty much an excuse for all of them to drink."

The partygoers were indeed showering themselves in booze, and the actual reason for the party had fallen by the wayside. The only things they were interested in were what alcohol was available and what food was accompanying it.

Jade held out his hand to Ruri, and Ruri took it. Then he tugged and reeled her over. It was an action so completely natural that Ruri simply submitted herself to it.

"I've been thinking…" Jade started. "What would I do if I wound up like Master Quartz? Human beings are weak. And if you were to die, would I wander around like Master Quartz in search of you?"

Realizing that Jade's gloominess came from his pondering, Ruri looked up at him and said, "We won't know that until the time comes. I plan to live a long life, so if you start worrying now, you'll surely go bald."

"Bald...?" Jade repeated, snapping out of his gloom.

"I doubt that will affect your suave, handsome looks, but I prefer you with a full head of hair, so try your best not to lose any follicles, okay?"

"...I'll make an effort, yes."

"Still, the time will come when we'll part ways. It's inevitable. And being a human, I'm sure I'll pass much sooner than you. But don't worry! We'll have plenty of kids, and they'll have grandkids, so I won't be leaving you all alone." Ruri hugged Jade tightly. "Let's make a *whole bunch* of memories, so we can part ways with a smile when the time does come!"

Ruri smiled, and it lit up Jade's heart. His lips naturally returned a smile as he said, "Yes, you're right. Let's fill our hours with each other's company."

"Yes, let's!"

Jade drew closer to Ruri and their lips met, almost as if they were exchanging vows.

Epilogue

With the party over, and with no further reason to stay in the castle, Chelsie decided to go back to the forest. Not only did Claus and Joshua come to see her off, but so did Quartz.

"Sorry for all the trouble I caused," Quartz said, apologizing to Chelsie for the mess he had caused when he'd kidnapped Ruri.

Chelsie smiled, albeit rather awkwardly, like a mother dealing with a fussy child. "You didn't do anything to me. If Ruri has forgiven you, then there is nothing I need to say. And it's not as though I couldn't understand how you felt either. It's just great that you were able to reunite with your mate."

"Yes, it really is great," Quartz said as he met eyes with Seraphie, who was standing a small distance away, happily grinning at him.

Chelsie was relieved to see Quartz looking so elated. Next, she turned to Ruri.

"Chelsie-san, are you going back so soon? You could always stay a little while longer."

"I only came here to check out the tournament. Well, and to check on you. Now that I know you're doing well, I'm going to head back."

Ruri had gone through so much that she hadn't been able to sit down and talk with Chelsie at all. She was displeased by this, and it showed on her face.

"Come now, child. All I have to do is come see you if I feel like visiting. Also, I suspect I'll be coming back soon enough anyway."

"Oh, why is that?" Ruri asked, not understanding what Chelsie was implying.

"For your wedding with His Majesty, of course," Chelsie explained, causing Ruri's cheeks to flush. "You get along with His Majesty, now. I'll come running to celebrate when the time comes."

"Okay, but I'll come visit you before that, so you'd better treat me to some of your home cooking when *that* time comes."

"Sure thing. I'll be waiting," Chelsie said. She then left, making her way back to the forest.

The tumultuous past few days had come to an end, and Ruri could finally take it easy and relax. It had been a long time since she'd enjoyed a nice comfortable sunbath in the garden with the spirits. The small spirits lay on Ruri as she used Kotaro and his big fluffy coat as a pillow.

"Mmm, it feels like forever since the last time I was able to relax this much!"

"*Yeah, yeah!*"

"*For sure!*"

Ruri had a feeling that the spirits were as relaxed and nonchalant as they always were, but it was cute to see them agree, so she took their words at face value.

"*Especially after all that business with Yadacain, Dark, and Light,*" Rin said, landing on Kotaro's head and staring off into the sky.

"Yeah, it was pretty hectic, but I sure am glad there was a happy ending to all of it."

"*That's true. You and the king have* finally *admitted your love for one another too,*" Rin added. "*Seeing you dawdle around forever and wondering when you'd eventually hook up with him was getting annoying. Isn't that right, Kotaro?*"

"*I'm fine with whatever Ruri desires—whether that means being the king's mate or refusing him,*" replied Kotaro.

"*Oh, my. You say that, but you were happy to hear the news, weren't you?*" asked Rin.

"*If Ruri is happy, then I'm happy,*" Kotaro stated, sounding like an extremely faithful canine companion. His tone caused Ruri to giggle.

"Humph, if he picked a brat like you as his mate, then I doubt his tastes."

Of course, the one to put a damper on the mood was the individual sitting beside Kotaro—Heat. Ruri furrowed her brow and grunted. Heat, who would normally be chasing tail, was joining Ruri and the others on a whim.

"Humph, you're the last person I want to hear critiquing people's tastes, considering your *very* loose standards in women," Ruri retorted.

"Don't get the wrong idea. Not just anyone will do for me. I evaluate whomever it is and attempt to romance them. Which is why I haven't attempted to romance *you*."

"And I'll have you know that I'm perfectly fine *without* you making passes at me, Heat-sama. I already have Jade-sama."

"Hah, then you'd best keep hold of him. If you let him get away, you'll lose the one man in the world willing to court you."

"Grk, what I'd give to punch you," Ruri murmured, clenching her fist. She resisted the urge to deliver a knuckle sandwich to Heat's face.

Rin chuckled and said, "*You stand there and tease Ruri with all those sarcastic quips, but you were terribly worried about her when she was kidnapped. You actually do like Ruri when all is said and done, don't you, Fire?*"

"Have you gone daft, Water?" Heat spat. "Why would I worry about a brat like her?" He stood up with a "hmph" and turned to walk away. However, he stopped, adding, "Well…maybe just a little. I'd be out of sorts without the brat around to provide her *insightful* and snippety back talk."

That was all Heat said before taking his leave. Ruri watched him walk off, stunned.

"Was that Heat-sama's…sweet side?" Ruri uttered, blinking in disbelief. She had just witnessed an astonishing turn of events.

Rin then asked her, "*Ruri, weren't you going to go see Time?*"

"Oh, I almost forgot!" Ruri cried, suddenly sitting up. All of the small spirits who'd been lying on her body rolled right off.

"*Huh~?*"

"*Eeek!*"

"*I'm falling~!*"

Carrying tea and snacks, Ruri headed to Lydia's place for a little girls-only gathering. Lydia seemed happy since it had been such a long time since their last tea party. As they ate pastries, their friendly conversation veered toward Jade, Ruri's new romantic partner.

"*Tee hee hee, my heart sank when I heard that you'd been kidnapped, but perhaps it wasn't such a bad thing if it gave you the courage you needed.*"

"Well, I guess you could say that."

"*So, tell me, Ruri. Are you happy now?*"

Ruri had been summoned to a strange new world with no one to rely on, cast into the forest, and left with no way to return to home. Be that as it may, here she'd met Jade, Chelsie, Lydia, and the other spirits—so many people who she considered near and dear to her. She might not be able to return to her world ever again, but Ruri's heart was filled with satisfaction.

"Of course I am!" Ruri replied with confidence, a sparkling smile stretching across her face.

Ruri and Jade had officially confessed their love to one another. The spirits were pleased, but no one was more pleased than Agate and the other elders, the very group who'd been trying to arrange a wife for Jade for years. Tears streamed from their eyes when they heard the good news, and they jumped for joy.

"Oh, Ruri, we are so glad… We are so *very* glad that you've made up your mind. There was a good moment there where we fretted over how you might respond… Alas, none of that matters now. Your joyous time as a royal mate has finally come. At long last, His Majesty has a mate!"

"Yes! We would admonish His Majesty till we were blue in the face, but he showed no interest! Now he has a mate!"

"Yes, there was a time when we worried his romantic interests might lie with men instead! Now he has a mate!"

"Oh, this is a delight!"

The elders all cheered and reveled in their good fortune— all the while paying no mind to Jade, who was growing increasingly perturbed.

"Oh, how should we express this joy?! We must notify the people of the castle of this posthaste!"

"Let's celebrate!"

"With liquor all around!"

"There'll be no sleeping tonight for sure!"

Though the elders were overjoyed at the news, Ruri felt uncomfortable.

"Right, everyone, now is the time to unveil what we've had in store!"

"Yes, the time has come!"

"Excellent idea!"

The elders stormed out of the room, chattering excitedly down the hall.

As soon as the gaggle of gray-haired vassals left, everyone in the office let out a long sigh of relief. They'd known that the elders would be happy, but they seemed so giddy that they would eventually collapse where they stood, which was…concerning, to say the least. It was time for them to start acting their age.

Despite how trying it was, their crazed display was a testament to just how much effort they'd poured into finding Jade a suitable partner. From what Ruri had heard, Jade had been desperately trying to stop the elders from playing matchmaker ever since they'd learned that he had given Ruri his dragonheart. He had been worried that they would sour things if they meddled too much.

Jade definitely felt that their interference had forced his efforts to take some convoluted detours, so he'd made a wise decision to rein them in. However, their euphoric state now was the release of all of their pent-up frustrations from having been relegated to the sidelines. Then again, they had indirectly involved themselves by going through with wedding preparations and renovating the queen's room.

Jade stayed extremely cool, assuming that the elders would calm down in due course. In the meantime, he held Ruri in his lap—in human form instead of her usual cat form—which put him in an *extraordinarily* good mood. While the elders were thrilled that Ruri had officially become Jade's mate, no one was more genuinely thrilled with all of this than Jade.

Ruri wouldn't have minded sitting on Jade's lap in her cat form, but doing so as a human was mortifying enough to make her want to get off. Nevertheless, Jade insisted on keeping her near, emanating an aura of happiness all the while.

She glanced at him, and he looked back at her with a sugary sweet smile. She flusteredly averted her gaze, unable to look at him or his grin directly.

Euclase, who was also present, said, "Albeit not to the degree of Agate and the elder vassals, but I'm honestly glad that you've become His Majesty's mate, Ruri."

"You are, Euclase-san?"

"Well, of course. His Majesty *did* hand you his dragonheart without your approval. A dragonheart can be removed from a dragonkin's body once, and *only* once. If you had refused, then His Majesty wouldn't have been able to have a mate. Also, if you had chosen some other man instead, His Majesty surely would have gone on a rampage."

"And the only person capable of stopping His Majesty should he ever go on a rampage would be Master Quartz," Claus said with a chuckle.

Ruri laughed at Euclase and Claus's jokes, thinking that would have never happened. Still, they were both very serious. The strongest dragonkin, the Dragon King himself, going berserk would have been terrible. The reason they could all laugh it off now was because Ruri had become his mate.

Before long, Agate returned to the royal office with his vassals—with goods in hand.

"Feast your eyes on our masterpieces," Agate said, presenting several glittering pieces of jewelry and accessories. There was a tiara and necklace, both with huge gemstones surrounded by a large number of smaller gems. A pair of earrings completed the look. The accessories' designs were the definition of grace and beauty. Ruri was captivated by the custom-made, matching set. The gemstones were quite large, and the thought of how much this one set had cost made her head spin.

"What are you doing with these, Agate?" Jade asked quizzically. He seemed to be unaware that Agate and the others had been making these.

"We received the gemstones from Lord Spirit of the Earth and had them made."

That reminded Ruri that she had asked Chi to make some gemstones for her. She had wondered what they were going to make with the leftovers, but now it made sense. However, when Agate had first asked for the gemstones, she'd had a bad feeling. He hadn't said anything about it being for her or the wedding.

"Oh, and we've made these as well," Agate added, taking out a small box and opening it to reveal two matching rings. "Ruri happened to tell me that it was customary to exchange rings at weddings in her world."

"Is that so?" asked Jade.

"Yes, I said that, but I'm surprised you remembered," Ruri replied.

"Heh heh heh, an ode to our perfect research so we can make this wedding the best it can be," quipped an elder.

"All right, now to get right to preparing!" shouted Agate.

The rest of the gung ho vassals pumped their fists into the air and yelled back in reply, "Here here!" No one in the office had the means to stop them from pressing forward.

"Yeesh, things made an awful lot of progress while I was away, eh?" commented Joshua. "Since when did you and His Majesty get so intimate?"

After things in Yadacain had wrapped up, Joshua had finally taken a vacation. When he returned, he'd stumbled upon the elders making a huge to-do out of Ruri and Jade's wedding.

Joshua naturally had already known about Jade's dragonheart adorning Ruri's neck, so he'd known how Jade felt. But Ruri's feelings had still been up in the air. He could really feel that he'd been gone a long time since the marriage talks had already progressed considerably by the time he came back.

"Well, you *were* gone the entire time," Ewan said. By comparison, he had spent a lot of time with Ruri. That also meant that he understood why Ruri had been so awkward and indecisive about Jade. "It's been really rough, I'll tell you."

Ruri didn't think that Ewan had anything to do with her situation, but apparently Ewan thought he did.

"All I did was accompany Ruri as her bodyguard, but His Majesty gave me the stink-eye like mad. 'Oh, you're getting too close.' 'Oh, you two sure are having fun chatting.' 'Oh, you're spending more time with Ruri than I am.' His eyes said it all," Ewan explained.

Finn, who was standing next to Ewan, patted Ewan on the head for a job well done.

Ruri looked at Jade, but Jade quickly averted his gaze. She wondered if Ewan was referring to when she had intentionally avoided Jade. While it was true that she'd spent more time with Ewan, she never would have imagined that Jade would get jealous of *Ewan* of all people.

"Jade-sama…" Ruri said, exasperated, but Jade still avoided eye contact.

Admittedly, it was uncouth of Ewan to divulge that here and now, but the situation must have been problematic enough for him to go airing it out to begin with.

"A dragonkin's jealousy ain't nothing to scoff at," Joshua said.

"I'd say so," Ewan agreed.

Both were fellow dragonkin, meaning they could comprehend how Jade felt.

"Welp, it's better than spurring his jealousy and getting confined to the castle," Joshua commented with a chuckle, though in reality it was no laughing matter. "Anywho, congrats, Ruri."

"Yes, we're glad you two wound up together," Finn added, congratulating them in turn.

"Thank you!" Ruri replied with a soft smile.

In contrast to the jubilant elders, there was someone who cried at the news of Ruri's marriage.

"Hngh, this is unbelievable. Just when I finally get to see my daughter again, she's getting married!" lamented Kohaku, Ruri's father. It was a natural complaint for any father with a daughter to have, but it wasn't that he unsparingly disapproved of their union; he was just sad.

"Don't moan about it, dad," chided Ruri.

"She's right," Riccia chimed in. "What's there to complain about? We'll be gaining a dreamboat of a son-in-law, so I absolutely approve." She'd called him "son-in-law" despite the fact that Jade was technically older than Ruri's grandfather.

"And I doubly approve if he's a strong man!" Beryl added.

In stark contrast to Kohaku, the two of them were extraordinarily pumped.

Ruri had safely reunited with her parents at the castle. She'd assumed that they would be exhausted from being trapped on a mysterious island, living in an unfamiliar environment for months, but much to her relief, her parents had more pep than she'd expected. In fact, Riccia had *too* much pep in her step. She was bursting at the seams with tremendous vigor. Whereas Kohaku, who wasn't as brazen or outspoken as Riccia, had probably been a nervous wreck this entire time. He looked to have lost some weight as well, but now that he was living a calmer life at the castle with all of the family together, he seemed to be back in good spirits.

"Actually, dad, are you sure you should've come here? I mean, you threw away your entire career."

"What are you talking about? There's nothing more important than family." Ruri felt touched by his fatherly comment, but Kohaku suddenly glared at Jade and leaned in close to the happy couple. "But are *you* sure, Ruri, that this is the right man? And Jade, will you be able to make my Ruri happy?"

"That's not quite my intent, good sir," Jade replied. "I want to be with Ruri because being with her makes me happy. That said, I will expend every effort to make Ruri happy as well. After all, she is the only woman I will ever love."

Riccia squealed in delight, Ruri blushed, and Kohaku humphed. He seemed a tad frustrated, but he didn't object. It wasn't every day that a girl found a husband with such high marks across the board. A part of Kohaku probably accepted that this was what Ruri wanted most of all.

"When's the wedding? Have you already picked a dress?" Riccia asked, barely stopping for breath.

"No, not yet. Agate and the others are going to take care of the entire ceremony."

"Oh my! That won't do! A wedding is every woman's lifelong dream. You should be more vocal about your requests. You *are* the star of the show."

"Of course I'm going to make requests, but Agate and the others are *way* more passionate about all this."

"And why are you yielding to *them*? Don't worry. I'll go have a little talk with them. This is my daughter's wedding. There will be no compromises," Riccia stated.

"Yeah! This is for my granddaughter, so I'll fight too!" Beryl added.

"Hold on, Riccia!" Kohaku cried, following after Ruri's mother and grandfather as they rushed out of the room like bats out of hell.

Ruri looked at Jade and smiled awkwardly. "I'm sorry that my family can't…settle down."

"No, it's good that they're so lively."

Ruri and Jade looked into each other's eyes, leaned into one another, and wrapped their arms around each other.

"I was worried about meeting your parents because I didn't know if they'd like me, but I take all of that as them approving of the marriage?" asked Jade.

"I think it's fine. Mom and dad are the type to say they're opposed to something if they really are."

"Well, I'm glad to hear that. Still, marriage, huh? I would have never imagined this would happen when I first met you, Ruri."

"Yes, well, I was a cat at first. That reminds me; I haven't been a cat as of late. You must be going through cuddle withdrawal by now?"

"Now that you mention it, I haven't pet you in your cat form as of late, have I?"

Ruri figured now was as good a time as any to pull out her bracelet. She put it on and transformed into a cat.

"*You can pet me all you like,*" Ruri said, rubbing her nose against Jade.

Jade smiled at the adorable gesture. He lifted Ruri in his arms, sat in his chair, and placed her on his lap.

As he gently stroked her head, she felt herself getting drowsy. She yawned, curled up into a ball on Jade's lap, and drifted off to sleep.

Jade watched in delight as Ruri fell into a graceful slumber.

Side Story: Jade's Wedding

Jade awakened to the light of early dawn. It was rare that he would wake up feeling so refreshed, but perhaps that was because today was an auspicious day. He sat up in bed and looked to his side to see Ruri still sleeping soundly. The mere sight of her was enough to bring Jade joy as his lips pushed up into a smile.

"Ruri, it's morning. Wake up."

"U-Ungh," Ruri groaned. She wasn't going to wake up without a fight.

Jade figured that she hadn't been able to sleep last night because she was so nervous about today.

Yes, today was the long-awaited day.

"Ruri, today is the wedding. We need to prepare."

Ruri's eyes snapped open and she sprung up. "I almost forgot!" she exclaimed as she peeled off the comforter and jumped out of bed.

"Let's have breakfast for the time being," Jade suggested. "Today is going to be a busy day, so you need to eat up or you won't make it through."

"Ugh… But I'm so nervous that it might not go down."

"What's the point in being nervous now? Nothing has even started yet," Jade pointed out.

"Well, yes, I know that, but…"

Today was Ruri and Jade's wedding ceremony. It was understandable that Ruri would be too nervous to keep any food down. But since today was going to be busy, if she skipped breakfast now, she might not have time to eat later, which meant breakfast was essential. Jade dragged Ruri off to eat before it was too late.

It felt like everyone in the castle was on the edge of their seat, excited for today's proceedings. The royal capital was probably in a similar mood; they had even held a pre-wedding celebration the night prior. It was a union between a King and a Beloved, after all. The town likely looked like a festival, with tons of food stalls lining the streets and people celebrating in grand style.

Even Jade was quite ecstatic that this day had finally arrived. He had hoped to have the wedding earlier, but between Agate and the other elders wanting to plan every detail and Ruri's mother adding her thoughts, the plans had grown more and more meticulous. It became clear that everything was behind schedule. Jade cared more about making Ruri his wife as soon as possible, but he found himself submitting to the intense drive of Agate and the others.

Nevertheless, the big day was finally here. He was being careful not to let anyone see him grinning like a lovesick fool, but a smile would end up appearing anyway. Ruri had said she was nervous, but Jade simply wanted the ceremony to start already. However, there was no need to rush; in a few short hours, his wishes would be granted.

After breakfast, Ruri and Jade went their separate ways to get ready. In general, women took longer to prepare than men, which meant that as soon as they finished eating, a crew of attendants whisked Ruri away.

As Jade was getting dressed, the elders came to check on him. They were choking on their tears, seeing Jade in his full wedding garb.

"At long last, gentlemen, the day is upon us!"

"Oh, how we have longed for this day!"

"My, it seems like an eternity ago that you were burning the portraits of bridal candidates, telling us that you had no need for a queen."

"Yes, but now we can reminisce about that fondly."

Jade wearily sighed. "If you're all going to cry, go someplace else. You're bringing me down."

The elders paid no mind to Jade's brusque words. It was the day that their king was to be wed, so nothing would spoil their mood.

"Everything is in order!"

"We shall make this the best ceremony anyone has ever seen!"

While it was nice of them to put so much effort into the ceremony, Jade was worried that they were spinning their wheels for nothing.

Suited up and ready to go, Jade waited in front of the wedding hall. The attendees were inside, doubtlessly waiting on bated breath for the ceremony to start.

It wasn't long before Jade saw Ruri, slowly and gracefully walking toward him. She was wearing a lacy, snow-white dress and a mantilla veil that draped down her back. Her cheeks were slightly red, and she was smiling bashfully. The white dress, which she had insisted on for the wedding, fit her extremely well. It gave her an aura of purity and elegance.

Jade found himself transfixed by her beauty, but he quickly came to his senses and offered her his hand. She timidly took it. Jade could tell her from her expression that she was racked with nerves.

"Ruri, deep breaths," Jade instructed.

Ruri complied and went through a few repetitions of inhaling and exhaling, which helped calm her down slightly.

"Let's be off," Jade prompted.

"Yes, let's!"

The doors slowly opened and the two were ushered inside.

The ceremonial hall used for dragonkin weddings had stained glass windows that sparkled in the sunlight. Guests were seated on either side of the room. A large number of people were in attendance, including Ruri's parents, several acquaintances, and royal visitors from other kingdoms.

Perhaps intimidated by all the eyes on her, Ruri tightened her grip on Jade's hand. Jade smiled at her to relieve her tension as he walked slowly down the red carpet in the center of the room, making sure to match Ruri's pace.

They walked their way to the front of the slightly elevated altar, where Agate was already standing. After much in-fighting among the elder vassals about who would be the one presiding over the ceremony, Agate had taken the honor for himself.

Once they stopped in front of Agate, the wedding was officially underway. Agate proceeded to recite lines at length. Jade wasn't really listening to him, though, because he was more focused on Ruri, who was standing at his side dressed to the nines.

"Now then, for the exchange of dragonhearts," Agate said.

Those words brought Jade's attention back to the proceedings. Agate presented him with the dragonheart, which was sitting atop a pedestal. Jade took the dragonheart and faced Ruri.

"I give this dragonheart to the woman who will become my one-and-only, my mate," Jade said.

If this were a wedding between two dragonkin, then both of them would have exchanged dragonhearts. But since Ruri was a human, Jade was the only one with a dragonheart to give.

After Ruri received the dragonheart, per the instructions she'd been given before the ceremony, she placed it in her mouth and swallowed it, albeit with some difficulty. Almost immediately, Jade felt his own mana from the dragonheart dissolve completely into Ruri.

With that, their marriage was officially solidified. Slowly but surely, the realization kicked in, and it filled Jade with joy. However, there was still a ceremony to get through, so he controlled himself and straightened his face so he wasn't grinning at everyone around him.

Normally, a dragonkin wedding ceremony would end here, but they were also going to include the traditions of Ruri's homeland for this ceremony. Two rings sat on the ring pillow—the same rings that Agate had shown them before.

Ruri had made sure to explain how to exchange rings beforehand. At first, Jade had thought this was a strange custom, but considering that he couldn't actually exchange dragonhearts with her, he was glad to make a tangible exchange like this.

Jade took Ruri's ring and slid it on her finger. Ruri took the remaining ring and placed it on Jade's finger in turn.

The ceremony had concluded. As they left the hall, Ruri looked up at Jade and smiled shyly, saying, "So, that makes me your wife now, right, Jade-sama?"

Ruri's gestures were so adorable that Jade couldn't help but take her in his arms. He honestly wanted to go someplace where they could be alone, but they needed to change for the wedding reception.

"Ahem, ahem." The assistant standing behind Jade cleared their throat, prompting both of them to hurry up.

(*Dammit...*) Jade spat in his mind, clicking his tongue as he let go of Ruri.

After they changed, they both headed to the reception hall. The reception was basically just a chance to sit down and enjoy a meal in everyone's company, so it helped put Ruri more at ease. Agate and the others had put a lot of thought into the entertainment, and just as they had confidently boasted, they were able to entertain the guests without a single bored face in sight.

The one thing that wasn't enjoyable was the number of wardrobe changes that Agate and the others had insisted on. Ruri had said one was enough, and Jade hadn't thought it necessary, but Ruri had been coerced into agreeing to three whole changes. Considering that they initially wanted *five* changes, three seemed like a compromise.

By the third change, Ruri was already sick and tired of it. In addition, she grew weary when Agate and the others complained about not getting five changes out of her. Five separate wardrobe changes was *nothing* to sneeze at.

After the reception, they all moved to a separate hall. The reception was for entertaining the guests from other countries, but this party was for the domestic attendees—out with the elegant yet stern atmosphere and in with the rowdy drinking and singing extravaganza.

With the more relaxed atmosphere, Ruri was finally able to release her tension, and she started smiling in delight.

Since Ruri was the main attraction, everyone around her kept offering her more and more alcohol, which got her tipsy. Jade was also offered alcohol, but in greater supply.

The alcohol started to steadily dwindle. While some were lifting whole barrels of wine to their mouths, drunks were mass-produced by the sip. People were drinking themselves onto a spot across the floor, but everyone was smiling happily.

Then came Celestine.

She was drunk, tottering on her feet and scowling with glassy eyes. Ruri had a bad feeling and, sure enough, Celestine's eyes locked onto her. She slowly got closer, and before Ruri knew it, Celestine was tugging at her cheeks.

"Vhat are foh doin?!" Ruri asked.

"Face your just punishment for stealing Master Jade away from me, you cur!" She pinned Ruri down and glared at her with intense rage. But in the next moment, her eyes began to water and she moaned, "Why, when I loved Master Jade more than youuuu?!"

It seemed that Celestine still had the habit of being a wreck when she was drunk. Then again, it was only natural that she would want to drink to drown her sorrows. After all, Jade, the man she loved, was now married to someone else.

"Aah. Okay, okay. Celestine-san, you've had too much to drink. Here, have some water," Ruri said, wasting no time to get her a glass.

Just then, someone called out to Ruri in a big bombastic voice. It was Ruri's mother, Riccia.

"Hey, Ruri! Let's take a photo for the occasion!"

"You brought a digital camera, mom?"

"Why, yes. And I brought a tripod."

"Wow, there's being prepared, and then there's *this*..."

While Kohaku was hurriedly setting up the camera, Riccia gathered everyone together.

"Jade-sama, let's go," Ruri prompted.

"Sure thing." Jade didn't understand what was going on, but he allowed Ruri to pull him over to stand in a row.

"Okay, I'll be taking the picture now. Don't move, everyone," Riccia said as she pressed the shutter. "All right, for the next one, just Ruri and His Majesty."

This time, only Ruri and Jade remained, huddled close together as they were instructed.

"My, what a beautiful shot," Riccia commented.

"Show me, show me!" Ruri said. She peered at the digital camera with her mother and squealed. She turned the screen toward Jade so that he could see. "Look, Jade-sama, a beautiful shot."

Jade was a little concerned that his expression might have been a bit too smiley—almost to the point of looking goofy. However, all he saw on his face was happiness, and no one was going to ridicule him for it. And though it was a delayed reaction, the happy smile he saw on Ruri's face as well really drove home the fact that the two of them were wed.

Jade could feel the joy slowly rising from within him. Unable to control his welling emotions, he lifted Ruri in his arms.

"Ruri, from now on, we will always be together."

"Yes, let's live our lives. Together."

Jade drew closer to Ruri and softly kissed her on the cheek.

Side Story: Honeymoon Trip

It had already been a month since the wedding. Ruri and Jade were smack-dab in the middle of their lovey-dovey honeymoon like a couple of good newlyweds.

Jade had been visibly happy, consistently in a good mood. He wouldn't let Ruri leave his side during work and wouldn't allow her to leave any other time either. It was no exaggeration to say that Ruri had spent nearly all of the day by Jade's side.

Jade was utterly entranced by Ruri. He fed her all of her meals by hand, as a sign of dragonkin love. Everything he did for Ruri was sweet—so sweet that she wanted to scream to the capital, "Yeesh, I'm getting cavities!" It was comparable to a stack of pancakes loaded with tons of whipped cream and jam, with a heaping pile of powdered sugar on top—sweet up the wazoo.

His behavior made her back itch. She was getting more than enough of a reminder about how much dragonkin loved their mates.

Jade was doting on her so much that Ruri couldn't help but worry that people would gawk at them. But this was apparently the norm for newlywed dragonkin, so no one paid it any mind. Even so, she tried resisting since it felt way too awkward to be so close to him all the time. So far, she hadn't been successful in escaping. Resigned, she decided to give in to his doting. Besides, there was something else giving Ruri enough problems.

"Ruri, are you bearing children yet?" Agate asked as soon as he and his starry-eyed group of elders walked into the royal office.

Tired of being asked the same question, Ruri replied the same way she had time and time again. "Not yet! You *just* asked that yesterday!"

"B-but, but~!" stammered Agate.

"You can whine all you want, but it won't make any difference."

Her current problems came from these elders. After years of meddling and interfering in Jade's marital affairs, the elders were sure to mellow out after he got married, right? At least, that's what Ruri had thought. Instead, they aimed their intensity at Ruri and pestered her about having children. They had only been married for a month. The daily inquiries were becoming an issue.

"I'm sure you two will have a child. And what a beautiful child it will be."

"We'll raise them from scratch."

"Uh, sure, sure. Just try not to take away from the mother's work, okay?" warned Ruri.

Ruri had been prepared to deal with these busybody fathers-in-law once she married Jade, but they were honestly getting on her last nerve. She didn't think there was any need to rush to have children when these old men would be running around healthy for another century.

"First off, we've only been married for a month. And second, we didn't spend much time as lovers before we got married, so we'd like to spend some more time in each other's company. Isn't that right, Jade-sama?" Ruri asked, looking up at Jade.

He looked back at her with kind eyes and a gentle smile. "That's right."

The old codgers were not happy with Jade's answer.

"Grrrrrrr!"

"We're not getting any younger! We want to see a child sooner rather than later!"

"I suppose we have no choice but to set the mood so they'll be in...well, *the mood?*"

The elders huddled together and started whispering among themselves. Ruri couldn't hear them, but she hoped that they wouldn't go butting in where they didn't belong again.

Meanwhile, Ruri was still confined to Jade's lap. She thought that she might be getting in the way of his work and tried to get off, but Jade's arm tightened around her waist once she did.

"Jade-sama, I should get down since I'll get in your way."

"You will not," Jade promptly replied, almost cutting off her sentence in the middle.

That was when someone handed Jade a letter. Ruri stared at him from the side as he scanned it.

Jade's behavior was probably natural considering they were in the honeymoon phase, but Ruri was a little worried that he might keep her by his side indefinitely. It wasn't that she didn't want to be around him, but she didn't want to stay like this *forever*. There were things that she wanted to do as well. She wanted to go into town, for one. It didn't seem likely, though, that Jade would allow any of that right now. This was an issue. Ruri had heard that dragonkin were very possessive, but she wanted some free time to herself. While she couldn't blame him for getting carried away by the moment, she would need to talk to him if this continued.

"Oh, by the way..." Ruri started, as if the word "honeymoon" had reminded her of something important.

"What's the matter?" asked Jade.

"That's right, Jade-sama! We haven't taken a honeymoon trip!"

"Honeymoon trip? What is that?"

Apparently, the idea of a honeymoon trip was a foreign concept in this world.

"Where I'm from, when you get married, you're supposed to go on a trip afterward."

"Oh-ho, that's a concept in your world, eh?" Jade mused. However, he was the king, and a king couldn't just up and leave on an impromptu getaway. "Hmm, I see. A trip…"

By the manner in which Jade was contemplating the idea, Ruri had the disappointing feeling that it was a no-go.

"I take it that it's not possible?" Ruri asked.

"No, it's perfect timing," Jade replied, tapping on the letter he had been reading.

"Who is that from?"

"It's from the Spirit King of the Nation of the Spirit King. It's an invitation addressed to you to visit their castle."

"Wait, me?"

"The Spirit of Trees residing in the Nation of the Spirit King apparently wishes to see you since you've contracted with their brethren."

"Wow, you don't say…" Ruri muttered.

"How about a 'honeymoon trip' to the Nation of the Spirit King?" Jade suggested.

"Wow, really? You mean we can? That would be great!"

As such, Ruri traveled to the Nation of the Spirit King to see the Spirit of Trees. Though it was a honeymoon trip, the kingdom couldn't let its ruler and its Beloved go alone, so they naturally sent security detail. In addition, the supreme-level spirits—Kotaro, Rin, Chi, and Heat—said they wanted to see the Spirit of Trees as well. The party ended up being bigger than expected, turning the romantic trip into more of a regular excursion. Nevertheless, they just had to play the hand they were dealt.

The Nation of the Spirit King's royal castle was a chalk-white structure that floated atop a lake. Behind the castle was the forest where the sacred beasts—one of which Kotaro was using as his host body—dwelled. The white castle reflected dazzlingly on the lake's surface, giving the structure an even more beautiful luster. On foggy days, it looked almost fantastical. It was also a famous location. Painters flocked there to capture its majesty.

Unfortunately, it was cloudy the day Ruri and Jade arrived, but that didn't detract from the white structure's beauty.

"Wow, what a beautiful castle!" Ruri exclaimed. Riding on the back of Jade's dragon body, Ruri had an unobstructed view of the structure from the sky.

Ruri had tried to ride Kotaro as usual to get to here, but that dragonkin possessiveness flared yet again and Jade adamantly refused to allow her to ride on anyone but himself. She'd had no choice but to ride on Jade. But unlike the soft and fluffy Kotaro, Jade's draconic skin was hard; her rear end was sore by the time they arrived.

When they landed at the castle, officials of the Nation of the Spirit King, including the Spirit King himself, greeted them. The Spirit King was Awain, the only pure qilin in this world. His eyes were as blue as the ocean's depths, and his straight, shoulder-length hair was a blueish silver. Although the look in his eyes was sharp and ferocious enough to force you to grovel for forgiveness, his look wasn't born of anger. That was simply the way he normally looked.

Although Awain wasn't directing any anger at her, Ruri ended up cowering behind Jade all the same. She had met Awain at the wedding, but one meeting was hardly enough to get used to his face's destructive power.

313

"So good of you to come, Jade, Beloved," Awain greeted.

"Yes, haven't seen you since the wedding," Jade replied.

"Good afternoon," Ruri added.

It wasn't clear whether Awain was aware of the effect his face had on others, but he didn't seem too concerned about Ruri's reaction.

"You must be tired. I'd suggest having a cup of tea and relaxing."

Jade agreed, saying, "Yes, I'd appreciate it."

As they were shown around the premises, Ruri walked with her mouth agape. The castle was white, inside and out. This much white meant that Awain had some sort of fixation on the shade.

As her heels clacked along the white marble floors, Ruri suddenly felt a gaze on her. She looked around to find a man staring—or rather, glaring—at her with deep blue eyes. His gaze was just as fierce and intense as Awain's. Ruri had no idea why this mysterious man was staring daggers at her, but she clung to Jade's arm nonetheless.

"Ruri?" Jade asked, noticing she was acting strange. He traced her line of sight until it reached the pillar, where the scowling man could be seen.

When Awain saw that Jade and Ruri had stopped walking, he naturally stopped as well. He noticed the man they were both staring at and asked him, "What are you doing over there, Lapis?"

Ruri looked confused, so Jade explained, "He's the Beloved of the Nation of the Spirit King and Awain's son."

That made sense, considering that his intense eyes had made her wonder if the two were blood relations.

With all eyes on him, the Nation of the Spirit King's Beloved, Lapis, marched his way up to Ruri without taking his eyes off of her and suddenly took her right hand. He stared at Ruri with what could easily be mistaken for an antagonistic glare, but before she could imagine what he would say to her, he simply stated, "I've fallen for you. Be my bride."

"Pardon…?"

The air instantly froze over—mainly from where Jade was standing. His face was obscured from view. In the next instant, he used his hand to chop through Lapis's grip and separate the two. Then he grasped Ruri in his arms.

"With all due respect, she is my mate. You should find someone else."

"I don't want to. I want her. She's mine."

"Ruri is mine. I would never give her up."

"You do realize that I'm a Beloved, don't you? Are you sure you want to say that to m— *Gaah!*"

Awain put an end to their childish argument by hitting the top of Lapis's head with his fist.

"Yowch! What're you doing, old man?!" Lapis complained.

Awain replied, "It's called educational guidance, my foolish son!"

"Quit butting in. I've met my soulmate."

"You need to stop falling in love at the drop of a hat!"

"I'm serious this time. This meeting is the last one for sure."

"You said the exact same thing two weeks ago to the new maid, you idiot of a son! 'Last time,' indeed! How many 'soulmates' must you meet before you're satisfied?!"

As the father and son bickered with each other, Jade wiped off Ruri's hand—the one that Lapis had held—with a handkerchief.

The Spirit King's aide, who watched the seemingly endless father-son spat with disappointment, decided to guide Jade and the others instead. According to him, their bickering was a common occurrence and no one would try to step in and break it up.

The aide showed Ruri and the others to a room where they took a breather with some tea. Once everyone had relaxed, the aide said, "The Spirit of Trees is looking forward to meeting with you. If you'd like, I shall take you to see them."

"Yes, I would appreciate that," replied Ruri. Meeting with the Spirit of Trees was her original reason for coming here. Taking Kotaro and the other supreme-level spirits with her, Ruri had the aide show her to where the Spirit of Trees was.

In the center of the castle, there was a large tree with lush, verdant leaves that seemed to cover the sky. That was the Spirit of Trees. This gigantic tree, which had been in place since the founding of the Nation of the Spirit King, towered over the people as if watching over them. It was a sight nothing short of spectacular.

"Amazing..." Ruri uttered, looking up at the tree with a mixture of surprise and excitement.

Just then, an old man with a transparent body appeared from the tree. With his long white beard, he looked like a mountain sage of some kind.

"*Good of you to come, Beloved of the Nation of the Dragon King and contract-bearer of my brethren.*"

"Erm, might you be the Spirit of Trees?" Ruri asked.

"*Indeed I am. Though I believe I invited only you, I see that you've brought along quite the entourage,*" the Spirit of Trees commented, looking around at Kotaro and the others.

"*Oh? And where's the harm?*" said Rin, flying up to him. "*It's not like it's every day that we have so many of our brethren in one spot.*"

"*You have a point. How many millennia has it been since this many of us have gathered together, I wonder.*"

"Do supreme-level spirits not see each other that often?" Ruri inquired.

"*Aye, that's right. I may stay exclusively in the Nation of the Spirit King, but not many of my other brethren stay in the same place for years on end. Fire and Wind there especially.*"

"Heh, wherever there are beautiful women, that is where I'll be," Heat said in a haughty tone, though nothing he said was anything to be proud of.

"*I was taken aback when I heard that Wind made a contract with a human in spite of his lack of interest in them. But I see he's changed quite a lot in the short time since I last saw him.*"

"*Yes, Kotaro has seen the most change,*" said Rin.

Kotaro protested, "*Well, I don't think I've changed all that much...*"

"*No, you have,*" Rin insisted.

"*Oh, yeah, big time,*" Chi chimed in.

Though three of his brethren were telling him so, Kotaro didn't seem too willing to accept it.

"*Beloved of the Nation of the Dragon King, are you getting along well with Time?*"

"Yes, I think we are, at least."

"*I see. That's good, then. I was curious about what kind of person you were since you made contracts with two spirits who normally have no ties with humans, but if you're getting along with both Wind and Time, then that will do. I ask that you continue to take care of my brethren.*"

"Oh, no, I am absolutely indebted to all of you," Ruri said with emotion.

It seemed that the Spirit of Trees was just worried about his brethren. He'd heard that they had made contracts with a human, so he wanted to check what kind of human the contract-bearer was.

317

The day after they met with the Spirit of Trees, Kotaro and the other supreme-level spirits were still chatting about their first reunion in years.

Ruri was about to go into town with Jade to enjoy their honeymoon, which was the other purpose of their trip. Ruri's heart was bouncing with joy since a date in town wasn't something they did—not even back in their own kingdom.

"Are you ready, Ruri?" asked Jade.

"Yes, all set!" she replied.

Just as Ruri was about to take Jade's outstretched hand so that they could be on their way, her body was suddenly lifted up, and someone took her into their arms.

Ruri blinked, dumbfounded. "Huh…?"

Jade was equally flabbergasted, but he shook it off and quickly tried to reach for Ruri. However, a literal wall of spirits stood in his way.

"*No!*"

"*Nuh-uh!*"

"*You're not getting through here!*"

"The rest is up to you guys!" said the person.

"*No problem!*" the spirits replied in unison.

The only one who could control this many spirits was a Beloved, and the only other Beloved here aside from Ruri was Lapis. As Jade tried to get past the wall of spirits, Lapis sprinted off like a jackrabbit. He ran all the way to town, where he finally let Ruri down.

"Jeez, what are you doing?!" Ruri angrily asked.

"All right, where'd you like to go now?"

"Where'd I'd 'like to go' nothing! I was about to go out with Jade-sama!"

"Okay, let's go to my favorite restaurant, then."

Lapis wasn't listening at all. Ruri tried to fight back, but he took her by the hand and refused to let her get away. With no other choice, Ruri reluctantly followed him.

Ruri wasn't sure why this was happening. Up until a second ago, she was giddy about going on a date with Jade, but now instead of being with the person she loved the most, she was with some frumpy-faced cretin. This was the absolute pits.

Though discontent and displeasure were written all over Ruri's face, Lapis was oblivious to it. It was just the two of them—not a bodyguard in sight. Ruri wondered if it was okay for a Beloved to go out without security, but Lapis walked the crowded streets without a care, as if he had done this a million times. The townspeople weren't overreacting to seeing Lapis either. They greeted him cheerfully, in fact.

"You don't come out with bodyguards?" Ruri asked.

"Why would I need those? These are my stomping grounds. No one would dare try to harm me here. And if someone did, the people around here would help me out."

The people of the Nation of the Spirit King were very religious, like the Nation of the Beast King's people. But instead of revering spirits as gods, the people here loved the spirits with a sense of familiarity, and they treated their Beloveds as well as they would their own family. Lapis being the son of the Spirit King, a wise and lauded ruler, probably also played a large part.

As they walked through the town, Ruri grew a little envious of the goodwill she felt from the townspeople. She wished she could be like this in the city of the Nation of the Dragon King. She was immensely frustrated with Lapis, but she reconsidered, thinking that he might not be such a bad person if this many townsfolk liked him.

Forced to change her initial plans from a lovey-dovey, sightseeing date with Jade, Ruri walked around the city. But just when it seemed like they would be leaving, she felt a chill run down her spine. Lapis felt the same chill and stopped dead in his tracks.

"Well, aren't *you* having fun?" said a voice packed with rage, as if echoing from the very bowels of hell.

Ruri and Lapis both slowly turned around, their faces pale.

Ruri gasped. Staring at the both of them with a sharp look— one that rivaled Awain's—stood Jade with his feet firmly planted and his hands on his hips.

Jade grabbed Lapis by the head with so much force that you could almost hear a cracking sound.

"Eep!" Lapis looked like a timid frog trapped in front of a leering snake. His face went deathly pale.

"I told you. I told you that Ruri is my mate. But it seems you'd like a one-on-one lesson about how immoral it is for someone to make a pass at a male dragonkin's mate."

Lapis's legs were quaking like a frightened fawn's.

"Come, we're going back. I would most likely end up killing you if I went any further, so enjoy being raked across the coals by Awain," Jade said as he dragged the scared Lapis back with them to the castle.

Awain was standing in wait, and as soon as they returned, he clocked his son right across the head.

"You foolish excuse for an offspring!"

"Gaah!"

Awain proceeded to give him a lengthy and stern talking-to.

Jade also ended up scolding Ruri. He said that she could have escaped if she'd felt like it. She defended herself by saying that theory and actually having a stranger lead you everywhere by the hand were two different stories.

Ruri averted her gaze from Jade and noticed that the Spirit of Light, who had said she'd be staying behind in the Nation of the Dragon King to take care of business, was also there. When Ruri asked why she was here, she said that she had finished her business and had come to see the Spirit of Trees herself.

While Ruri conversed with the Spirit of Light, Lapis shoved Awain away in the middle of his fatherly lecture. As Awain stewed in anger and confusion, Lapis walked up to the Spirit of Light, took her hand, and said, "I've fallen for you. Be my bride."

Just then, Awain's fist came crashing down on his head once again.

Ruri and Jade couldn't help but be shocked and disappointed. What was even the point of all the fuss he caused today? They could have done without any of this.

"I finally have a trip with you and look what happens," Jade vented, frustrated by the unnecessary interruption.

Ruri hadn't expected this to happen either. It was their first time out on the town in a long while, but this had squandered the entire day for them.

"Well, we can always try again tomorrow," Ruri offered, taking his hand.

Jade's temper finally petered out, and his expression began to soften. "That's right. And I swear I won't let anyone get in our way tomorrow."

"Why don't we just go by ourselves while we're at it? When I was in town today, it seemed safe enough for two Beloveds to be out on their own, so I don't think we need a procession of bodyguards around if you're there, Jade-sama."

"Just the two of us, huh? I see. A leisurely stroll without worrying about threats around us...just the two of us..."

"Yes! Then it would make it feel more like a date! I learned about a lot of good eateries today, so I'll show you tomorrow," Ruri said, trying to contain her excitement.

"I'm not exactly thrilled that you learned about them from another man, but oh well. I suppose I'll keep my hopes up."

"Of course! Just leave it to me!"

The two of them leaned close and smiled at each other. Tenderness filled the air around them. They'd had their fair share of problems along the way, but it looked like they would be able to enjoy their initial plan of a lovey-dovey honeymoon trip after all.

Author: **Kureha**
Illustrator: **Yamigo**

FINAL VOLUME
ON SALE
JANUARY 2023!

The
**White Cat's
Revenge**
as Plotted from the
Dragon King's Lap

6

Author:
SATORU YAMAGUCHI
Illustrator: **NAMI HIDAKA**

11

VOLUME 11
ON SALE NOW!

My Next Life
as a VILLAINESS:
ALL ROUTES
LEAD TO DOOM!

VOL. 1-6
ON SALE NOW!

Tearmoon Empire

Nozomu Mochitsuki
Illustrator: Gilse

Bibliophile Princess

Novel + Manga Available from All Major Ebook Stores

Author: Yui
Ilustrator: Satsuki Sheena

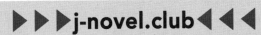

J-Novel Club Lineup

Latest Ebook Releases Series List